The Daily

Modern M

Also by Jonathan Goodman

Crime History

The Killing of Julia Wallace
The Burning of Evelyn Foster
The Stabbing of George Harry Storrs
The Slaying of Joseph Bowne Elwell
The Passing of Starr Faithfull
Bloody Versicles: The Rhymes of Crime
Posts-Mortem: The Correspondence of Murder
The Trial of Ian Brady and Myra Hindley (*re-issued as*
The Moors Murders)
The Trial of Ruth Ellis (*with Patrick Pringle*)
The Crippen File
The Oscar Wilde File
Acts of Murder
Underworld (*with Ian Will*)
The Black Museum (*with Bill Waddell*)
Murder in High Places
Murder in Low Places
Anthologies: The Pleasures of Murder, The Railway
Murders, The Seaside Murders, The Country House
Murders, The Christmas Murders, The Vintage Car
Murders, The Lady Killers, The Art of Murder,
The Medical Murders, The Supernatural Murders,
Masterpieces of Murder, The Daily Telegraph Murder File

Novels

Instead of Murder
Criminal Tendencies
Hello Cruel World Goodbye
The Last Sentence

Verse

Matinée Idylls

Others

Who He?: Goodman's Dictionary of the Unknown Famous
The Master Eccentric: The Journals of Rayner
Heppenstall, 1969–81 (*editor*)

The Daily Telegraph
Modern Murder File

Edited by
JONATHAN GOODMAN

Mandarin

Picture acknowledgements:

The Hulton Deutsch Collection Ltd provided the following
illustrations in the picture sections: 2nd page, top;
5th page, top; 6th page, both; 8th page, both; 12th page;
13th page, top; 14th page, both. Some of the other pictures
are from the editor's own collection or from those of fellow
crime historians, and the remainder are from the *Daily* or
Sunday Telegraph. The cartoon on page 41 is reproduced
by permission of the cartoonist, Willie Rushton.

A Mandarin Paperback
THE DAILY TELEGRAPH MODERN MURDER FILE

First published in Great Britain 1995
by Mandarin Paperbacks
an imprint of Reed Books Ltd
Michelin House, 81 Fulham Road, London SW3 6RB
and Auckland, Melbourne, Singapore and Toronto

A CIP catalogue record for this title
is available from the British Library
ISBN 0 7493 1970 4

Printed and bound in Great Britain
by Cox & Wyman Ltd, Reading, Berkshire

Contents

Introduction

I was pleased when I was invited to edit a companion volume to *The Daily Telegraph Murder File*, which is a sampling of that paper's reports and comments on murder cases between its inaugural appearance in 1855 and the (quite unconnected) abolition of capital punishment for murder in Great Britain about a hundred years later. But my pleasure dwindled, almost evaporated, when I learned that what was wanted was not a concurrent companion but a consecutive one – comprising reports and comments on cases during the thirty years that separate the final hangings (in 1964: two at the same time for the same murder) from the present day. I came close to turning down the invitation – so close that, now that I have done the job and thoroughly enjoyed doing it, I honestly can't recall what the single pro was that overcame the several perceived cons.

Among the latter was my abhorrence of 'instant' true-crime books, of which there has been an epidemic lately: books cobbled together by typists rather than authors, industrious while a case is proceeding, then spending as long as five minutes on a last chapterette reporting the outcome, and faxing that to a printer who, having set the earlier stuff, is champing to meet a publication deadline only days away. These instant books, as well as being tatty, are downright harmful, for they lessen the chance of getting decent books on the same subjects. I know of many, too many, instances of a proposal for a retrospective examination of a criminal case being turned down by a publisher for the simple reason that there has already been one book on the case, and (*the editor speaking*:) 'how many – or rather, how few – of the people who bought the first book are likely to fork out for a second? – the market has been blighted' – by catchpenny trash.*

---

* 1995 was heralded in with the news that Frederick West, the Gloucester builder accused of murdering a dozen young women, had been found hanged in his

Addendum to that objection (and now I may be speaking only for myself – none of my monographs has covered a case that made front-page news more recently than 1931), I believed that, just as there is a forty-year rule for nostalgia – presently being proved by 1950s-recalling fashions of one sort or another – there is a no-fewer-than-twenty-years rule for being quite sure that a murder case is truly memorable, not merely loitering in some minds because of shock-horror extraneities. And, further to the addendum, it seemed to me, a taker of newspapers but a negligent reader of them, that there were nowhere near enough recent and still-interesting cases to fill a book.

But after trawling through the *Telegraph*'s post-UK-abolition reports, I confess that there are exceptions to the no-fewer-than-twenty-years rule – and that, glittering amidst the midden of thud-and-blunder affairs, there are twenty or so cases, and a couple of events resulting from murders, that deserve to be recalled. Or so it seems to me.

Perhaps because I have only rearranged some of my prejudices against modern cases, I feel that they (the last thirty years' worth) have produced fewer piquant titbits than those of earlier similar portions of time. But still, I was intrigued by a number, including these:

● The crazy sort of poetry of a snatch of a letter
written by a serial-killer: '. . . huge drops of lead
poured down upon her head until she was dead – yet
the cats still come out at night to mate and the
sparrows still sing in the morning' – which is quite
as lyrical as some of the terminal utterances of
Dutch Schultz, delirious before dying from bullet-

---

prison cell. The following day, the *Telegraph*'s 'Peterborough' column contained the cheerier news that West's death was 'a setback to a number of writers [who] have been beavering away on books scheduled for publication straight after [his] anticipated trial. An unnamed publisher was quoted as saying: 'Had West gone to trial, the whole thing would have been paraded through the newspapers in great detail, heightening public awareness and making for a better book' (a pity that he had not been asked to define 'better'). One of the beavers was reported as saying that he was 'pondering whether to proceed with his project,' and adding the pious comment (unintendedly wounding to players of the Hunt-the-Ripper game): 'One cannot write a book about charges alleged against a man who isn't alive to answer them. That would be malicious.'

wounds inflicted by other gangsters in the autumn of
1935: 'Oh, oh, dog biscuit. And when he is happy he
doesn't get snappy. . . . A boy has never wept nor
dashed a thousand kim.'
- The response from a British habitual killer, following
his arrest, to a stranger's offer to look after his dog
and return it as soon as he was free: 'Well, who'd
want an eighty-year-old dog back?'
- A murderer's explanation – claimed to be explicable
only by his counsel and, of course, *of course*, by
psychiatrists – that three inoffensive sentences in a
modern novel, nothing to do with crime, had
triggered his gun.
- The coincidence of two unconnected killings by
different persons on one small farm in Hertfordshire
– which surely dents the notion that, simply because
John Reginald Halliday Christie committed a
number of murders at his flat in West London, then
Timothy John Evans, tenant of a flat in the same
house, must have been innocent of the murder of
both his wife (the crime for which he was executed in
the spring of 1950) and his daughter. (Anybody who
has been led to believe that there are reasons other
than the coincidental one for *knowing* that Evans
was wrongfully hanged should read John Eddowes's
book *The Two Killers of Rillington Place* (republished
as a paperback earlier this year), which shows that
certain 'Evans was Innocent – OK?' propaganda is,
let us say, economical with truths and lavish with
errors of fact that just happen to give ostensible
support to the propagandists' arguments.)

There is no clear-cut answer to the question, When was
capital punishment for murder abolished in Great Britain?
In 1957, a majority of members of both Houses of Parlia-
ment voted for the ludicrous Homicide Act, which retained
the death penalty only for five categories of murder: in the
course or furtherance of theft; by shooting or by causing an
explosion; in the course of or for the purpose of resisting or
avoiding or preventing a lawful arrest, or of effecting or
assisting an escape or rescue from legal custody; any murder

of a police officer acting in the execution of his duty or of a person assisting a police officer so acting; in the case of a person who was a prisoner at the time when he did or was a party to the murder; any murder of a prison officer. The death penalty also applied to persons convicted of murder on a previous occasion, and to persons convicted on the same indictment of two or more murders done on different occasions. Then, in 1965, came the Murder (Abolition of Death Penalty) Act, which officially suspended capital punishment for 'an experimental period' of five years, but which to all intents and purposes ended it. In 1969, shortly before the Christmas recess, the Commons affirmed the abolitional resolution, and, a day or so later, so did a majority of those Lords who had bothered to turn up.

Throughout their campaign, the Abolitionists had insisted, brooking no argument about it, that capital punishment was not a deterrent to murder. Which was nonsense, of course. Capital punishment may not deter (for instance) certain psychopaths, sexual perverts, sadists, and underworld thugs; nor will it have much, if any, effect on the number of murders occurring during domestic brawls, which make up by far the largest percentage of killings. But there is no doubt, not the slightest, that the fear of an executional consequence will cause *some* people who are contemplating murder to have second thoughts. And it is equally certain that that fear will dissuade *some* robbers from carrying firearms which, intended only as 'frighteners', may go off accidentally – or be fired haphazardly – with lethal effect.

It is worth repeating, with slight rearrangement, something that appeared as a footnote in the first of these *Telegraph* books:

Though there was an enormous increase in the volume of types of crime other than murder (by over 300 per cent between 1930 and 1959) from the middle of the nineteenth century until the Murder (Abolition of Death Penalty) Act was made permanent in 1969, the annual tally of murders remained much the same. These are Home Office figures for offences initially recorded as homicide:

	Annual average	*Per million population*
1900–09	306	9.0
1910–19	275	7.5
1920–29	284	7.3
1930–39	321	7.9
1940–49	353	8.2
1950–59	315	7.1
1960–69	336	6.5
Post-Abolition:		
1970–79	512	10.4
1980–89	687	12.4

In 1969, 395 offences were initially recorded as homicide, but 63 of them were subsequently reclassified (leaving a total that equalled 7.3 homicides per million population); firearms were used in 50 burglaries and 464 robberies.

In 1993, 675 offences were initially recorded as homicide, but 69 of them were subsequently reclassified (leaving a total that equalled 11.8 homicides per million population); firearms were used in 235 burglaries and 5918 robberies.

I think it is fair to say that the Abolitionist politicians, with their spoutings about 'the sanctity of human life', are proved to have been – and to be – accessories before the fact of a kind of mass-murder. Killers' lives have been – and are being – saved at the expense of an increase in the number of people killed.

I have no idea which of the stories I have selected from the past thirty-seven years will – or will not – be of much interest in thirty-seven years' time. Ages ago (Heavens! – can it really be as long as a quarter of a century?), I outlined just some of the elements that might or undoubtedly would make certain murder cases stick in my mind, and I am pleased by the surprise of seeing that what I wrote then holds true.

In a vicarious and, of course, law-abiding sense, the crime of murder exerts different fascinations on different people: one man's meat-axe is another man's poison; a particular case, a favourite with one person, may appeal not at all to another, simply because its ingredients, singularly or as a mixture, are not to his criminous taste.

Most murder cases are caviare to the general. There appears to be a single factor common to those rare cases that capture and hold a wide interest, and this is that they are both appropriate to and evocative of the ambience of their period and place. The Ripper crimes of the late 1880s, for instance: one feels that if they had never happened, they would need to have been invented to fill the gap left by their unintended absence, so perfectly do they fit the context of the times and the grim and grimy milieu of the Whitechapel slums. And the Crippen case, which gives a clearer picture of London and Londoners in 1910 than a whole shelf of social history books.

All murder cases (and the *all* is not a thoughtless over-statement) reveal something of their ambience, and this is one of the fascinations of studying them; one of many. There is also the fascination of trying to solve the puzzle inherent in so many of the cases – less often who-did-it than what-made-him-do-it; of watching a great advocate in action, recognising his tricks of rhetoric and presentation, comparing his style in one case with or to his style in another; of seeing a small-part player (the 'pig woman' in the Hall-Mills case is a prime example) suddenly become the star, the headline-maker.

A lot of my own homicidal fascinations are on the outskirts of cases: the 'crhymes' they inspire (or used to inspire, in what I am reactionary enough to call, without lowering my voice, the 'good old days'); the post-trial lives of the protagonists; the minutiae of investigations, such as the police lists – pathetic and surprising Salinger-parodies – of the contents of victims' and suspects' pockets.

But what fascinates me perhaps most of all is the way in which murder (other crimes, too, but murder especially) invests ordinary, everyday things with a terrible significance: the tatty raincoat in the Wallace case, the 'rising sun' post-card, the paper flowers in the McKay outrage. A murder is committed, and suddenly these unimportant articles are transformed, are given a new and vital identity, become clues in an investigation, exhibits at a trial.

Just as the contents of this book are only a comparatively tiny sampling of the *Telegraph*'s 'murder file', each chapter – and I am speaking even of each of the long ones – is made up of only a little of what the paper had to say on that

particular murderous subject. I have made textual altera-
tions throughout and have transposed paragraphs in a
number of the reports; no more than once or twice have I
thought it really necessary to signify an elision, by inserting
triple points; some of the dates of publication are not quite
accurate, in that I have sometimes switched paragraphs
from one report to another; I have kept explanatory and
updating footnotes to the minimum.

I am grateful to David Ward, who, unlike most researchers, did not simply provide bundles of photocopies but told
me of his serendipitous observation of things that he
thought (usually rightly) would interest me; and, for specific
information, to Albert Borowitz, Jeffrey Bloomfield, Neil
Darbyshire (chief crime correspondent of the *Daily Telegraph*), Drs Lewis and Jean Gavin, Wilfred Gregg, Andrew
McCooey, Mrs Georgina McMasters, James Morton, Robin
Odell, Richard Whittington-Egan, and members of the
Public Relations Branch of the Home Office.

1958 . . .

Saturday, November 29:

DEATH FROM HIRE-PURCHASE

Edward Donald Garlick, a 21-year-old factory worker, and his 19-year-old wife Wendy, who were married on Boxing Day last year, had piled up heavy debts from hire-purchase by the second week of September, when they moved into the top flat of a house in Mosslea Road, Penge, South London. A fortnight later, on September 26 – by which time they owed the landlady, Mrs Stoneman, £9 5s 3d* (two rent payments of £4 a week, together with cash and the cost of groceries borrowed from her)

– they were discovered in the gas-filled kitchen of the flat, Wendy dead and her husband unconscious from the fumes.

Yesterday, at the Kent Assizes in Maidstone, Garlick, who had pleaded not guilty to murder because he and his wife had entered into a suicide pact, was found guilty of manslaughter and put on probation for three years, a condition being that he was to remain in a mental hospital for up to a year.

Saturday, February 2, 1963:

With one curt word, 'Life,' Mr Justice Paull at the Old Bailey yesterday sentenced Edward Donald Garlick, a 25-year-old storeman, of Princes Park Lane, Hayes, Middlesex, for the murder of Carol Ann White, a 16-year-old assistant at a Woolworth store, whose body was found on waste ground at West Drayton [just west of Hayes] on Thursday, October 11, last year.

At about nine o'clock the previous night, she had left her home to await a call at a telephone box, West Drayton 2101, from her boyfriend in Guildford. When she had not returned after an hour, her

father walked to the box, where he found her purse and ballpoint pen. At 4.30 p.m. on October 11, Edward Garlick, apparently distressed, stopped a van near the waste ground and told the driver that he had stumbled upon a girl's corpse while walking there with his wife. The body of Carol White lay in a ditch close to an unlighted road – 600 yards from the telephone box. Five of seven stab-wounds had pierced her lungs. In the opinion of the examining pathologist, a piece of cloth used as a gag had been pressed so firmly inside her mouth that it would have been sufficient to

* At the start of 1995, the purchasing power of the 1958 £1 was about £9.

cause death from asphyxia. The pathologist also stated that sexual intercourse had taken place shortly before death, with the girl a consenting party.

Partly because of lies told by Garlick, he became the main, and eventually sole, suspect.

Lie No. 1: He told the police that he did not know the surname of his aunt Alice, whom, so he said, he was intending to visit at her home in nearby Harmondsworth when he found Carol's body.

Truth: The police discovered that he knew that her name was Ford because he had visited her eight times during the previous year.

Lie No. 2: He said that he had started off on the shortest route to Harmondsworth.

Truth: Detectives walked two routes, and ascertained that he had taken the longest way round, thereby passing the place near Cherry Lane where the murder was committed.

Lie No. 3: He claimed that he had found the body after his landlord's dog, which had followed him on the walk, ran into the field to avoid being put on a lead in a heavy traffic area.

Truth: Sipson Row, where Garlick first showed the dog the lead, carried little traffic.

Lie No. 4: He said that when he chased the dog into the field, he did not see the body until he stood up after 'tripping over something'.

Truth The body could be seen from 10 yards away.

Lie No. 5: His alibi for the time of the murder was that he had called at four public houses in two hours, trying to buy

headache tablets for himself and his wife.

Truth: The tablets he said he needed were stocked at two of the public houses he claimed to have visited.

In addition, the police received vital information from Jeanette Coleman, an 18-year-old neighbour of the Garlicks, who on the night of the murder was out driving with a friend. At 10.25, in Gould's Green, two miles from the murder scene, the car's head-lights had picked out Garlick.

At first, he denied having, or ever having had, a knife of the stiletto type that had been used for the killing. Then he said that he had had such a knife, but had given it to his stepson. Later, he admitted that he still had the knife but insisted that he could not remember what had happened to it.

After being interviewed again, on Monday, October 29 – 18 days after claiming that he had 'found' the body – he was taken back to his home, where, in the hearing of detectives, his wife asked him, 'Did you do it?' and he replied: 'Yes, I did.'

He then showed the detectives where he had buried the knife and, at the police station, demonstrated how he had stabbed the girl. In a statement, he said: 'I did not force her out of the phone box. She came running. She asked me for a light. We chatted and then she said she knew a place down the road. We walked up the road. I showed her my knife. She was not frightened. She laughed and put it in her bag. [After having sexual intercourse in the field,] she said I wanted practice. I went mad and I shoved the knife into her. I first met her seven months earlier.'

Towards the end of the trial, Dr Fraser Brisby, the chief medical officer at Brixton Prison [called by the defence], said in cross-examination by Mr Mervyn Griffith-Jones that Garlick was under his care at Brixton in the autumn of 1958 while on remand following the death of his first wife: 'When he came into prison, he was suffering from a form of insanity from which he recovered by the time he stood trial. I think he was suffering from toxic confusional insanity owing to carbon monoxide poisoning.' He was acutely ill for five or six days, and within 14 days was fit to be interviewed. At the trial, after being found guilty of manslaughter, he was placed on probation on condition that he received treatment in a mental home. He did so well at the home that he was released after five months, in April 1959.

Garlick, the only son of elderly parents, married his present wife Barbara at Uxbridge in March 1961. They have two children.

Friday, October 2, 1981:

Edward Donald Garlick, a double killer, put his head on a railway line and then turned to face death as a train thundered towards him, an inquest at Devizes heard yesterday. Dr William Kennard, a Home Office pathologist, said that Garlick, who was 44, had drunk so much that he should already have been dead from alcohol poisoning.

His headless corpse was found in Box railway tunnel, near Chippenham, Wiltshire. He had been given leave from an open prison in Gloucestershire, where he was serving a life sentence passed in 1963. An after-care officer testified that Garlick was depressed because he was not allowed to visit his children. 'He said that there was no point in living if he could not see them.'

The coroner recorded a verdict of suicide.

1960 . . .

Monday, December 12:

BRENDA NASH FOUND MURDERED

The body of 12-year-old Brenda Nash was found yesterday by three small boys on common ground in the Hampshire village of Yateley, 20 miles south-west of where she was last seen six weeks ago, on the evening of Friday, October 28, close to her home in Bleriot Road, Heston, Middlesex, to which she was returning after a Girl Guide meeting. The body, still dressed in Guide uniform bearing the insignia of the Fifth Heston Company, was covered with grass and leaves, indicating that the killer had attempted a makeshift burial. A post-mortem examination conducted by Dr Keith Simpson, the Home Office patholo-gist, has revealed that the child was strangled; though she was not raped, disarrangement of her knick-ers and vest indicated that a sexual assault was attempted.

Yateley, which is on the Camber-ley-to-Farnborough A327 road, little used at night, is in the vicinity of the route taken by 'a scar-faced man' who, on the Friday seven weeks before the abduction of Brenda Nash, kidnapped an 11-year-old Girl Guide from Twicken-ham, close to Heston, drove her to a secluded spot and raped her, after-wards driving her back to Twicken-ham.

The police believe that one man was probably responsible for both crimes, and the inference is that a particularly dangerous sex maniac is at large. A factor that detectives have to consider in repetitive crimes is that the criminal may strike at regular intervals. As next Friday will be the end of the second seven-week cycle, it is feared that the maniac may then strike again.

Wet weather over the last few weeks has meant that few people have passed the spot, 30 yards from the road, where the body of Brenda Nash lay. Uniformed policemen were last night questioning drivers and passengers of cars and buses passing through the village, and house-to-house inquiries were in progress.

Dusk was falling over the neat terraced home of Mr and Mrs James Nash in Heston when they heard that a girl's body had been dis-covered. Mrs Nash, who had never given up hope that Brenda might be found alive, collapsed when she heard the news. Later, Detective Sergeant Fred Malyon, who has been closely concerned with the couple during the inquiries, drove them to Norwood Green police station, so that they could be kept fully informed. After an hour and a half, they were driven back to their council house, where relatives were gathered to try to comfort them.

Friday, January 13, 1961:

WITNESSES HEARD IN PRIVATE

The press and public were excluded from the magistrates' court at Feltham, Middlesex, yesterday during the hearing of part of the evidence against Arthur Albert Jones, a 44-year-old fitter-welder, of Ely Road, Hounslow, Middlesex, who is charged with raping an 11-year-old girl (referred to only as Barbara) who returned to her home in Twickenham at about 1.30 on the morning of September 10 in a distressed condition, suffering injuries from a sexual assault and also, according to the doctor who examined her, from having been 'half-strangled'.

Before the first of the police witnesses was called, Jones's counsel, Mr Michael Hoare, asked for the court to be cleared, saying that it was impossible to conceive that any jury who would try the case, if it were committed for trial, would not already have some idea of the facts and of what the evidence was going to be. In his submission, he read part of the summing-up by Mr Justice Devlin at the trial of Dr John Bodkin Adams at the Old Bailey in 1957:

'I would like to say this, and I say it with the authority of the Lord Chief Justice. . . . I think it would have been wiser in this case if the preliminary proceedings before the magistrates had been held in private, because when you have a case which arouses widespread discussion, it is inevitable that reports should appear in the press. As I reminded you [the jury] at the beginning of the case, the committal proceedings were quite different from the proceedings as they emerged in this court. They would be read by the public consequently – and by members of the public who might be asked to serve on the jury.'*

The magistrates decided that the hearing should proceed in public but that Mr Hoare could object at any stage. Having accepted that decision, defence counsel objected when the first police witness was called, and the court was cleared.

---

* In April 1957, Dr Adams was acquitted at the Central Criminal Court on a charge of murdering one of his patients in his general practice at Eastbourne. At the committal proceedings, the prosecution had led evidence of the circumstances in which two other patients of Dr Adams had died, but that evidence was not given at the trial. Two months later, as the result of Mr Justice Devlin's comments, the Home Secretary, R. A. Butler, appointed Lord Tucker to be chairman of a departmental committee on Proceedings Before Examining Justices. In its report, published in July 1958 (HMSO Cmnd. 479), the committee recommended that 'unless the accused has been discharged or until the trial has ended, any report of committal proceedings should be restricted to particulars of the name of the accused, the charge, the decision of the court and the like'. An amended form of the recommendation (allowing restriction of media coverage at the request of the defence) became law, and is presently embodied in section 8 of the Magistrates' Courts Act, 1980.

Thursday, March 16:

BEAUTY-PARLOUR GOSSIP THAT BROKE AN ALIBI

Yesterday at the Old Bailey, at the end of the trial of Arthur Albert Jones for the rape of a 12-year-old Girl Guide referred to only as Barbara, he hung his head as the foreman of the all-male jury, Mr Christopher Winn, the former Oxford and England rugby player, accounced the verdict of Guilty, which had been arrived at after nearly three hours of deliberation. Jones's teenage son and married daughter were sitting beside the dock, but his wife Grace was in the matron's rest-room. Mrs Jones broke down when she was told the verdict.

It was gossip which broke the alibi fabricated by Jones, with the help of his wife and sister-in-law. The three had agreed to say that on September 9, at the time of the offence, Jones was with his sister-in-law, Mrs Ivy Eldridge, at her home in Beckenham, Kent. But later, after all three had made statements to that effect, Mrs Eldridge's daughter Veronica, who works at a beauty parlour in Curzon Street, Mayfair, confided in another assistant that her mother had lied to the police. On December 28, the colleague telephoned Scotland Yard, and Jones was arrested as he left work that evening. Shortly before, senior investigators, having combed through hundreds of statements taken from men in the Twickenham and Hounslow areas, had begun to suspect that Jones's alibi was false – for, as one detective has explained, 'We felt that the actors in this alibi story seemed just a little bit too well rehearsed.'

At the time of Jones's arrest, the police had started tracing and questioning the owners of black Vauxhall Wyvern cars throughout the country. Motor taxation authorities had told them that of some 199,000 Vauxhalls registered between 1951 and 1954, about 44,000 were painted black.

It was learned that, from the time of the attack on the child, Jones had pursued his lone-wolf life. Every Friday at 4.30 p.m., he would leave his workshop at the firm of F. F. Deveta, in Hounslow, where he earned £18 a week as a fitter, and drive home in his black Vauxhall, FAN 342. At the well-furnished council house where he had lived for 10 years, he would put on one of his five suits and, at about half-past seven, set out for Henekey's bar in Hounslow for his three pints of draught cider. Usually by ten o'clock he was on his way into the West End, where, as he admitted during the trial, he had on at least one occasion picked up a prostitute. Friday night over, he was a home-bird for the rest of the week, mending radios and watches, doing odd jobs around the house, and making more cider in his alcohol-still.

His neighbours considered him stand-offish. They would see him cleaning and polishing his car at weekends, but words were seldom exchanged. It was the same at his work, where few of his mates could regard him as a friend.

A native of the Kent seaside town of Folkestone, he joined the Army, giving a false age, when he was 15, but was discharged after two years, when his real age was discovered. Between that time, in 1933, and soon after the start of the Second World War, six years later, he worked for 15 engineering firms. In 1940 he joined the Royal Army Service Corps as a driver, and served, mostly in Britain, until his discharge in February 1946, when he resumed working as a fitter-welder.

The vital evidence against Jones was given, both before the trial and during it, by his young victim, Barbara. Detectives have nothing but praise for how, soon after her ordeal, she gave them an accurate description of the man and of his car. She never wavered from her statement, and it led to the dramatic moments on March 7, the first day of the trial, when, sitting at a table beside Mr Justice Hilbery, she was asked by Mr Mervyn Griffith-Jones, prosecuting, if she could see her attacker. Pale-faced but looking straight at the man in the dock, she pointed at him and said: 'Over there.' The judge then ordered the defendant to stand up. Jones – ruddy complexioned, with black hair brushed diagonally back from a centre parting and wearing a smartly-cut grey suit and suede shoes – got to his feet, and the judge, in a kind voice, asked Barbara: 'Is that the man?'

Barbara answered softly through a microphone: 'Yes.'

Mr Griffith-Jones: 'Any doubt about that at all?'

Barbara: 'No.'

Earlier, Mr Griffith-Jones had said that, in her description of her attacker, Barbara had said that the man had a scar on his right cheek. After the judge had examined a long diagonal scar on the lower part of Jones's right jaw, an usher escorted Jones over to the jury box, where he turned and showed the jurors the scar, then returned to the dock.

Mr Norman Skelhorn, QC,* defending, did not object to the Crown's leading Barbara in her evidence. Later, he said that he might seek leave to recall Barbara – but the judge, interrupting, said: 'I am not going to have Barbara brought back for anyone. A child of that age ought not to be harassed and examined and cross-examined more than necessary.'

The Crown case was that at about 9.15 on the evening of September 9, when Barbara was cycling towards her home after a Girl Guides meeting, a man standing beside a car stopped her and said: 'Do you think you can help me? I'm a policeman. Would you like to see my badge?' He held out a wallet, which she felt, noticing only that it was embossed with some kind of badge. He then told her that he was investigating the theft of a bicycle and that her bicycle looked like the stolen one. He told her to leave it against a tree and get into his car, saying that he would drive her home and then to the police station. He did not drive her home.

Once she was in the car, he produced a revolver. After driving for several miles, they reached a level-crossing, where he offered her a mint sweet from a cubby-hole in the dashboard. She took it and put the wrapper in her blazer pocket. The man also took a wristwatch on a 'whitish' strap from his pocket and showed it to her.

After driving into a lane and parking, he raped her inside the car, having punched her in the face when she tried to struggle free. He seized her by the neck, and Barbara thought that she was suffocating. When Barbara asked him why he had done that, he answered: 'I wanted to frighten you.' Then he forced her out of the car, took a grey blanket from the boot, forced her on to it, and again raped her. Mr Griffith-Jones said that 'they struggled for some 10 minutes before he told her to get back into the front seat of the car. And then, having finished his filthy purposes, he drove the little girl back to the outskirts of London.' On the way, he told her to keep her head down as he did not want to get into trouble. When he dropped her off near her home, he said to her: 'Do you think you would recognise me again?' She said that she would not.

Barbara ran home, arriving there at about 1.20 a.m. As her mother greeted her, she sobbed: 'Oh, Mummy, it was horrible! He tried to strangle me.' Mr Griffith-Jones said that the child's lips were swollen, her mouth was covered with blood, her eyes were protruding, her face was bruised, and there were scratches down her leg. She was laughing hysterically.

A doctor who examined her shortly afterwards was of the opinion that full intercourse had taken place 'recently'. Her clothes were handed to the police for examination, and a very small fibre of an unusual yellow colour was found in the hem of her skirt.

It was not until November 24 that Jones was interviewed by a policeman, Detective Sergeant Walter Nicholson, who saw him at his home. The sergeant noticed that on the front seat of Jones's Vauxhall car was a check rug, and on the back seat a greenish one. A packet of mints, not of the kind that had been accepted by Barbara, was also in the car. Jones said to the sergeant: 'I know I answer the description of the man described in the newspapers, but I can be definite that on that night I was at the home of my sister-in-law at Beckenham. I'm sure of that because we returned from our holiday on Saturday, September 3, and on the following Friday I took my wife and son to see Mrs Eldridge. It was the first time since our return from holiday that we had visited Beckenham.'

'As you will hear,' Mr Griffith-Jones told the jury, 'that was a false alibi, and it was this defendant, with a scar on his face, and owning a black Vauxhall car, who was putting it up. He himself has since admitted that it was not true.' Jones was told by the police that inquiries would have to be made at Beckenham, and he was warned not to communicate with Mrs Eldridge until that had been done. 'It would appear that the police had hardly turned the corner outside than that the defendant, ignoring the warning, went hot-foot to see Mrs Eldridge to arrange for her support for the false alibi he had given. By the next morning, when the police arrived to question Mrs Eldridge, Jones and his wife had been to see her, and she gave a statement to the police which certainly put them off the trail.'

The inquiries continued until December 28. That evening, when Jones was questioned by Detective Superintendent Frederick Hixson, he repeated the alibi he had given on November 24. His home was searched. Among the things found there were a plastic wallet bearing an embossed badge, a wristwatch with a broken strap of white metal, and a box of .22 ammunition – but no gun. Later, Jones's clothing was examined, and yellow wool fibre, identical to the fibre found in the hem of Barbara's skirt, was found on one of his jackets.

When questioned, Jones admitted that he had not seen Mrs Eldridge on the night of September 9. After being cautioned, he sat silent for a moment, staring at the floor. Then he said: 'I don't remember now what happened.' Later, when he was charged with rape, he said: 'I don't want to say anything now. I'll wait and see my solicitor before I say anything.'

While he was on remand, his wife visited him in a cell at Feltham magistrates' court, and said to him in the presence of a policeman: 'The police have turned the house inside out, looking for things. They've searched everywhere. They said they were looking for your revolver, but they didn't find it. What have you done with it?' Jones replied: 'I don't know. I can't remember.' She advised him to tell everything to his solicitor, Mr Matthissen. He then broke down and sobbed 'uncontrollably'. Later, when he was visited by two policemen in the cell, he said: 'These terrible things that I have done are getting on my nerves. I want to tell somebody about it now, but I've promised my wife that I'll only tell Mr Matthissen when I see him next week in Brixton prison. I don't want to break that promise.'

On January 4, the solicitor handed the police a statement made by Jones. It said that on the night of September 9 he had gone to Henekey's public house in Hounslow High Street, and at about half-past nine, after speaking to his friend Charlie Silvester, had gone to another public house at Shepherd's Bush, west London, leaving there at about 10 p.m. He was just sitting in his car, lighting a cigar, when a pretty half-caste girl tapped on the window. She told him that the police were around, and he let her get in. Saying that she was 'on the game', she invited him home for £2. He went with her, and afterwards they left her flat and drove to a night-club in Soho. The girl told him that he had better not come in with her as the man who looked after her was there and might cause trouble. After leaving her, he drove around until he came to a restaurant which had a sign saying 'Chicken Barbecue'. He went in for a meal and then drove home, arriving at 12.30 a.m. His wife was in bed but awake. She was very annoyed, and wanted to know where he had been. He told her: 'I've been out with a few of the boys.' Next morning, his wife would not speak to him, and she remained annoyed for several days. During that time, and afterwards, he was ribbed by fellow-workers because he owned a black Vauxhall and had a scar on his face. He realised that he could not substantiate his story about being with a prostitute on the night of the crime. He and his son talked about it, and he eventually thought of saying that he was at Beckenham. He spoke to his wife about the proposed alibi, and she agreed to speak to her sister, leaving it up to her to decide whether or not to help him out.

During his summation, Mr Justice Hilbery said that it was difficult to find adequate or appropriate adjectives for the attack on Barbara, a child who was not very well developed, rather frail to look at — but highly intelligent. 'If a malign fate has created a man other than the defendant, who is about 40 years of age, is heavily built, has thin lips, dark hair and a scar on the side of his face, and who owns a black Vauxhall car in which he carries mint sweets, two rugs, and so on, it is an overwhelming disaster to the accused that he himself fits that description. Unless there is another such man, it would seem, would it not, that the accused must be the man who committed this crime?'

As soon as the jury had given their answer to that question, the judge said that he had seldom listened to a clearer case or heard more overwhelming evidence than that which had convicted Arthur Albert Jones of 'this atrocious rape'.

Those who had had to listen to all the details knew how foul a crime it was. 'Nothing but a severe sentence can be adequate in such a case, where the rape was accompanied by such horrible details and committed with such brutality on a child of such tender years.' The sentence imposed by Mr Justice Hilbery was 14 years' imprisonment.

Wednesday, May 17:

JONES FOR TRIAL
AFTER SECRET HEARING

At Bow Street yesterday, Arthur Albert Jones, smartly dressed in a grey-striped suit, white shirt and red tie, stepped into the dock of No. 1 Court at 10.31 a.m. Before any charge was read out to the Chief Metropolitan Magistrate, Sir Robert Blundell, Mr T. H. K. Berry rose and said: 'I appear to defend, and before the proceedings open, I have an application that I should like to make in closed court.' And so, at 10.33 a.m., the court was cleared. Six minutes later, the public and the press were re-admitted, and the magistrate announced:

'In this case, I am asked by Mr Berry to exercise my powers under the Magistrates' Courts Act to say that the hearing should be in private. In ordinary circumstances I should not accede to the application, but having regard for the reasons which have been put forward to me, they appear sufficient, and I shall accede to the request.'

Again the court was cleared, and evidence from the Crown witnesses was taken in camera until 5.20 p.m., when the court was re-opened. Only one person, a bespectacled elderly woman, was in the public gallery to hear the formal committal of Jones for trial at the Old Bailey, accused of the murder of 12-year-old Brenda Jean Nash.

Court officials at Bow Street could not recall an earlier occasion when the whole hearing of committal proceedings involving a murder charge had been heard there in camera.

Tuesday, June 20:

'TWO CRIMES EVIL BEYOND ALL ADJECTIVES'

A 3-inch piece of tarnished jewellery chain, dangled by Crown counsel on the first day of the trial of Arthur Albert Jones for the murder of Brenda Nash [June 12], and the courage of a young hairdresser, were the two vital factors in the case.

The chain, exhibit No. 7 at the trial, was found in the grass under the child's head after her body was found at Yateley on December 11. Jones knew that district from his period as an Army driver at Aldershot during the Second World War. The police are convinced that he dropped the chain unknowingly from the pocket of his blue blazer as he knelt to lay Brenda's body in the undergrowth on Yateley Common, having driven her there dead in the boot of his 1952 black Vauxhall, FAN 342. In a search of his home after his arrest on December 28, two pieces of chain were found, one wrapped in a sheet of newspaper in a drawer in the back bedroom, the other on top of the wardrobe, and forensic scientists established that those pieces of chain were identical in pattern and of the same chemical composition as the piece dropped at Yateley.

Jones may now regret his passion for hoarding everything, which was connected with his boastfulness that no do-it-yourself repair job was too difficult for him. For months he had carried those pieces of chain on him, meaning to link them together for his 16-year-old son Martin, who likes wearing chains round his neck. Jones's well-furnished council house at Hounslow was stacked with all kinds of things he had collected: radios, watches, car-parts, motors and much else.

It was Lesley Carruthers who led the police to Jones. Once she did so, the evidence of the matching pieces of chain convinced them that he was the man who had raped the little girl called Barbara and killed Brenda Nash. On October 31, Miss Carruthers was chatting over coffee in the rest-room of a Curzon Street beauty salon with her colleague Christine Eldridge, when Christine let slip that her Uncle Arthur had called at her home in Beckenham on two occasions, each time to plead with her mother to support a false alibi – one for the night of September 9, the other for the night of October 28. The gossip meant nothing to Lesley at the time, for Brenda Nash was then only 'missing'. Within a week, she left for another job; but on December 28, 16 days after the first reports of the finding of Brenda Nash's body, 'something clicked in her mind,' and she at once told the police of her conversation with Christine Eldridge. Mrs Ivy Eldridge, who had previously been questioned by detectives and had supported both of her brother-in-law's false alibis, was questioned again. Now she admitted that she had lied on his behalf.

A senior detective has said: 'No doubt, in the end, we would have got back to Jones, but the public spirit of Lesley Carruthers in coming forward shortened our task by many months. She might indirectly have saved another life.'

Once in custody, Jones admitted the falsity of his alibis, but insisted that on the night when Brenda Nash was abducted, he was with a prostitute in the West End (and that for the latter part of the night when Barbara was raped, he was with another prostitute). Some of his few acquaintances confirmed that it was his habit on Friday nights to drive into London for that purpose. Even his wife said that, and during the trial she claimed that the only reason she agreed to support his false alibi was to prevent his Friday-night activities becoming generally known.

There was ample evidence to charge him with the rape of Barbara, and that was duly done. But the Director of Public Prosecutions ruled that there was insufficient evidence for a murder charge. Therefore, teams of detectives were sent to London prisons to find men who had talked with him while he was on remand in Brixton on the rape charge. Among 60 prisoners who were interviewed, 16 were to be convicted of murder.

One of the prisoners, 26-year-old Ian James Roberts, gave evidence for the prosecution. He stated that he had a long criminal record, that for periods he had been certified as insane, and that, having recently been convicted of obtaining money by false pretences, he was 'waiting to go in for mental treatment at Wormwood Scrubs prison'. He testified that in March, while he was in the hospital at Brixton prison, he had a conversation with Jones: 'I think he was under the impression that I was in for murder, and he asked me if I was doing life.... I asked him if he was the man who was questioned about the Brenda Nash murder, and he said he was .... He said something about various spots on his clothes that would

not match, and also that the police would never find enough evidence to pin it on him.... He said he had done or did it – I'm not sure which. He had rather a kind of smile on his face.'

Under cross-examination by Mr Norman Brodrick, QC, Roberts agreed that he had considered retracting his statement about Jones's confession, and when re-examined by Mr Griffith-Jones, he said that that was because 'I had enough trouble and worry of my own. A prison officer said it was my duty to say what I did, but I didn't consider it was my duty, because I'm a criminal myself.'

MR GRIFFITH-JONES: All that the jury are concerned to discover is whether or not the conversation with the defendant took place. Are you telling the truth today?

ROBERTS: So far as I can remember, yes. I've not got a very retentive memory.

There was also evidence from three men, each of whom identified Jones as a man they had seen standing by a parked car near Brenda Nash's home on the night of October 28, only a minute or so before she was due to pass close to that spot after attending the Girl Guides meeting.

Yesterday, towards the end of his summing-up, Mr Justice Sachs referred to 'the curtain which the law imposes around conversations between solicitor and client,' and went on to say that he thought that the advice to Jones from his solicitor, Mr Matthissen, was 'If you are pressed, tell more lies'. The judge continued: 'I must say that I never heard of a solicitor giving that advice before, and I hope I won't again. You, members of the jury, must not blame Jones if you think he acted on that advice, although what impression it makes on a man to be told to tell more lies as long as it suits him, I don't know.'

Mr Justice Sachs completed his summing-up at 24 minutes past noon, and the jury of three women and nine men retired to consider their verdict.

The judge and most of the counsel had left the court, and police officers were chatting outside, expecting a long wait, when the word spread: 'They're coming back.' Mr Norman Brodrick, who had not even left the court, raised his eyebrows in surprise. Court officials were hurriedly recalled, and at 12.32 p.m. the jury returned.

Jones, standing between two warders, bowed his head at the verdict of Guilty. When asked if he wanted to say anything, he answered loudly: 'No, sir.'

It was at this stage, when everyone was expecting Mr Justice Sachs to pronounce the formal sentence of life imprisonment, that he created legal history.

He called Superintendent Hixson into the witness-box and asked him: 'What is the present position regarding the prisoner?'

The detective replied: 'He is serving a term of fourteen years' imprisonment passed on him in this court on March 15 for unlawful sexual intercourse with a girl aged 11.'

The JUDGE: Was it a case which had any affinity to the present one?

The DETECTIVE: It was on all fours with the present case. The only difference was that the child did not die.

The JUDGE: Was she a Girl Guide?

The DETECTIVE: Yes, she was, but not of the same troop.

The judge then entered into discussion with counsel as to whether he could pass a life sentence to follow a term already being served, rather than concurrently. Mr Brodrick submitted that he could not.

Then the judge passed sentence:

'Arthur Albert Jones, you have been found guilty now of two crimes evil beyond all adjectives. It is proper that you should serve your sentence for the first crime and that neither as a matter of fact nor of appearance should it cease to be operative. In these circumstances, I will pass on you a sentence according to statute, that you be sentenced to life imprisonment.

'For the protection of the public I think, firstly, that it should be consecutive, to commence on the expiration of your existing sentence, and secondly, that it would be lamentable indeed if, on the sentence that I have just passed, you did not serve a far longer time than on the first.'

The judge paused for a moment, then said curtly: 'Take him away.'

The main ground of Jones's appeal, which was heard on July 25 and 26, was that Mr Justice Sachs had allowed him to be cross-examined upon the similarity of the stories he had told of his actions on the night of the rape of Barbara and on the night of the abduction of Brenda Nash, which might have conveyed to the jury that he had been convicted of a similar offence. The Court dismissed the appeal, giving its reasons on October 5: significant similarities between the two cases would have rendered admissible at the murder-trial evidence as to the circumstances in which the offence of rape was committed; before putting the questions to Jones, Mr Griffith-Jones had invited the judge's discretion, and in the Appeal Court's opinion, the questions were admissible in law. The appeal against the consecutiveness of the sentences was also dismissed, 'since the practical effect between the sentences being consecutive or concurrent was the same'.

The appeal on the admissibility of the cross-examination was carried to the House of Lords, where it was heard between November 2 and 7 by Viscount Simmonds, Lord Reid, Lord Denning, Lord Morris of Borth-y-Gest, and Lord Devlin. Having reserved judgment until February 7, 1962, they then dismissed the appeal.

1966 . . .

Wednesday, May 7:

BRADY AND HINDLEY GAOLED FOR LIFE

'Calculated, Cruel and Cold-Blooded' Killings

Life sentences were passed at Chester last night on Ian Brady, 28, and Myra Hindley, 23, found guilty of murder in the 'Bodies on the Moors' trial.

For what Mr Justice Fenton Atkinson called 'three calculated, cruel and cold-blooded murders,' Brady was sentenced to three concurrent terms of life imprisonment. His victims were Edward Evans, 17; Lesley Ann Downey, 10; and John Kilbride, 12.

Brady's mistress, Hindley, received concurrent life sentences for 'two equally horrible murders,' having been found guilty of the Evans and Downey murders and not guilty of murdering Kilbride. She was also given a concurrent seven-year sentence for harbouring Brady, knowing that he had murdered Kilbride.

The bodies of the children were uncovered on the Pennine moors seven months ago. Evans was killed with an axe in a council house at Hattersley, Hyde, Cheshire.

Brady stood with his arms folded, staring straight ahead, as the jury foreman replied 'Guilty' to the murder charges.

The Judge told him: 'In your case, I pass the only sentence which the law now allows: three concurrent sentences of life imprisonment.'

Without a sign of emotion, Glasgow-born Brady, a lean, thin-faced figure, was led below after sentence, followed by Hindley, the shorthand-typist who was 'infatuated' with him.

The sentencing of Brady and Hindley came almost as an anti-climax to the 14 days of drawn-out horrific evidence. It was all over within seven minutes after the jury returned from their smoke-filled retiring room.

The case opened exactly seven months ago today after 18-year-old David Smith witnessed the axe-murder of Edward Evans.

The jury took three of the 186 exhibits with them when they retired: Brady's notebook with the name of John Kilbride written inside, the 'murder plan' for the disposal of the body of Evans, and Hindley's shoes spotted with his blood.

The Judge had a special word of praise for the police after passing sentence: 'These matters were only brought to light by a police investigation of the utmost skill and thoroughness.'

The discovery of a left-luggage ticket tucked down the back of Hindley's Communion Prayer Book was typical of the thoroughness which had led to the case. The ticket was for two suitcases containing pornographic books, nude pictures of Lesley Ann Downey, and the 'harrowing' tape-recording of the dead girl's voice.

The Home Office said last night that a person sentenced to life imprisonment was liable to be detained for the whole of his natural life, but the Home Secretary had powers to release such a person on licence. The Home Secretary could release a life-sentence prisoner after reviewing the case and consulting the Lord Chief Justice and the judge concerned in the trial. 'Obviously, public safety would be considered in any review of a life sentence for murder.' A judge could recommend a minimum period of years a person must serve.

No reference to a minimum sentence was made by Mr Justice Fenton Atkinson when he passed sentence on Brady and Hindley.

Detective Chief Superintendent Arthur Benfield, head of Cheshire CID, who led the police investigation of the case, said last night that police chiefs from several forces would be meeting shortly to examine their files on missing young people.

Among the names in the files are Keith Bennett, nine, and Pauline Read, 16, both of Manchester, who disappeared some time ago and who were mentioned during the Moors trial. Brady said in court that he had been questioned about the two children.

WORSHIPPER OF NAZIS AND HIS WILLING PUPIL IN MURDER

Ian Brady, who during phases in his life was known as 'The Undertaker' and 'Dracula,' was the product of Glasgow's Gorbals area, an illegitimate child. He idolised Hitler, Nazism and horror, delighted in reading about perversions, and was so convinced of his own superiority that he thought he could dictate to Fate. Perhaps he believed that he had such influence when he met Myra Hindley.

She became a willing and efficient pupil to this teacher, whose textbooks were on murder, torture and sexual perversions.

Brady went through three phases in his life, showing viciousness as a child, then a period of retraction within himself, and finally the demented philosophy which led him to the dock.

Hindley's life also followed a three-phase pattern, but her story might well have been very different if the 'million-to-one chance' that brought them together in 1961, when she was 18, had not materialised.

A war-time baby from a Manchester slum area, her association with Brady brought out and developed an inhuman streak. This changed her from a young woman with natural maternal instincts into a sadist who took pleasure in watching a child being subjected to vile practices before being murdered.

Her phases of life went through a

Who goes where?

One of these two has his eye on the distance. Correct—it's the character in the pale suit, which in fact is made of a Tergal/cotton mixture in very narrow blue and white stripes, not only crease-resistant but literally washable! Self belt, pleatless trousers. He's heading for Santander and all stations south, will probably wind up in Vera Cruz or Honolulu, heavily sun-tanned but just as elegant as you see him now.

The other, who likes real beer and a proper breakfast, is driving north on Friday next. His slim-fitting jacket of covert cloth, in fawn, has what tailors call "hand-swelled" edges. His trousers, lightweight tweed, has what weavers call "windowpane" overcheck—dark brown on a golden cigar colour.

They are no longer on speaking terms as you can see. But you may pick up ideas from either, without taking sides.

Tergal/cotton slim fitting suit, in black/white or blue/white stripes. Sizes 36"—42". £18.17.6.

Poplin shirt with round collar in blue, pink, fawn, or dark grey. Sizes 14½—17. £2.19.6.

Covert cloth hacking jacket with centre vent. Sizes 36"—40". £18.10.0.

Lightweight windowpane check tweed trousers in brown or black/white. Waist 28"—34". £8.8.0.

Lightweight check poplin shirt with round collar, available in fawn/black, red/black or blue/black. Sizes 14½—17. £3.5.0.

reasonably normal childhood until she saw a child drown. Then came a phase of religious fervour before the complete degradation as the more-than-willing tool of Brady.

It ended with her accepting the Nazi 'ideals' and the philosophy of the Marquis de Sade, posing for pornographic photographs, and choosing the infamous Irma Grese, female 'Beast of Belsen,' as her 'heroine' and even carrying Grese's photograph with her.

Brady was born in a Glasgow maternity hospital on January 2, 1938, the son of Margaret Stewart, a tea-room waitress. He was soon sent to foster-parents, Mr and Mrs Sloan, with whom he lived in Camden Street, Hutchesontown.

He had a bad temper and is remembered as a baby who threw tantrums if he did not get what he wanted. He was a 'terrible heartbreak' for his foster-mother, and, as he grew older, would bang his head against a wall when in a rage. He developed a cruel streak, delighting in torturing cats.

Mr Frank Flanagan, who lived immediately below Brady's home at the time, said: 'Once Ian threw a cat out of a top-floor window, and on another occasion boasted he had buried a cat under a gravestone because he wanted to see how long it would live. We released the animal.'

Outside school, Brady took little interest in the play of other children. Local people recall how he was absorbed by horror films and would spend his pocket-money on going to see such films over and over again. This earned him the name 'Dracula'.

When he was 11, he moved with his foster-parents from the dingy tenement to spacious, airy surroundings on a new estate at Pollok. He seemed to have left behind his cruel streak, and is remembered as 'the boy with little to say and who did not attract attention'.

Meanwhile, Hindley was living in Bannock Street, Gorton, Manchester, with her grandmother, Mrs Ellen Maybury. She did well at school, being above average intelligence.

She was 13 when she saw the boy drown. Deeply moved by the accident, she organised a collection for a wreath and then started attending a Roman Catholic church, taking the name 'Veronica' and attending Mass regularly.

She kept the prayer book given to her after her first Holy Communion, and it was in this that police found the ticket for two suitcases left at a Manchester railway station. The cases contained the tape-recordings, documents and photographs which weighed so heavily against herself and Brady in court.

Brady, having completed his education at 15, was going through another phase of trying to settle down. He worked for a short period as a messenger-boy at a local butcher's shop and then at a shipyard. Meanwhile, his mother had moved to Manchester, and in May, 1950, married Mr Patrick Brady.

A year later, her son first came under police notice. He appeared in Glasgow Sheriff Court on charges of housebreaking and attempted theft, and was put on probation for two years. In July, 1952, he was admonished in Govan Court on charges of housebreaking and theft. Then came nine charges of housebreaking and theft, for which he received two years' probation, a condition of the order being that he went to live with his mother in Manchester.

He changed his name to Brady and found work with his step-father while living at Cuttell Street, Gorton, but he slipped back to crime. In December 1955, he appeared on a theft charge and was sent to Borstal.

Upon his release, early in 1958, he joined his mother, who had moved with her husband to Westmoreland Street, Longsight. After working for eight months in a brewery, he went to Millwards Merchandise, a small chemical distributing firm in Levenshulme Road, Gorton, where two years later he was to meet Hindley.

Between school-leaving and joining Millwards in 1961, Hindley had several boy friends, but her closest attachment was with Ronald Sinclair, formerly of Dalkeith Street, Gorton, to whom she became engaged. This friendship lasted almost three years. Hindley broke off the engagement after just over a year because, she said, 'he is too childish'.

She then revealed an interest in Germany and obtained application forms for joining the NAAFI so that she could go there. This was before she met Brady. When she met him, she gave up the idea and 'set her cap' at Brady.

He had already lost most of his friends at the firm because of his 'Hitler was right' and 'Britain is decadent' attitudes. He was anti-British, anti-religion and anti-convention. He openly expressed admiration for some of the German war-leaders, bought records of Nazi speeches and German martial music, and made tape recordings of similar material.

He ignored Hindley when she joined the firm, and it was almost a year before she 'won through' and they had their first date.

Brady called Hindley his 'Myra Hess'. They spent holidays together in Scotland and travelled to and from work together; when Hindley moved with her grandmother to an overspill estate at Hattersley, Cheshire, Brady began living with her.

It was at that house, 16 Wardle Brook Avenue, that police found the body of Edward Evans on October 7, 1965.

The change in Hindley after the beginning of her assocation with Brady was noticeable. Her emotionless reaction to murder and her enjoyment of degrading practices show how complete was the change. Her one stable emotion was love of her dog Puppet.

Brady, too, had now become completely perverted. He still thought he was better than everyone and that no one could or dare laugh at him. He did not know that there were two sisters who lived near his mother's home at Longsight who thought him a figure of fun. He used then to wear a long dark overcoat reaching almost to his ankles. They laughed at this and, because of it, nicknamed him 'The Undertaker'.

Leading article:

ULTIMATE CORRUPTION

Avarice, fear, lust, jealousy, revenge – the common motives for murder are so related to the temptations to which all human flesh is subject that few sensitive spirits can exclude moments of sympathy and pity for the prisoner in the dock. The terrible fascination exerted by the 'Moors' trial over the public mind throughout this country and far beyond reflects the sense that here has broken into the human life we know a thing utterly inhuman; that we have had a glimpse of naked evil, unashamed. Nevertheless, these two pitiless child-killers are not satanic creatures from another world, but examples of human nature reduced to extreme corruption; and the evidence has indicated something of the process of their descent into depravity.

'Sadism' is cruelty rooted in sexual perversion, or exercised as a stimulant to perverted erotic sensation. In this case, the actual works of the Marquis de Sade, with much else of a similar tendency, were the drugs with which Ian Brady and Myra Hindley poisoned their minds. Other malign figures exercised a spell upon them: they appear to have soaked themselves in the mythology of Hitler and the bestial Nazi crimes against humanity. Our generation has reacted strongly against the principle of literary censorship, and a single dreadful example is not a ground for repudiating the belief in the free circulation of ideas, even those most repellent to the normal mind. Nevertheless, this appalling case is a salutary reminder that the printed word can deepen depravity which other things, including horror films, may have started. It is a case not to be forgotten in discussion of issues affecting the exposure of susceptible minds to corrupting influences.

A secondary point needing public consideration in the light of the trial arises from the revelation that David Smith, the leading witness for the Crown [present at the murder of Edward Evans], by contracting with a newspaper [the *News of the World*] for the conditional publication of his story, had acquired a vested interest in the conviction of the accused. The judge did not think this in fact vitiated his evidence, but held this new development of 'cheque-book journalism' (which generally buys only the memoirs of the criminal himself) to be obviously undesirable. Plainly, it must stop.

'Way of the World' column, May 10:

WAIT FOR IT

As soon as the verdict in the 'Moors' case was given, I began wondering which progressive public figure would be the first to announce that the whole community, and all of us personally, shared in the murderers' guilt.

It must have been touch and go. But this time the honour of making this age-old announcement has fallen to Mr Leo Abse, Labour MP for Pontypool, who has duly declared to a meeting of Cambridge University Labour and Liberal groups that the whole community is ultimately responsible for Brady's terrible deeds.

His fellow-progressives should not repine too much at having missed the chance of getting in this crack at the doctrine of Original Sin before he did. Another big opportunity for progressive utterance is coming up.

Who will be the first to declare that anyone, from President Johnson downwards, who does not unreservedly condemn the American campaign in Vietnam, shares the guilt of murder a thousand times worse than the crimes of Brady and Hindley, those passive victims of an ill-organised society?

Saturday, November 30, 1985: Ian Brady, who is now 47, was transferred yesterday from Gartree Prison, Market Harborough, Leicestershire, to a secure mental hospial, Park Lane Special Hospital, near Liverpool. He is understood to be suffering from paranoid psychosis, hearing imaginary voices and having hallucinations, and his weight has dropped from 13 to eight stone.

In making the announcement of the transfer, the Home Office stressed that it would not cut short his life-sentence.

Wednesday, November 19, 1986:

HINDLEY SPEAKS OUT

Myra Hindley last night broke her silence about two children who have been missing for 21 years. After being interviewed for the second successive day about the disappearances of Pauline Reade, who was 16, and Keith Bennett, who was 12, and as police prepared to renew their search of Pennine moorland, she dictated a statement to her solicitor, who had visited her in Cookham Wood Prison, Kent:

'I received a letter, the first ever, from the mother of one of the missing children [Keith Bennett], and this has caused me enormous distress. I have agreed to help the Manchester police in any way possible, and have today identified, from photographs and maps, places that I know were of particular interest to Ian Brady, some of which I visited with him. I have searched my heart and memory, and given whatever help I can give to the police.

'I'm glad, at long last, to have been given this opportunity, and I will continue to do all that I can. I hope that one day people will be able to forgive the wrong I have done, and know the truth of what I have not done. But, for now, I want the police to be able to conclude their inquiries, so ending public speculation and the private anguish of those directly involved.'

Hindley's solicitor said later that contempt for Brady was one of the factors which had led his client to decide to help the police: 'I think that the feeling of contempt has been working away over the years, and it became something she could not contain any longer.'

Lord Longford, the social cam-paigner, has defended Hindley's right to be considered for parole on the grounds that she has been con-verted to Roman Catholicism and now regrets the killings.

Wednesday, November 26:

Ian Brady was interviewed by a detective for two hours yesterday in the presence of his solicitor, Benedict Birnberg, in Park Lane Special Hospital. Afterwards, Mr Birnberg said that Brady had become 'a changed man' since being committed to hospital, and was fully conscious of happenings in the past week: 'He sees television, he reads newspapers – and the whole media circus, which is the term he uses, does affect him.'

The renewed search of Saddle-worth Moor by police, who are using dogs trained to sniff out buried bodies, continued yesterday in rain and mist. Initial discussions have been held between the police and Home Office staff about the possi-bility of Hindley's being allowed to join the search.

Wednesday, December 17:

Myra Hindley directed police to a new area of Saddleworth Moor yes-terday after being flown there to help in the hunt for the graves of the two missing children.

The operation, involving hundreds of police, began before first light. Hindley was driven at high speed from Cookham Wood Prison. Then, as road-blocks were set up around the moor 200 miles away, she was transferred to a Scot-land Yard helicopter for the journey north. By the time the helicopter landed at 8.40 a.m., after flying over the area of the search, all roads leading to the moor were sealed off; dogs and guns faced anyone who thought of trying to break the cordon, and the police were so anxious to prevent any photographs of Hindley's return to the scene of her crimes that officers themselves had been warned not to carry personal cameras.

Two figures emerged from the helicopter, one carrying a shoulder-bag, and they were met by a convoy of police vehicles which escorted them to the mobile headquarters on the moor. Throughout the day, Hindley wore dark-blue waterproof clothing and a balaclava, just like the police who surrounded her, and it was hard to pick her out in the swirling mist.

As police dug up spots she indicated, Ian Brady watched TV and listened to radio news-bulletins on the search in the secure hospital on Merseyside where he is kept. His lawyer, who spent 20 minutes on the phone to him, described Brady's attitude as 'non-committal'.

After spending eight hours on the moor, Hindley was taken back to the prison in Kent.

Saturday, April 4, 1987:

Myra Hindley has confessed to having killed the two children whose bodies police are still seeking on Pennine moorland. Though she has been taken to the moors twice to pinpoint the area to search, she had previously only hinted at her involvement.

'I admitted my role in these awful events, and said that I consider myself to be as guilty as my former lover, Ian Brady, although our roles were different,' she said in a statement issued through her solicitor.

'I know that the parents of the missing children may never be able to forgive me and that no words of mine can ever express the remorse I now feel for what I did, and my refusal for so long to admit the crimes.

'I hope that my actions now in making my confession to the police will speak louder than any words. I want nothing more than to help find the bodies so that their poor relatives can at last have the comfort of giving them a Christian burial.'

She added that her request to the Home Office not to be considered for parole in 1990 should prove that she was not making the confession in the hope of an early release, and her solicitor pointed out that she could face additional murder charges.

Thursday, July 2:

Yesterday, police searching Saddleworth Moor found a body in a peatgrave in the Hollin Brown Knoll area above Oldham, close to the spot where Brady and Hindley buried one of their victims, 10-year-old Lesley Ann Downey, in 1964.

Saturday, July 4:

Yesterday, Ian Brady, a gaunt figure handcuffed to two detectives, spent nearly 11 hours in the bleak landscape of Saddleworth Moor. His return followed the discovery of the body of 16-year-old Pauline Reade in an area identified by his accomplice, Myra Hindley.

He was taken at dawn from the Park Lane Special Hospital to the Shiny Brook part of the moor. Plain-clothes policemen, some with guns, were stationed at key points overlooking the moor as Brady pointed out spots where bodies may have been buried.

His solicitor, Benedict Birnberg, afterwards said that, though the search was not successful, information Brady had given 'should enable the police to resolve the matter more quickly. He has expressed a wish to be given a second chance to go back and help further.'

Leading article:

The discovery of the body of Pauline Reade on Saddleworth Moor has provoked a new orgy of media attention upon both the police excavations and the criminals concerned. It is now being said that Ian Brady, who last year was alleged to be in a deteriorating mental condition, is willing to co-operate with police; Myra Hindley likewise.

We suggested some months ago, when the police search on the moors was resumed, that it was difficult to perceive any legitimate public interest being served by pursuing the operation. Nothing has happened since to change our view. It has been widely presumed for many years that the missing children were victims of Hindley and Brady. There is an argument that the bereaved parents deserve to know for certain what happened to their children. Yet we find it difficult to believe that the comfort to be gained from this knowledge outweighs the pain from the dreadful weight of new publicity and morbid curiosity that has now descended upon the families.

Some senior policemen give the appearance of being obsessed with the resolution of the outstanding Moors cases. Yet there is little doubt that those responsible for these crimes are already behind bars. It would seem infinitely more profitable to deploy the large police resources committed on the Moors to the pursuit of uncaptured criminals, who daily commit violent crimes in Greater Manchester. Plainly, now that a body has been found, there will have to be an inquest upon it. But it would be a scandalous misuse of public funds and resources if there was to be any suggestion of a new murder trial. The time has come for a halt to police excavations, and to visits by the murderers to the Moors in the glare of publicity which could please only the least admirable of policemen. There must also be no more discussion of any kind about the possible release of Brady or Hindley. Their own moral regeneration has nothing to do with the matter. What they did was simply too dreadful for society to contemplate granting their freedom.

Tuesday, August 4:

At the opening of an inquest in Oldham yesterday, it was stated that tests on the remains of Pauline Reade have established that her death was a crime.

In a faltering voice, the child's father, Amos Reade, said that he had been able to identify her from the pink and gold dress, white shoes and gold-coloured necklet she was wearing when she left their home, then in Wiles Street, Gorton, Manchester, on July 12, 1963.

The Coroner granted permission for the burial of Pauline's body on Thursday.

Tuesday, August 25:

The search for the body of Keith Bennett was called off last night. The detective who has led the nine-month excavations said that inquiries into the killing will continue.

Friday, January 15, 1988:

The Director of Public Prosecutions, Mr Allan Green, QC, announced yesterday that Ian Brady and Myra Hindley will not stand trial for the killings of Pauline Reade and Keith Bennett. His decision is believed to be based on his belief that neither of the murderers is ever likely to be released and his wish not to distress relatives of the victims unnecessarily. It is also probable that Brady would have been ruled unfit to plead had a trial been ordered.

Even if the Parole Board eventually recommended the release of either prisoner, the final decision would rest with the Home Secretary, and according to a Home Office source: 'It would take an extremely brave Home Secretary to allow either of those two out.'

Leading article; Saturday, March 19, 1994:

LIFE FOR A LIFE

The Home Secretary should countenance an important change in the law, which could go far to reconcile public opinion to the absence of capital punishment for murder. Legislation should be amended to ensure that in a relatively small number of the most serious cases, life imprisonment really does mean confinement until death. At present, a life sentence is almost invariably a piece of rhetoric, decreed with empty solemnity upon the conviction of a man or woman for taking another life. The real sentence served is at the discretion of the Home Secretary of the day. By one recent count, a total of 3106 prisoners were serving average periods of 11 to 12 years of their 'life sentences' in British prisons, before release on licence. The 28 years so far served by Moors murderer Myra Hindley is quite exceptional.

Having created a 'life means life' category, the Home Secretary should place Hindley in it. That would end, once and for all, the vexatious repetition of calls for her release. Her hopes are frequently lifted by allies outside, who raise the prospect of a favourable parole-board recommendation, which is dashed when the Home Office is reminded that public sentiment would still not stand for it.

Public revulsion and anger remain intense about the Moors murders three decades ago. Arrayed against public opinion, however, is a small group of liberal lawyers and prison reformers who reject the concept of permanent punishment for heinous crimes. Last year it was announced that their legal costs were being met by David Astor, former editor of *The Observer*, as a protest against the tabloid treatment of Hindley's case. But the public mood cannot be blamed on tabloid newspapers. It merely reflects the fact that most decent people vividly recall the details of this most repugnant of cases.

Yesterday, Lord Longford, who has befriended Hindley in prison, again demanded her release, declaring that no one should remain in prison indefinitely unless they are dangerous. His campaign indulges his personal pursuit of redemption at the expense of society. Life imprisonment is not an exercise in gratuitous sadism. It is simply right that when a crime of sufficient gravity has been committed, its perpetrator should be deemed to have forfeited the right to freedom in this world, whatever remission they might achieve in the next. Murderers may be granted forgiveness by the Church, by Lord Longford, by David Astor and by liberal opinion, but in the most grievous cases they should never again be granted liberty. Judges should be given the power to pass a literal life sentence upon conviction, in appropriate cases. This would obviously remain subject to review by the Appeal Court, but should thereafter be irrevocable.

'Way of the World' by Auberon Waugh; Monday, October 31:

Easing the Pain

Esther Rantzen, the television personality, has decided that the time has come to execute Myra Hindley and Ian Brady. Nearly 30 years after the crimes for which they were convicted, Rantzen feels that 'these people are almost like a different species. . . . I don't want them in the world'.

This change of heart has come about after a meeting with the mother of one of the victims on a

radio chat-show. The victim concerned would now be nearly 40 years old, but Rantzen feels that the mother's continuing anguish must be partly due to the fact of Hindley's and Brady's presence, still alive, in prison:

'Two days ago I would not have felt like this,' she told the *Sun*. 'I was always against capital punishment but now I think we don't need them in the world. Just take them away. . . . This is not about revenge. It's the only way of easing the pain.'

Well, if Esther Rantzen has decided that they should be executed, I suppose we had better get on and do it, or have it done. She has obviously given considerable thought to this, and nobody in politics or anywhere else in this country wants to pick a quarrel with one of our foremost television personalities.

It will add a certain something to the daily lives of all long-term prisoners if they know that they can be taken out and hanged at any time – even after 30 years – if an important television presenter like Esther Rantzen suddenly changes her mind about a case.

Thursday, December 8:

TELEVISION
Channel 4

9.00 p.m. Witness – 'Myra Hindley: A Life Sentence.' Examines arguments for and against Myra Hindley's release from prison, and includes a written statement from her.

Leading article; Friday, December 9:

WHEN LIFE MEANS LIFE

Given his track-record, it is inconceivable that the Home Secretary, Michael Howard, would be moved to release Myra Hindley because of her latest plea for mercy, made on television last night. So inconceivable is it, indeed, that those who have advised her to issue this appeal must have had some other purpose in mind. They think that public feeling against her is whipped up by certain newspapers which harp on the horrors of the Moors murders for cynical reasons of their own. Her supporters believe that this feeling might eventually be reversed by an appeal to the public's better nature. Thus would Mr Howard (or more likely a future Home Secretary) find himself under growing public pressure to free her.

These are delusions that do not belong in the real world. Hindley, who has served nearly 30 years, belongs in that tiny category of life prisoner who can never be released, as Mr Howard has more or less implied. That is the public's overwhelming view, which newspapers do not create but merely reflect. Those who want to be kind to her should be helping her to accept that fate, not endlessly encouraging her to hope otherwise. For the Earl of Longford to call her a political prisoner is both ludicrous and immoral. She was the co-author of one of the most horrific crimes of the century, not the innocent victim of political or religious persecution.

Such mercy as she can expect, she already has. The abolition of capital punishment was the extension of state mercy to all murderers: no longer were they called upon to pay for the lives they had taken with their own. She is humanely treated in prison – she would be in more danger out of it. Nor is it difficult to detect a hard edge of arrogance in the words of her appeal. Those who are really sorry do not demand to be forgiven. If she was as deeply remorseful as she says, she would see that, short of the death penalty, no punishment inflicted on her would ever be equivalent to the suffering and loss she inflicted on others. It is clear from the response of Mrs Anne West, mother of Hindley's victim Lesley Anne Downey, that her pain and grief is as intense as ever. Hindley and her campaigning friends are merely adding to it. Few of those who remember the Moors trial will ever be entirely free of its shadow.

Hindley asks to be judged as she is now, not as she was 30 years ago. But she was not judged for what she was; she was judged for what she did. Though one may take leave to doubt it, she may be a reformed woman in all respects. But that does not earn her freedom. Punishment, not rehabilitation, is the issue here. It is essential for justice that the range of judicial sentences should continue to envisage the ultimate case: the murder so foul that its perpetrator can never be let out. If the Moors murders are not in that category, nothing will ever be.

1966

Wednesday, August 2:

THE TEXAS SNIPER

On Monday, a sniper stationed on the 26th 'observation' floor of the University of Texas in Austin shot dead 12 people and wounded 34 others. The shooting started at noon and was cruelly accurate, even at distances of some 500 yards. The sniper frequently changed his firing position from one side of the slender tower to another. At times he fired in staccato bursts, and at other times there were single shots, about 30 seconds apart.

The sniper (arrowed) on the University of Texas building

Fire engines and police using rifles with telescopic lenses ringed the tower as a hundred or more bullets whined into the grounds. Ambulances were brought from all parts of Austin, and an armoured van was called in to pick up the injured lying on lawns and footpaths. After a siege lasting an hour and a half, a white flag appeared on the tower, and then a man was dragged struggling from the building. He died from bullet-wounds on the way to the hospital. He was named as Charles Whitman, a 24-year-old former Marine who was studying architectural engineering at the university.

As doctors fought to save the lives of some of the wounded, police forced an entry into Whitman's home. There they found the dead bodies of his wife and mother, apparently shot before the university massacre began. In three notes which he left beside the bodies, he wrote that he hated his father 'with a mortal passion' – a hatred perhaps engendered by the fact that his parents separated five months ago. Of his mother, he wrote: 'If there is a heaven, she is in heaven. But if there is no heaven, she is at least out of her misery.' After writing those words, he added a matter-of-fact notation: '3 a.m. Both mother and wife dead.'

To most of those who knew him, Whitman fitted perfectly into the mould of the 'All-American Boy'. He was clean-cut, clean-living, patriotic and friendly. He grew up in a typically middle-class family with a God-fearing and loving mother and a firm but generous father – now working as a plumber in Florida. He became an altar-boy, an Eagle Scout at 13, an honour student at school, and later a scoutmaster.

But recently, something had begun to trouble him. Few of his friends were aware that he had consulted a psychiatrist at the university about severe headaches, overwork and mental strain. It appears that no one other than the psychiatrist knew that he had spoken of 'going up on the university tower with a rifle and shooting people'.

The pathologist who examined Whitman's bullet-ridden body found a small tumour close to the brain. This could have caused pressure on the brain and contributed directly or indirectly to his actions on Monday.

Whitman worked until mid-morning, carefully assembling his arsenal, including a 6 mm sporting rifle with a telescopic sight, a Remington 0.35 rifle, a Magnum pistol and hundreds of rounds of ammunition. He packed these weapons, with food, water and containers of petrol, in a metal trunk, and then set off to buy yet another gun. He obtained this, on credit, from a branch of a mail-order firm, sawed off the end of the barrel, and put it in the trunk.

Then he headed for the university tower . . .

New York has a 'mad litterbug' in its midst. He struck again yesterday.

Police are certain that one deranged person has been responsible for laying carpets of rubbish in the streets at frequent intervals. The litterbug makes his sorties in the quiet hours before dawn, leaving trails of neatly-cut newspapers and telephone directories, two or three inches deep in places.

'It's been going on like this for a couple of years,' said a street-cleaner as he tackled the latest mess outside the New York Public Library on Fifth Avenue. 'I notice that there's a full moon,' he added.

1968 . . .

Tuesday, December 3:

THE CASE THAT SHOCKED THE SCOTS

Mrs Sheila Garvie (née Watson) is an attractive Scotswoman of 33, with brunette hair dyed blonde. Her father, a stonemason, worked for some of her childhood on the Royal estate at Balmoral; she lived there for three years, and at the age of 13 played the part of Queen Victoria in a pageant watched by members of the Royal Family. She left school two years later, and, after a short spell working at a telephone exchange, returned to Balmoral, first as a maid, then as assistant housekeeper. She then took a job in a coal merchant's office in the 'granite city' of Aberdeen, on the east coast of Scotland, and it was at that office that she met Maxwell Garvie.

An only son, Garvie had been educated at boarding school and at an agricultural college, and in the early months of 1955, when he was 21, had taken over the running of his father's 200-acre farm, West Cairnbeg, on the road between Fettercairn and Stonehaven, just over 20 miles south-west of Aberdeen. He ceased to be one of the most eligible bachelors in the area on June 11, 1955, when he and Sheila Watson were married.

Their first child was born in 1956, and the second, another daughter, in the following year; much later, in 1964, they had a son. By the early 1960s, Garvie was so interested in flying that he had become known as 'the flying farmer'; he spent about £6000 on forming a club at nearby Fordoun, providing it with a twin-seater German-built Bolkow Junior, and became its first president. He also joined the Scottish National Party, and eventually became secretary of the Stonehaven branch and vice-chairman of the Angus constituency group. His wife, too, joined the SNP, and it was at party meetings in Stonehaven, some 12 miles from their home, that the Garvies met and became friendly with a dark and handsome young man named Brian Tevendale.

As a boy, Tevendale had lived at the Bush Hotel, a few miles from West Cairnbeg, which was owned by his father, a retired Army officer who held the Distinguished Conduct Medal and was at one time Provost Marshal for Scottish Command and, at another, commander of the Bridge of Don barracks in Aberdeen. Brian Tevendale attended Montrose Academy and then joined the Royal Army Medical Corps – though not for long because, during training, he and another recruit went absent without leave and stole a car; after being arrested, he was court-martialled, dismissed from the service, and given two years on probation. Within weeks he was sent to a detention centre for smashing windows in Stonehaven.

Following his release, he grew a beard and developed an interest in Scottish Nationalism.

Maxwell Garvie invited Tevendale to West Cairnbeg at weekends, where he did odd jobs around the farm, and in the evenings went with the Garvies for drinks at local hotels. In September 1967, soon after becoming friendly with the couple, Tevendale introduced Garvie his elder sister, Trudy Birse, who lived with her husband, a police constable, in Aberdeen. She, too, became a regular visitor at West Cairnbeg, and while Maxwell Garvie often went into Aberdeen to see her, Sheila Garvie was often seen out with Tevendale, who by now was employed as a barman at a public house, the East Neuk, in Aberdeen. Meanwhile, Tevendale had become acquainted with a 20-year-old motor mechanic named Alan Peters.

In March 1968, Mrs Garvie went off with Tevendale. Her husband, clearly distraught, traced them to Bradford and persuaded her to return.

On Tuesday, May 14, Garvie attended an SNP meeting in Stonehaven. When he left, at about 10 p.m., he said something to the effect of 'I mustn't keep them waiting'; he also mentioned that he intended to fly to a place in Perthshire the next day but would be back for an SNP meeting on the Thursday. He then drove off towards West Cairnbeg in his white Cortina 1600E saloon car.

On the following Sunday, his sister, Mrs Hilda Kerr, called at Laurencekirk police station, saying that he was missing. Later that day, in a telephone conversation between his wife and an officer at the station, Mrs Garvie said that she was sure he would turn up for a meeting of the Fordoun Flying Club on the Monday – but on that Monday night she phoned to say that he had not returned and that she wished to report him as a missing person.

His car was found straddled across the flying club's runway. The police began searching fields and copses around West Cairnbeg, wells were dredged, and messages sent to flying clubs both in Britain and abroad.

His wife, still insisting that she had no idea where he might be, gave the police information that formed the basis of a remarkable description of him which appeared in the official *Police Gazette* on June 14:

'Spends freely, is a heavy spirit drinker and often consumes tranquillisers and Pro-Plus tablets when drinking. Is fond of female company but has strong homosexual tendencies and is often in the company of young men. . . . Deals in pornographic material and is an active member of nudist camps. . . .'

On Friday, August 16, Sheila Garvie's mother, Mrs Edith Watson, arrived at Laurencekirk police station in a hysterical state and made certain allegations, as a result of which a call was put through to police headquarters at Bucksburn, near Aberdeen. Shortly afterwards, Mrs Garvie was taken there by car. Later that day, Brian Tevendale was arrested at the East Neuk bar and charged with the murder of Maxwell Garvie. Early next morning, Garvie's body was discovered in an underground tunnel at Lauriston Castle, near St Cyrus – close to the Bush Hotel, where Tevendale had spent his childhood. The next day, Alan Peters (who had married since Garvie's disappearance) was arrested.

Six weeks later, on November 8, the three – all charged with murder – attended a pleading diet in the

Sheriff Court at Stonehaven. Mrs Garvie gave notice (as she had to under Scots Law, so that the Crown had warning) that she intended to attack the character of her late husband 'in respect of his unnatural and perverted sexual practices'. She also lodged a special defence, that of 'impeachment of one or other or both' of her co-accused – in other words, claiming that Tevendale and/or Peters had committed the murder. This defence had been used only twice before in Scotland in the past hundred years or so: by Jessie M'Lachlan, who, at her trial in 1862 for the murder of a servant-girl, unsuccessfully accused James Fleming, the elderly father of the girl's employer, of the crime; and by the serial killer, Peter Manuel, who, at his trial in 1958, claimed that three of the eight victims had been murdered by a man named William Watt. Alan Peters' agent also lodged a special defence, pleading that Maxwell Garvie was not murdered by Peters but by Tevendale and Mrs Garvie, and that 'any acts done by Peters in connection with the murder were on the coercion' of Tevendale.

Sheila Garvie's mother, Mrs Edith Watson, should have been one of the first prosecution witnesses at the trial, which began on Tuesday, November 19, at the High Court in Aberdeen, but as she collapsed before giving her evidence, she did not enter the witness-box until the following day. Breaking down several times during the questioning, she said that after Garvie's disappearance she had got the impression from her daughter that he was dead: 'She asked me about tides and seemed worried about the body being washed up and discovered.' After saying that she had wanted to protect her daughter, she said: 'I decided to go to the police when Sheila talked of buying a house in Aberdeen and taking the children with her. I had promised Maxwell that if anything happened to him, I would look after the children and not let them anywhere near Tevendale. I had to put Tevendale into the hands of the police, and to do that I had to involve my daughter.'

Questioned by Mr Lionel Daiches, QC, defending Mrs Garvie, Mrs Watson said that she understood that Garvie had been making unnatural sexual demands on her daughter. On one occasion, he had twisted his wife's arm up behind her back and thrown her against a bedroom wall with all his force because she refused to called Tevendale 'a bastard,' even after being forced to her knees and having jagged glass pushed against her face. 'Maxwell told me that he didn't mind who Sheila slept with as long as she came back home. He told me that he and Tevendale had once tossed a coin to see who would sleep with my daughter first.'

A farmer at St Cyrus testified that, early on a day in May, he had been got out of bed by two men – Tevendale and Peters – who wanted him to use his tractor to get their car out of a deep rut in a road leading to a nearby quarry. On August 17, he had helped in opening up an underground tunnel leading from the quarry and had seen the decomposed body of Maxwell Garvie.

The Reverend Kenneth Thompson, of the Manse of Fordoun, said that Mrs Garvie had told him that she had been subjected to perverted acts of intercourse during her married life. He had not, however, heard that West Cairnbeg was known locally as 'Kinky Cottage'.

The victim's skull was produced by a medical witness, explaining injuries to it, and as soon as it was returned to its cardboard box, Mr Daiches said that his client was 'feeling slightly indisposed' and requested a short adjournment, which was granted by the judge, Lord Thomson.

When the court reconvened, one of the star-witnesses, 31-year-old Mrs Gertrude ('Trudy') Birse was called. She told how she had become Garvie's mistress, visiting him at his home and having intercourse with him there. 'Maxwell, who showed me books on sexual techniques, said that he had encouraged the friendship between his wife and my brother Brian because he wanted Sheila to become a better lover for him – Maxwell.'

She said that, shortly after Garvie's disappearance, she had found a pile of dirty clothing on her kitchen floor and asked her brother about it. He had eventually told her: 'It's been done. It's over. Max is dead.' On the Sunday after Garvie disappeared, she had asked her brother what had happened. 'I wanted to know whether Maxwell had been left suffering or had been killed outright. My main concern was that he had not suffered. Brian told me, after a lot of hesitation, that Alan Peters had struck Max with a steel bar, and that when he, Brian, believed Maxwell to be dead, had shot him.' She understood that her brother and Peters had been let into the West Cornbeg farmhouse by Mrs Garvie, and that they had waited upstairs until she told them that Garvie was in bed.

Under cross-examination, Mrs Birse said that she had first met Garvie when he came to her home with his wife in August 1967. She agreed that she was immediately attracted to him, adding that she had made a note in her diary that she had 'felt electricity' that night.

The following night, Tevendale and Garvie had gone for a walk, and she and Mrs Garvie had joined them later: 'That was the first time I saw my brother and Sheila embracing. I turned to Maxwell and said: "Don't you mind?" He said: "No, I like to see them enjoying themselves." Not only did he encourage the relationship – he nourished it.' She said that Garvie enjoyed hearing details about the sex-play between his wife and her brother. He had shown her lewd photographs and pornographic literature.

Detectives gave evidence regarding statements made by the three accused. When Mrs Garvie was charged, she said: 'I didn't shoot, kill or cause any injury to my husband.' Afterwards, she said that Tevendale and 'another man' had taken her from her bedroom when she was asleep with her husband and 'hustled' her into the bathroom. Tevendale was carrying a gun. She heard 'terrible thumping noises' coming from the bedroom, and about five minutes later Tevendale came to her and said: 'You won't have any more of him to put up with.' She said that she saw Tevendale and the other man pulling her husband's body out of the bedroom, wrapped in a groundsheet. Some time later, Tevendale phoned her to say that he had taken Garvie's clothes to Mrs Birse, who would get rid of them.

When Alan Peters was charged, he replied: 'I know I didn't shoot him. Can I make a statement?' He then said that when he and Tevendale arrived at the house, Mrs Garvie let them in and Tevendale got a gun from behind the door. They went into the sitting-room, where Mrs Garvie gave them a drink and showed them to a room upstairs, where they waited until Garvie came home and went to bed. Shortly afterwards, she came to

them and said that her husband was asleep. 'Brian hit him on the back of the head with the butt of the gun. Then he shot him with the gun.' Peters said that he and Tevendale then took the body to 'the place where we left him'.

In a statement made by Tevendale shortly after he had led detectives to where the body was hidden, he said that he had seen Sheila's doctor and spoken to him about her husband's sexual demands. After the doctor had spoken to Garvie, the latter had twisted his wife's arm. On the night of the murder, Tevendale said, he had visited Sheila and found her in 'a terrible state'. She had said that Garvie had been shot when they were fighting for a gun. 'This was where I came in. I put the body in the car and drove away with it. I remembered the tunnel where I used to play as a boy, and dragged the body to it.' Tevendale said that one night, when Garvie had begun to make 'strange advances' to him, he had told Garvie that if he didn't stop, he would hit him. On another night, Garvie had suggested that they should toss up to see who should sleep with Sheila; Tevendale had won the toss, but when he woke up the next morning, Garvie was in bed with them, and Sheila told him that her husband had tried to have 'kinky sex' with her. Tevendale also alleged that Garvie had told him that he was going to try 'a new type of sex' with Sheila, and if she didn't like it, he would break her neck. He said that, one night in Aberdeen, he had been attacked in an alleyway and slightly slashed by a man who had cried out: 'That's a present from Skipper' – which was a name that he, Tevendale, had given to Garvie. 'When I told Garvie of the incident, he said I wouldn't get a chance to run next time.'

The Crown case was closed on the morning of the sixth day of the trial, and 20-year-old Alan Peters was called to the witness-box by his counsel, Dr R. R. Taylor, QC.

He said that he had first met Tevendale in November or December 1967, when they were both working for a firm called Aberdeen Motors. Tevendale had once said 'something about getting rid of a bloke,' but he had not thought anything about it. After admitting that he had driven Tevendale to West Cairnbeg in his own car on the night of May 14, he stuck closely to the account he had given to the police when he was charged, but he now said that after Mrs Garvie had come into the upstairs room to say that her husband was asleep, Tevendale had told her to follow, and all three of them had crossed the landing to the bedroom; Tevendale had then struck the man several times with the butt of the gun, put a pillow over his head, and fired through it. 'I was horrified,' Peters testified. 'I didn't say anything. I just felt sick.' In answer to another question from his counsel, as to why he had not interfered, he replied: 'I might have got the same, for all I knew.' He said that when he and Tevendale had returned to the house after carrying the body down to his car, which he had parked in a garage, Tevendale had said that he and Mrs Garvie were going to make coffee. She had previously been fully dressed but was now wearing a dressing-gown. She and Tevendale had left the room for half an hour. He and Tevendale had then driven the body to St Cyrus, put it in the tunnel and covered it with stones, after which they had returned to the car and, finding that it was stuck, knocked up a farmer, who had pulled the vehicle out with a tractor.

Cross-examined by Mrs Garvie's counsel, Peters agreed that Tevendale had been his best man when he was married on July 26. Mr Daiches enquired: 'This is the man of whom you walked in terror?' and Peters replied: 'Yes. I didn't want to appear to be avoiding him.'

Sheila Garvie, dressed in the powder-blue suit she had worn from the start of the trial, replaced Peters in the witness-box. She said that her marriage was happy and normal until her husband was attracted to nudism in 1962. This had caused her to need psychiatric treatment. She had not wanted to accompany him to nudist clubs, but after arguing with him, she had finally agreed to go. He had insisted that she and their children should go to a naturist place in Corsica for a holiday, and had afterwards opened a nudist club in Aberdeenshire. He had wanted her to perform the opening ceremony in the nude, but she had refused and had cut the tape fully dressed.

She said that her husband was by then drinking heavily and mixing with a different type of person to that of his former farming associates; he was also going about with younger men. 'He seemed to get sex out of all proportion, and sent for sex literature and books of pornographic pictures. He wanted to take pictures of me in the nude. After he accused me of being inhibited, I posed for him one night. I then discovered that he had shown the pictures to other people. I was shocked, but he seemed amused.' She said that he had encouraged her friendship with Tevendale and suggested that she should have intercourse with him. She had finally done so after he began associating with Trudy Birse. 'When he began the affair with Mrs Birse, I was very upset, but he said that

this was 1967 and people did that sort of thing. He was seeing a lot of Mrs Birse, and his sexual demands on me became greater because he said he had done things with her, and if she could do them, then I could do the same. I lost all respect for him, and physically felt nothing at all.' In the few weeks before the murder, things had become much worse for her, and her husband had taunted her that she needed mental treatment. She said that her state of mental stress was due to the fact that her husband's unnatural sexual demands had 'increased terribly'.

Often speaking in whispers, she said that on the night of the murder she had read fairy-stories to her four-year-old son before he dropped off to sleep. Her husband had arrived home towards the end of *The Avengers* television programme. He had been drinking, and they had begun arguing about sex pills. She had finally taken two sleeping tablets and gone to bed at about midnight. He had come to her bedroom, they had had intercourse, and she had then fallen asleep. The next thing she remembered, she told the jury, was being awoken by someone pulling at her arm. She had thought it was one of the children, but had then recognised Tevendale's voice telling her to get up.

'I was terribly sleepy, but I got up out of bed and was led by Brian to the bathroom. I saw another figure standing there. Brian told me to stay there. I was in a daze. I had no idea what Brian was doing there – no idea what time it was. A few minutes after the terrible thumping noises, Brian opened the bathroom door and said: "He won't worry you any longer." He told me to hold on to the handle on the children's bedroom door to keep it closed. When I held on to it, I was on my knees, because I couldn't stand.' She said that she had not seen the body being taken away and had never known how it was disposed of. She had subsequently asked Tevendale how he thought he could get away with the crime, and he had told her that if she said anything, she would be implicated and would get twenty-five years in prison. As the weeks of deception had gone on, she had decided to commit suicide and had made a will leaving everything to her children. Asked by her counsel how she could have continued the association with Tevendale, she replied: 'I was in love – and still am in love – with Brian, and want to protect him. I looked at it this way: Brian did this to protect me, and I felt I could not betray him.'

Dr R. R. TAYLOR (representing Peters): You were afterwards sharing the bed of this man who you knew had murdered your husband?

Mrs GARVIE: That is right.

Dr TAYLOR: And yet you say that you were not a party to the murder?

Mrs GARVIE: I was not.

In his cross-examination of Sheila Garvie, the Solicitor-General, Mr Ewan Stewart, asked if it were true that she had started writing a life-story entitled *Death Slave* and completed a short story called 'Life with a Kinky Husband who Came to a Bloody End'. There was a long silence when he asked her for the title of the short story, and when he finally put it to her, she replied: 'I'm not sure if that is what I wrote. It was written in the first few days of my imprisonment, and I was feeling very bitter towards myself and everyone.' She claimed that she had no recollection of reminding Tevendale that he had always said that the *News of the World* would pay well to hear 'all the gory details of her sex-life'. When asked about the nude photographs of her that had been found in Tevendale's

possession, she said that she had given them to him after the murder because she did not want them lying about in her husband's office.

After saying that she had no interest in money, Sheila Garvie added: 'All the money I have known these past years has only brought destruction.' She was unaware of life assurance policies that would give her £37,000* if her husband died, although, as she admitted, she must have had to sign proposal forms.

Speaking of the time of the murder, she said that she did not think of screaming to awaken her husband or the children, of picking up the children, or of throwing herself across her husband. She agreed that there must have been a carefully laid plan to allay suspicion about Garvie's disappearance, and said that she had no idea how Tevendale could have known that Garvie would be returning to the house that night.

In re-examining her at the end of her nine hours in the witness-box, Mr Daiches asked what she had experienced since May 14.

'A great deal of anxiety and unhappiness,' she whispered.

Looking very tired, she walked back to the dock and sat next to Brian Tevendale. His counsel, Mr Kenneth Cameron, son of the Scottish High Court judge Lord Cameron, who had earlier intimated that he did not wish to cross-examine Mrs Garvie, now announced that he would not be leading any evidence.

During the closing speeches, Mrs Garvie heard herself described by various counsel as Lady Bountiful, Lady Macbeth, and Lady Chatterley. Yesterday, Lord Thomson, in his summing-up, said that the court was not a court of morals. In some ways, he said, it had been a sordid case, but the jury were not to decide whether any person was moral, immoral or amoral. 'You have heard a great deal about sexual peculiarities and perversions, but you must exclude from your deliberations all considerations based on sympathy or emotion.'

The jury of nine men and five women† took 58 minutes to reach their verdicts. There was a majority verdict of Guilty against Sheila Garvie, but the same verdict against her 22-year-old bearded lover, Brian Tevendale, was unanimous. The case against 20-year-old Alan Peters was found Not Proven, and the judge told him: 'You are free to go.' As soon as Peters had stepped nimbly from the dock and hurried out of the courtroom, Lord Thomson turned to the other defendants and, speaking rapidly, said: 'Sheila Watson or Garvie and Brian Gordon Tevendale, according to the law of the land, the sentence for murder is prescribed. I sentence both of you to life imprisonment.'

There were gasps in the court. Mrs Garvie closed her eyes and gripped the rail of the dock. Tevendale stood motionless. The trapdoor opened and the lovers walked – the woman first – down the stairs to the cells.

A few minutes later, outside the courthouse, a crowd of some 400 booed Mrs Gertrude Birse as she entered a waiting taxi-cab with her husband Alfred, formerly an Aberdeen police constable.

---

* At the start of 1995, the purchasing power of the 1968 £1 was about £7 – and so £37,000 in 1968 would have become roughly equivalent to a quarter of a million.
† Scottish juries are composed of 15 persons, but during this trial a woman juror had been excused after being taken ill.

1969 . . .

RAYMOND MORRIS:
A KILLER TRAPPED BY HIS ARROGANCE

People who know Raymond Leslie Morris say that he is cold, calculating – and arrogant. It was that arrogance which led to his arrest 15 months after he killed seven-year-old Christine Darby.

One of the most intensive and expensive investigations in recent police history was directed by two detectives of Scotland Yard's Murder Squad, Superintendent Ian Forbes (since promoted to Chief Superintendent) and Sergeant Tom Parry. The investigation was unusual in several respects, but mainly because, firstly, it depended on routine police work, with forensic science playing little part, and secondly, because the police set out to identify the murderer by his character, temperament and mental outlook rather than by physical description or association with the victim.

The character-picture drawn by the investigators turned out to be correct. So did Ian Forbes's belief – which did not deflect him from spreading inquiries throughout the world – that the criminal was a local man.

In the early afternoon of Saturday, August 19, 1967, Christine Darby was playing with other children in the street where she lived – Camden Street, in the Staffordshire town of Walsall, north of Birmingham – when a man driving a grey Austin car pulled up, asking the direction of Caldmore Green. The children told him that it was no more than a hundred yards away, that he only had to turn right at the end of the street and he would come to it; but still, he asked Christine to get into the car and show him. She did so. The other children watched as the car pulled away – and were suddenly alarmed when they saw it turn, not right, but left. One of them, a boy, ran to Christine's home, where the door was opened by her grandmother, who as soon as she understood what had happened, hurried towards the end of the street; at the same time, Christine's mother Lilian, hearing the commotion from the kitchen, rushed out of the house to an off-licence, the nearest shop with a phone, and got someone there to call the police. The time was about twenty minutes past two.

A massive police search was organised, eventually involving officers from the West Midlands and Birmingham forces as well as men and women of the Staffordshire Constabulary, 400 in all, 50 of them with tracker dogs, and hundreds of soldiers from local camps.

On Sunday morning, a pair of

white knickers, subsequently identified as Christine's from some darning done by her grandmother, was found at Portal Pool, on the southern edge of the large area of forest and heathland known as Cannock Chase, some 14 miles north of Walsall; they were lying near the A34 road, which cuts through the Chase and passes close to the child's home.

Just after midday on Monday, a child's black right plimsoll, the lace tied tightly in a bow, suggesting that the shoe had been wrenched off, was found near the A34, some three miles farther north from where the knickers had been discovered. It was identified as Christine's by her mother and grandmother.

Late on Tuesday afternoon, one of the searching soldiers, a recently-recruited private of the Staffordshire Regiment, found the child's partly-clothed body lying in dense bracken on the Chase, a couple of miles east of the A34. She had been raped and strangled.

The Chief Constable of Staffordshire had already called in Scotland Yard, and Superintendent Forbes and Sergeant Parry were at the police headquarters when news of the discovery was received there.

The place where the body lay was about three miles north-east, across the A34, from a part of the Chase called Mansty Gully, where, in January 1966, the bodies of two missing children had been found. Five-year-old Diane Tift, who had disappeared from near her home in Walsall a fortnight before, had been suffocated after her woollen pixie-hood had been pulled down over her head and the free end used as a ligature around her neck. The body of Margaret Reynolds, who had disappeared at the age of 5 while on her way to school in the Birmingham suburb of Aston in September 1965, was lying in silt beneath that of Diane Tift, and was too decomposed for the cause of her death to be established. Officers from Scotland Yard had led the inquiry into the murders, but no arrest had been made.

Throughout the investigation into the murder of Christine Darby, there were never fewer than 120 police officers working on the case, and in the early stages the number was around 200. At Cannock police station, Chief Superintendent Andrew Mitchell, Detective Chief Inspector Pat Molloy and Detective Inspector Harry Fisher built up the organisation required by the men from the Yard. The 'murder room', under the direction of Sergeant Parry, eventually looked like the filing office of a large company; by the end of the investigation, the card-index contained 3½ million entries, and there were 12,500 items of correspondence, 31,000 notes of telephone messages, 50,000 reports of interviews with men in the Walsall district aged between 21 and 50, 14,500 statements, 39,000 house-to-house questionnaires, and 250,000 'special interview' reports. After witnesses' descriptions had established that the murderer's car was a grey Austin A60 or A55, about 1,375,000 road-tax files were examined, and 25,000 extracted as 'possibles'; by the time the case was solved, all but 2000 of the 'possibles' had been eliminated after inquiries in 17 countries.

Raymond Morris, who owned a grey Austin A55 with the registration number 158 BOC, was first interviewed on September 5, a fortnight after the discovery of the body. The interview, by two detectives, took place in his fourth-floor flat in Regent House, an eight-storey block in Green Lane, Walsall, overlooking the new West Midlands police divisional station. His wife Carol was present. Asked to account for his movements between 1 p.m. and 3 p.m. on Saturday, August 19, Morris said that he had knocked off from his work at Oldbury, about 18 miles from Walsall, at 1 p.m., and soon after arriving home at 1.45 p.m., had gone shopping with his wife in their car before going to visit his wife's mother in a suburb of Walsall. His wife confirmed his time of arrival from work and their activities afterwards.

Three days later, the same detectives went back to the flat. Morris and his wife said that they could not recall which shops they had visited on August 19, other than Marks & Spencer.

A week later, Morris sold the Austin and bought a Ford Corsair.

After publication of an Identikit picture, one of Morris's relatives told the police that Morris had similar features to those shown in the picture and that his character and temperament fitted the 'offender profile'.

On February 29, two other detectives visited Morris at his flat. He and his wife gave the same account of his arrival home and their subsequent movements on the afternoon of August 19, and Morris, becoming angry, said: 'If you think I'll tell a different story, I won't.'

Despite his apparent alibi, details of him were retained in the 'unsatisfactory' files on about 150 men who had been interviewed.

Morris, one of four children, was born into a good home on August 13, 1929; but even before he left school in Walsall at the age of 15, he was antagonistic towards his family. He was already vain about his dark good looks. Dissatisfied with his school-leaving report, he wrote his own testimonials when he sought employment.

In September 1947, he entered the RAF for National Service, and served as an aircraftsman second-class until June 1949. His overall conduct was assessed as 'very good', and his record showed no evidence of misbehaviour or trouble.

He worked at different jobs until May 1952, when, using skills he had learned in the RAF, he became a toolmaker at £20 a week with a firm at Oldbury. He stayed there for 11 years before leaving of his own accord.

Meanwhile, he married a girl whom he had known since his schooldays. After the birth of a second son, a spastic, the couple were divorced.

Having taken up photography as a hobby, Morris pretended that he was a professional photographer. Later, on business cards that he had printed, R. L. Morris was referred to as the 'Midland Representative' of 'Regent Studios (Birmingham)', with an address to which 'Midland enquiries' were to be sent. The address was in Birmingham, where the occupier believed that Morris was what he pretended to be.

In July 1964, Morris became a £25-a-week 'special salesman' with the West Midlands Gas Board. He was described as reliable and honest when he left of his own accord after a year. During that time – on August 22, 1964 – he remarried, and he and his new wife, Carol, a 21-year-old wages clerk, set up home in the flat at Regent House.

For a year, from May 1966 until he was made redundant, he was a foreman at a firm in Willenhall, just to the west of Walsall, earning £26 a week. He was described as an excellent and intelligent employee.

Shortly afterwards, he was taken on as works foreman with another firm in Oldbury. He earned £35 a week.* He was still employed by the company when the police began to take an interest in him.

At the end of August 1968, after a year of virtually night-and-day work on the case, Ian Forbes and Tom Parry returned to London. Superintendent Forbes made it clear that 'this does not mean that inquiries have come to an end. Just wait. We will get him. This is just the end of Phase One. You'll see, we will be back for Phase Two.'

On Monday, November 4, in Walsall, a man attempted to entice ten-year-old Margaret Aughton into a green Ford Corsair with a white roof. Mrs Wendy Lane, who lived at Cemetery Lodge in the town, witnessed the attempt and took a note of the car's registration number: 429 LOP. A search by police through road-tax records showed that Mrs Lane must have made a mistake, for that number belonged to a grey Ford Anglia whose owner was a Yorkshireman who had never been in Walsall. Three West Midlands detectives, Sergeant James Love and Constables Conrad Joseph and Terry Atkins, decided to permutate the number ... and found that of eight 'possibles', one – 492 LOP – belonged to a car that fitted both the make and the description. So as to be absolutely sure of the identification, detectives of the Staffordshire Crime Squad traced and checked every one of the other 998 vehicles in the LOP registration group. There were 24 Ford Corsairs; but none of them was green with a white roof.

The car registered as 492 LOP belonged to Raymond Morris.

Ian Forbes returned to Cannock, and on the morning of the following day, Friday, November 15, Detective Chief Inspector Pat Molloy arrested Morris as he was driving from his home towards Oldbury. Soon afterwards, Carol Morris was escorted from her workplace – first to her home, where she waited while detectives searched every room and removed boxes filled with her husband's clothing and other things, and then to a police station – not the one where Morris was being held.

There, during an interview conducted by Ian Forbes and local detectives, she admitted that she had not told the truth on the three occasions when she had supported Morris's alibi for the time of Christine Darby's abduction.

In the evening, Ian Forbes interviewed Morris, who had by then been charged with the murder of Christine Darby. Morris was at first aloof and arrogant. Mr Forbes thought it 'rather strange that he never denied [the murder] ...'. At one point, he remarked: 'Whatever I say will make no difference,' and when asked what he meant by that, said: 'I'm finished. My marriage. My life. My job. My whole future. What does it matter?' He was told that his wife had been interviewed and had said that he had not arrived home until 4.30 on the afternoon of the murder. According to Mr Forbes, 'He then became somewhat upset, put his head in his hands, and said: "Oh God, oh God, she wouldn't," and sat shaking his head for a time.'

He again became upset when he was asked to go on an identity parade, saying: 'No, no. No. Nothing will make me, and you can't force me.' He was asked four more times,

---

* Roughly equivalent to £250 at the start of 1995.

but continued to refuse.

Among the items found on Morris when he was arrested were photographs of Forestry Commission land on Cannock Chase. And in the search of his home, the police had found eight photographic negatives, nine prints and a camera with a time-delay device. The negatives and prints all pictured Morris, in a room of his flat, indecently assaulting a small girl. He was shown the photographs one by one, and each time simply said 'Yes'. The child was subsequently identified as Mrs Morris's five-year-old cousin.

On February 10, 1969, Morris appeared at Staffordshire Assizes. He pleaded not guilty to the murder of Christine Darby and to the attempt to take away a girl of ten by force on November 4, 1968, but guilty to the illegal assault on a five-year-old girl between August 9 and 19, 1968.

Among the prosecution witnesses were two women and a man, each of whom had separately been on Cannock Chase in the afternoon of Christine Darby's abduction. Both women recalled seeing a man driving a grey car, and one of them said that a small girl was sitting in the passenger seat 'too close to the door,' adding that she had subsequently recognised the child as Christine Darby from a photograph that she had been shown. The male witness said that, while walking his dog, he had seen a man standing beside a grey car. Each of the three witnesses was asked if the man they had seen was in court, and each of them pointed at the defendant in the dock.

Carol Morris, wearing an orange-coloured coat and a brown fur hat, chose to give evidence for the prosecution, although Mr Justice Ashworth made it clear to her that, as the wife of the accused, she did not have to do so against her will. Never once looking towards the dock, she told the jury of nine men and three women that Morris had arrived home on the Saturday at 4.30 p.m. and not at about 2 p.m., as she had originally told the police during their murder inquiries. In his cross-examination of her, Morris's counsel, Mr Kenneth Mynett, QC, pointed out that on three occasions she had supported her husband's alibi: 'That is part of the reason, Mrs Morris, why I suggest to you that if your evidence today is proved, you have told lies about this case.'

Mrs MORRIS: No, I didn't think it was him.

Mr MYNETT: Never mind what you thought. Whatever you may or may not have thought, you were telling the police what you say today is untrue?

Mrs MORRIS: Yes.

Mr MYNETT: Without beating about the bush, if your evidence today is true, you were lying?

Mrs MORRIS: I only agreed with what he said.

Mr MYNETT: You were lying to the police?

Mrs MORRIS: Yes.

Mr MYNETT: And you were quite deliberately lying to the police on a matter of great importance?

Mrs MORRIS: If a person comes home and acts normally and eats his meals and shows no sign of emotion, you can't believe. . . .

While giving evidence on his own behalf, Raymond Morris broke down and cried. This was after he had testified that, shortly after his arrest, Chief Superintendent Forbes had come into the cell where he was being kept and told him: 'Well, son, you are on your own now. Your wife has left you.'

Asked by Mr Mynett if there was anything unusual, so far as he could recall, in the events of August 19, 1967, he said that he had gone to work in the morning and clocked off at about 1.13 p.m.; that he had had a wash, checked the premises, and then handed over to his boss, who had been away for a week's holiday.

Mr MYNETT: At any time during that day did you go to Cannock Chase?

MORRIS: No, sir.

Mr MYNETT: Or anywhere near it?

MORRIS: No, sir.

Mr MYNETT: To your knowledge, had you ever seen the little girl Christine Darby in your life?

MORRIS: No, sir.

Morris insisted that he and his wife had given the police what they thought were correct answers regarding the time of his return from work. 'I had to refer to her to verify because I was not very sure. I was never very sure about any of the times.'

He said that on November 15, 1968, he left home shortly before 7.30 a.m. and was stopped by a police patrol car. He was asked for his driving licence, but then Detective Chief Inspector Pat Molloy came across, brushed the other officers aside, and told him that he was being arrested for Christine's murder. 'I could not say anything. I was just speechless.' He said that he did not speak on the way to the police station, but as soon as he was there he asked to see a solicitor in view of the seriousness of the charge. He was taken to a cell, where 'Mr Molloy pushed me against the wall and punched me in the stomach. I put my hands over my stomach and doubled up, and he punched me in my left-hand side. He said: "Now do you want a solicitor?" I was just doubled up in pain. He threw me down sideways on to a wooden bed and then went out and slammed the door.' (Mr Molloy had earlier denied during cross-examination that he had ever struck Morris.)

Morris said that Superintendent Forbes later came into the cell with three or four other detectives and asked if he knew why he was there. 'I told him I had nothing to do with it all. He just said: "Well, we know that you did it. We know you're sick in the head. Why don't you tell us why you did it? You won't see the outside of prison for 30 years."'

On the seventh day of the trial, the jury, who had been out for 90 minutes, found Morris guilty of the murder of Christine Darby, and he was sentenced to life imprisonment. He was also sentenced to three years concurrent for the attempted abduction, and to 12 months concurrent for the indecent assault.

As he left the dock, he stopped, turned and glared for several seconds at his wife, who was sitting in the public gallery, and she burst into tears.

The judge praised the 'tremendous efforts' of Superintendent Forbes, saying: 'There must be many mothers in Walsall and the surrounding area whose hearts will beat more lightly as a result of this case. There will be many who are truly grateful to you and to those who served under you.'

The man from Scotland Yard was cheered by hundreds outside the court.

Wednesday, January 21, 1970:

Ian Brady in Hot Water

Raymond Morris, at whom Ian Brady, the Moors Murderer, threw hot tea five weeks ago, has thrown a jugful of hot water at Brady, who was sitting reading a newspaper in the recreation room in the top-security wing of Durham Prison.

As a result, Morris has been confined to his cell for twenty-eight days, which is the same punishment as that given to the tea-throwing Brady, who, during his confinement, went on hunger-strike and was fed by tube.

Morris is one of five prisoners who are allowed to associate with Brady because of the nature of their crimes. Other prisoners are kept away from him for his own safety.

1969

Wednesday, March 5:

KRAY TWINS GUILTY OF MURDER

Thirty-five-year-old Ronald Kray and his twin-brother Reginald, who terrorised East London, were both found guilty of murder at the Old Bailey yesterday. Four members of their 'firm' were also found guilty of murder.

The jury was out for six hours and 54 minutes. The trial, lasting 39 days, has been the longest murder hearing at the Central Criminal Court. Costs of the whole case, in which 23 counsel were engaged, are expected to exceed £200,000. Three shorthand writers have recorded and transcribed nearly one and a half million words throughout the trial, in which all the defendants were legally aided.

Court No. 1 was packed when the jury returned. Women relatives of the 10 accused men were crying. But the father of the Kray brothers, Charles Kray Senior, sat impassively in the seat he had occupied since the start of the trial.

Strict security precautions surrounded the court while the jury was out. Cars were towed away from parking meters outside the building, extra uniformed police, with two-way radios, patrolled the nearby streets, and there were several policemen on the roof.

The defendants were summoned into the dock one by one, and stood flanked by three prison officers as the foreman of the jury gave the unanimous verdicts.

Ronald Kray, plump-faced and bespectacled, blinked repeatedly while the Clerk of the Court recorded the verdicts. He was found guilty of murdering George Cornell, 38, by shooting him through the head at the Blind Beggar public house, Whitechapel, on March 9, 1966, and guilty of murdering Jack 'The Hat' McVitie, 38, at a basement flat in Evering Road, Stoke Newington, in October 1967.

His brother Reginald was found guilty of murdering McVitie by stabbing him in the face, chest and throat nine times while Ronald held him from behind. He was also found guilty of being an accessory after the murder of Cornell by harbouring his brother.

John Alexander Barrie, 31, of no settled address, was found guilty of the murder of Cornell, the prosecution case being that he went with Ronald Kray to the Blind Beggar, and fired shots to distract customers.

Christopher Lambrianou, 29, of Queensbridge Road, Hackney, was found guilty of the murder of McVitie, whom he lured to the flat in Evering Road after getting him drunk at the Regency Club, Stoke Newington. Before going to the cells, he turned in the dock and called out to someone in the public gallery: 'See you later.' His brother

Anthony, 26, of Blythe Road, Bethnal Green, was also found guilty of murdering McVitie by luring him to the flat. As he left the dock, he made a thumbs-up sign to someone in the public gallery.

Ronald Albert Bender, 31, of Cubitt House, Milwall, was also found guilty of the murder of McVitie, by providing the carving knife used by Reginald Kray to stab McVitie to death.

The twins' elder brother, Charles James Kray, 42, of Rosefield Gardens, Birchfield Estate, Poplar, was found guilty of being an accessory after the murder of McVitie by organising some of the accused, including his brothers, and assisting in arrangements for the disposal of the body.

Frederick Gerald Foreman, 36, of the Prince of Wales public house, Lant Street, Southwark, was found guilty of being an accessory after the murder of McVitie by organising the disposal of the body. Cornelius John Whitehead, 33, of Bigland Street, Stepney, was found guilty of being an accessory after the murder of McVitie by assisting in cleaning the flat in Evering Road and harbouring the twins.

A tenth defendant, Anthony Thomas Barry, 30, part-owner of the Regency Club, was found not guilty of the murder of McVitie and was ordered to be discharged. The Crown case against him was that he had taken a gun to the flat in Evering Road.

Another defendant, Albert Donaghue, 32, of Devon Road, Bow, has pleaded guilty to being an accessory after the murder of McVitie, and will also be sentenced today.

The rule of fear created by a syndicate of gangsters in London's East End has been smashed by the verdicts passed on the Kray brothers.

'Protection' was a major source of income to them. Clubs were a natural target for this extortion – known to the Kray gang either as 'pensions' (regular payments of £50 a week or more) or as 'nipping', referring to lesser payments.

The savage, cold-blooded murders of two men, purely for prestige and to establish the supremacy of the brothers as gang-leaders, shocked even the inhabitants of an area already accustomed to violence. The Krays had tried to build up a legend for themselves similar to that of some other brothers in criminal history – men like Frank and Jesse James, infamous for their viciousness and contempt for law and order.

The Krays lived in an atmosphere unreal to ordinary people – an atmosphere varying from the lavish and hospitable to the laconic and sordid, with fear the main theme. The fear was instilled by their attitude to life and the belief that they were 'outside' all the rules and regulations as well as the morals and standards by which decent people live.

Ronald and Reginald Kray, who lived this unreal life with their elder brother Charles, liked to be thought of as 'down-to-earth' people. This attitude was illustrated when they were invited by the Cambridge Union to take part in a debate on the subject, 'The Law is an Ass'. They refused the invitation, saying that there was no point in talking about the law – it was there and nothing could be done about it. While accepting that the law existed, they hid the fact that they did not think that it applied to them. The law was for others.

The whole of their lives reflected their contempt for authority – at school, in the Army, and subsequently as members of the criminal fraternity.

In later years, to project an image of themselves as respectable but unique businessmen, they arranged for the preparation of a PR sheet, with their photographs on the front and a potted history of themselves on the back. They were shown tastefully dressed in well-cut suits, Charles in the centre and a twin on each side. The biographical notes told of their family-home in Vallance Road, Bethnal Green, in the heart of the East End, described its interior decoration, and referred to their maternal grandfather, Jimmy Lee, now in his 90s and once known in boxing circles as 'the Cannonball Southpaw'. The notes commented on the wide range of their legal activities and named East End public houses and West End clubs they frequented; mention was made of Charles and his wife Dolly, of Reginald and the girl he had married (who later committed suicide), and of Ronald – 'quite a famous bachelor'. The notes also contained a short but colourful character-assessment of the twins. Ronald, it was said, wore a heavy gold ring that matched his heavy character and temperament; he was taciturn almost to the point of being morose, and yet had flashes of humour. Reginald was said to be of different temperament, with a permanently worried expression and an attitude which gave the impression that he was always anxious to please. He was softly spoken compared with Ronald. The character of Charles was not described.

This montage – distributed on at least one occasion in the area of South London that was then ruled by the Richardson 'torture case' gang* – did not mention that the Krays' group of helpers included many men with criminal records. Nor did it tell of the fear that the Krays instilled in so many people, to such an extent that some of them went to extreme lengths to help them escape justice following two brutal murders – lengths which encompassed the disposal of McVitie's body, which has never been found. The organisation even included a woman who could, if necessary, 'take care of' potential female witnesses against the brothers: according to one of the trial witnesses, Ronald Kray had said that two women would be poisoned if they talked about the murder of McVitie, that he had a woman ready to do it, and that she was ready 'to do Cornell's wife as well'.

The Crown claimed that Cornell and McVitie were murdered because the twins wished to demonstrate how far each of them was prepared to go. Both Cornell and McVitie had 'got out of line' by defying the Krays. Cornell, who was an associate of the Richardsons, had openly shown his contempt for the twins – Ronald in particular, to whom he had made a derogatory remark concerning his sexual predilections. Ronald waited until Cornell was without the support of some of the Richardson men, who were being questioned by the police,

---

* In the summer of 1967, at the Old Bailey, Charles Richardson, his younger brother Eddie, and three members of their gang, all of whom had engaged in torture for business or pleasure, received prison sentences ranging from eight to twenty-five years, with Charles being treated most severely by Mr Justice Lawton; and in the winter of the same year, other Richardson gangsters were imprisoned for a large-scale parking fraud at Heathrow Airport.

and then sought his revenge. McVitie, too, found himself without the support of any associates, after the Krays had commented that he was 'getting too flash' and making them look fools, and he was tricked into going to the flat where he was murdered.

So far as Cornell was concerned, the twins, fearful of repercussions, went into hiding, having taken steps to protect their home in Vallance Road by sending two armed men there in case any of Cornell's friends should call. Although Charles was not present at either murder, it was to him that the twins turned for help after the killing of McVitie, as they had so often done before.

When the twins were born on October 24, 1933, in a small, drab house in Stean Street, Bethnal Green, their brother (then aged 7) little knew that in the years to come he would acquire the infamous reputation of being their 'trouble-shooter' – so much so that he stood in the dock at the Old Bailey accused of being an accessory after the murder of McVitie, for it was he the twins telephoned in the early hours of the morning after the killing to help them escape into hiding.

They were identical, Reginald being just 10 minutes older than Ronald. Their father was a 'wardrobe dealer', a man who bought and sold second-hand clothes, which provided a reasonable living for his wife and family. Before the twins were born, Charles David Kray had two children. His first son he named after himself, and his daughter he called Violet. The Krays were always considered a very close family. Shortly before the War, they moved to nearby Vallance Road.

The twins were educated at a local council school – a dull, Victorian building hemmed in by equally lifeless business premises and houses. There, they soon acquired a reputation for being rough and crude. Both in and out of school, their brash behaviour and spitefulness led neighbours to warn their children not to play with them.

Leaving school when they were 14, their reputation became worse. They were involved in a number of 'beating-up' incidents. Before long, the 'authorities' they so much despised took a hand. A probation officer suggested that they should take up boxing, and was pleasantly surprised at how readily they fell in with the idea. They started with the Mansford Club, now no longer in existence, and then went on to the famous Repton Amateur Boxing Club, which has produced a number of top-class fighters. As amateurs, they fought each other three times, with Ronald winning twice. At this time, they both weighed 9 stone 9 pounds, in the lightweight class. They left the Repton Club under a cloud because they would not or could not knuckle down to any form of discipline, and antagonised officials.

Having opened a second-hand clothing business, they supplemented their income by boxing professionally, appearing in six-round preliminary bouts at a number of major events. By this time, Ronald had moved up into the welterweight class. He fought six times, winning four bouts and losing two. Reginald was undefeated in his seven contests. They were not yet 19 years old. Some people who knew them at that time believe that if they had continued boxing, they might have accepted the discipline and the rigid training schedules; others feel that neither would ever have 'stuck it out'.

The decision was taken out of their hands when they were called up for National Service in the early 1950s. Even as soldiers, stationed for part of the time at the Home Counties Brigade Depot, Canterbury, they flouted authority. According to officers and men who were at the Canterbury depot during the same period, the twins spent most of their time under close arrest in the guardroom. While they were being punished for military offences and local escapades outside the camp, inquiries led to a liaison with other civilian police which resulted in an action concerning offences from their pre-Army days.

One of the depot's staff officers recalls: 'Even at that time, they were an absolute legend – the famous Kray twins – famous for their complete indifference to authority of any kind. On one occasion, I went into the guardroom while on fire-picket duty and was astonished to see the prisoners' cage festooned with small strips of red cloth. I was told that the Kray twins had seized the orderly sergeant, removed the red sash he wore on duty, torn it into pieces and arranged them around the wire-mesh. After seizing the sergeant, they had emptied buckets of slop over him.' The officer adds: 'It was a trick, whenever a newcomer was placed on duty as orderly officer, to let him go and inspect the Krays, without warning him of the pranks they would get up to, and see how he fared. The Krays would flout the usually severe guardroom discipline by greeting new officers with remarks such as "Oh, aren't you a lovely boy!" They exploded the myth that the Army can sort out anyone. You know the saying, "Wait until he gets into the Army, they'll knock some sense into him"? Well, even the Army could do absolutely nothing with the Krays, they were such extraordinary characters.'

On their return to civilian life, the twins received their first real introduction to clubland when they ran a billiards hall in the East End. There, they mixed with some of London's roughest characters, and their reputations as 'toughs' earned them grudging respect. It was here that the groundwork for their future leadership was laid.

In August 1956, Ronald was charged with unlawful possession of a loaded revolver. At the same time, he, Reginald and another man were charged with causing grievous bodily harm to Terence Martin, who had been stabbed with a bayonet outside a public house in Stepney. At the trial at the Old Bailey, prosecuting counsel said that it was only by luck that Martin had survived the attack. On Guy Fawkes Day, 1956, the twins were sentenced to three years' imprisonment, and Ronald was given a six-months concurrent sentence for the firearm offence. Sir Gerald Dobson, the Recorder of London, said that the three men had plunged part of the East End into 'an abyss of brutality'. They had, he said, set out on a punitive expedition to wreak vengeance on Martin, and had left him with two gaping wounds at the back of the head and two more wounds on a shoulder. 'It would seem,' he said, 'that there has existed a state of gang-warfare for some time, dangerous to all concerned – flouting and scorning the law, regardless of life.'

In February 1958, Ronald, who had been sent to Winchester Prison, was certified insane and transferred to Long Grove Mental Hospital at Epsom, Surrey; he was said to be suffering from persecution mania. While at Long Grove, he received frequent visits from Reginald, who had been released on parole. In May, Reginald and several other people visited him in the ward of the mental hospital, where the rule was that one visitor could go to the canteen for a jug of tea. By coincidence, the twins were wearing identical dark blue suits. It was Ronald who went for the tea, passing an unsuspecting attendant at the door. When he did not return, Reginald informed a hospital manager; but by then it was too late – Ronald was gone.

The following day, Reginald was quoted as saying: 'I am taking all possible steps to have my brother's case examined.' He added that Ronald had become worried about the possibility of an extra 17 months' treatment for his illness. An extensive search was made near the Krays' home, and the police warned the pubic that Ronald might use violence if approached. In fact, he offered no resistance when officers of the Flying Squad caught him in Bethnal Green. He maintained: 'I escaped to prove my sanity,' and insisted that he should not have been sent to a mental hospital. After he was returned to Long Grove, his case was reviewed by a special panel, which upheld his contention, and he was sent back to prison, from which he was released shortly before Christmas 1959.

Soon afterwards, the twins opened their first club, the Double R (the initials of their Christian names) in Bow Road, at the heart of Cockney-land. A lavishly appointed place, it became known as the most fashionable club in the East End.

Thinking that a change of image would do them no harm, the twins began a series of charitable activities on behalf of old people and retired sportsmen, and offered to assist with various national campaigns. One of the latter was the British Empire Cancer Appeal, from whom, in 1962, they bought tickets to the value of £200 for a show given by the Repton Club in aid of the appeal. They loved to be photographed with sportsmen, particularly boxers – among whom were Terry Spinks, a former Olympic medalist, Jack 'Kid' Berg, Ted Lewis, and Billy Walker. They became acquainted with three American former world heavyweight champions, Joe Louis, Rocky Marciano and Sonny Liston, and as well as entertaining them, arranged for them to visit clubs and attend sporting events when they were in England. Ronald claimed that he took Louis to Newcastle-upon-Tyne, Marciano to the Repton Club, and Liston on a trip to the West End.

Show-business personalities were also favoured by the twins. In March 1963, they held an unofficial party for the première of Joan Littlewood's comedy *Sparrers Can't Sing*, and two of its stars – Barbara Windsor and James Booth – turned up. Later, when *Sparrers Can't Sing* was being filmed in streets on the Krays' 'manor', several of the leading actors were frequent guests at the Double R Club, where they were entertained on a grand scale.

On April 19, 1965, when Reginald married Frances Shea (a sister of one of his close friends, Frank Shea) at a church in Bethnal Green, telegrams of congratulation were sent by several well-known personalities, including Judy Garland, Billy Daniels, Lita Roza, Barbara Windsor, and Lord Boothby.

A fortnight before his marriage, Reginald, together with Ronald and another man, had been acquitted at the Old Bailey of demanding money with menaces. One of the Krays' character witnesses was the Reverend Albert John Foster, who also officiated at Reginald's marriage.

The marriage did not last. After six months, an application for an affiliation order was made against Reginald by Miss Ann Zambodini, who had given birth to a child at a hospital in Bow in June 1965; the application was dismissed for 'lack of corroborative evidence'. Shortly afterwards, Reginald and Frances separated, and she reverted to using her maiden name. On June 7, 1967, she was found dead by her brother Frank at his flat in Wimbourne Street, Hackney, where she had been living for some time. At the inquest, the coroner recorded a verdict that she had taken her own life and that death was due to a massive overdose of drugs.

During this turbulent period, George Cornell was shot dead at the Blind Beggar. The twins were taken in for questioning, and were held for more than 24 hours – one at the police station in Commercial Road, the other at Leyton station – before being released. Ronald then gave an interview to reporters who had traced him to a flat above a barber's shop in Lea Bridge Road, Leyton. A burly, poker-faced guard stood at the door. As Ronald spoke, six of his associates, forming a half-circle around him, kept completely silent. Wearing a grubby white shirt, he said. 'I feel more dirty than anything else, and I am going to have a bath and clean-up. This is where they picked me up. We were having a little bit of a party in here.

'My brother Reggie is still inside at Leyton [*sic*]. I don't know why they are holding him. The coppers didn't ask me too many questions – hardly any at all. They told me it was about the George Cornell affair. They told me I was going on an identification parade. I was there 36 hours. There was another bloke on the parade. I don't know who he was or anything about him. There were two witnesses. They walked by and I heard one of them say,

"There is nobody here." The other man nodded his head.

'I was kept in the cells. They looked after me, gave me sausage and mash and a pie and tea when I wanted. I don't know what they wanted to charge me with. It may have been murder. I just don't know, they didn't tell me.'

Double-agents ... 'secret' conferences planned so that information would leak to the other side ... policewomen acting as market researchers ... and a final swoop carried out by more than 100 men who were not told what they had to do until minutes before they acted. ...

All these were part of the incredibly complex and thorough police investigation into the Kray gang, which for years had ruled the East End by force and fear and whose ambitions to take over London and the inner edges of the Home Counties were baulked by the Richardson gang of South London, most of whom are now in prison.

By a pleasing twist of fate, the removal of the Richardsons, which should have left the way clear for the Krays, started the inquiries which resulted in the twins, their brother, and several of their associates being arrested. During the Richardson inquiries, detectives were told of 'gang-warfare and anarchy', all of which they believed were part of the Richardson operations. But investigations showed that this was not so – that some of the stories, told by terrified men and women who refused to make official statements, in fact referred to the Krays.

With the Richardson men dealt with, Peter Brodie, Assistant Commissioner (Crime), the head of London's detective force, called in some of his top officers to plan a new inquiry, with the Kray brothers as the subject. Commander John du Rose, one of the country's most astute detectives, was chosen to start the project. He was given freedom to take whatever steps he thought necessary, the only proviso being that the inquiry should be top-secret. The cover he chose was one which he knew would keep brother officers away from the investigators: a 'No. 1 docket' – the term for a complaint against a policeman.

A superintendent and a sergeant from the Yard's central pool of detectives – officially designated Department C.1, but better known as the 'Murder Squad' – were assigned to open the investigation. They were told not to book in or out of their office, not to make up their work diaries, and to report directly to Commander du Rose. At first, they could make no headway because they were hampered both by reluctant witnesses and by the fact that they could not come out into the open about what they were investigating. They examined files of unsolved cases of violence, and, under various pretexts, drew out files on the Kray brothers and some of their known associates. From these they compiled a list of people involved; but because of the need to protect their cover, they had to trace acquaintances and associates three and even four times removed from the actual men they were interested in questioning. These frustrated, slogging inquiries went on for three months – until the superintendent, Ferguson Walker, was promoted and had to be moved to other work.

It was then that Detective Superintendent Leonard 'Nipper' Read took over, and the team was increased to four officers, still under the rule of secrecy. An office was set up for them at Tintagel House, a Metropolitan Police building between Lambeth and Vauxhall.

Soon afterwards, a criminal with reason for feeling bitter towards certain members of the Kray gang gave the detectives information about the gangsters' contacts. Then, after a further three months, another criminal came forward. Though the information he gave seemed important, the detectives suspected that he was a 'plant', hired by the Krays to find out what the secret police inquiries were about. It was decided to 'play him along', treating him as a double-agent. He was allowed to overhear snatches of conversation between officers – remarks such as 'We're not getting very far' and 'Nobody's going to say anything about anything'.

Meanwhile, progress was being made as members of the 'Tintagel Team' – now comprising a dozen officers – repeatedly visited contacts. Victims of the Krays' rule of fear began hinting where and how the detectives might get some of the evidence they needed.

One piece of information was to the effect that a list of some 10 men had been drawn up by the Krays for disciplining, and officers immediately concentrated on tracing the men. It was soon established that about half of them had been subjected to violence, mainly shootings; but there was no evidence to indicate who was responsible.

After more than 12 months' work, it was decided at a conference of senior officers and legal advisers that if corroboration of some of the evidence could be obtained, arrests could be made. The detectives set about the various tasks. It was to take them several months.

As the additional inquiries forced the officers to work more openly, the Krays and some of their men became alarmed, and it was learned that several of them were making arrangements to leave the country. The double-agent was 'carpeted' and told that his information was of such little value that it would not even help to convict a drunk. The ruse was successful: the tension building up among the gang eased off, and only one air-ticket was used; the man who left the country returned a few weeks later, confident that it was safe to do so.

At Tintagel House, Commander du Rose and the leaders of the team worked out plans for the simultaneous arrests of 18 men. It was decided that the main arresting force would be made up of 100 detectives of the No. 9 District Regional Crime Squad, operating from nine bases in the Metropolitan Police District. The plan included arrangements for assembling the force without arousing suspicions.

At 11 p.m. on May 9, 1968, the detective inspector in charge of each of the Crime Squad bases was telephoned and instructed to assemble his men, and at midnight was again telephoned with orders for himself and his men to drive to Tintagel House, none of the cars arriving together. Each group was given a different approximate time of arrival, and by half-past two on the morning of Friday, May 10, the entire force was present. The officers congregated in a large hall, where for the first time they were told what they were to do. The 100 men, together with members of the 'Tintagel Team', were divided into groups, each with a specific target. The whole operation was timed for 6 a.m. – on the dot. As soon as arrests had been made, reports were to be transmitted by radio, using a special frequency, to a communications centre at Tintagel House; those arrested were then to be taken to West End Central Police Station in Savile Row.

Fifteen of the suspected men were taken into custody, and two of the remaining three were arrested shortly afterwards. The charges were so various and complicated that they were not completed until the early hours of the following morning. As a result of the arrests, additional information flowed in, and it was decided to keep the Crime Squad officers on the inquiry, following up the new leads. There was now no need for secrecy, and so the nature of the investigation changed completely. Once-reluctant witnesses began to volunteer assistance, but there were still some who kept silent, believing that the Krays were capable of outwitting the police.

As some of the information indicated that George Cornell had been shot by Ronald Kray at the Blind Beggar, the police concentrated their efforts upon locating and interviewing people who had been in the public house at the time of the murder. Detective Chief Inspector Harry Mooney, one of the original team, was soon convinced that the key to the case lay with the barmaid. By gentle but persistent persuasion, he finally managed to overcome her fear of the Krays (which she subsequently admitted in court was why she had kept silent), and she identified Ronald as the murderer; she did not know the name of the man with him, but later identified him as John Barrie.

The next breakthrough came when Ronald Hart made a statement about the murder of Jack 'The Hat' McVitie, saying that he had been present when Reginald Kray committed the crime in a basement flat in Evering Road, Stoke Newington, in October 1967.

The police learned that, during the months between the two murders, the Kray brothers had been invited to visit crime bosses in America who were said to have links with the Mafia. There were reasons for believing that the 'contact man' who had suggested the meeting had interested the Krays in the idea of welding together various criminal gangs in this country into a Mafia-style organisation. The twins had gone to America and met men alleged to have links with the Cosa Nostra; Charles had flown to Canada but had been refused entry. The brothers had afterwards appeared to treat the whole idea of transatlantic co-operation as 'a bit of a laugh', although they had admitted concern about the existence in this country of gangsters already associated with American crime syndicates.

In the search for McVitie's body, many methods of disposal were considered, ranging from burial in a graveyard to encasement in newly-laid concrete on a building site; gravel- and sand-pits, lakes and rubbish dumps were checked, and inquiries were made at workplaces with large furnaces. As the police wanted to speak to people living in or near Evering Road without associates of the Krays finding out, in case attempts were made to 'influence' possible witnesses, the 'market research plan' was thought up. With the aim of identifying residents, women detectives posing as market researchers called at houses in the area – as well as in the vicinity of the homes of men named as being present during the murder – and asked for help in testing a new brand of detergent, which, so they said, entailed the completion of a questionnaire. An offshoot fact arising from the 'market research operation' was that there was a newly-puttied window in the basement flat where McVitie was said to have been murdered – confirmation, perhaps, of a statement that in his desperation to escape, he had tried to throw himself through a window.

After further inquiries, it was felt that there was sufficient evidence to justify adding charges relating to the murder of McVitie to those already brought against various members of the gang.

Towards the end of the trial, when Detective Superintendent Read was in the witness-box, he gave some idea of how he and his men had got round the difficulties of questioning convicts who were frightened of repercussions if they talked: 'It was essential to use subterfuge. For instance, I would not go into a prison under my police title, but would go in as a Home Office official or a prison visitor, so that the grapevine would not get to know that I was in the prison at all – would not get to know that a man had made a statement.' On other occasions, he went in late at night, when all the prisoners were locked in their cells. The men he wanted to question were called away for 'medical examination', and he would talk to them in the prison chapel and other 'unofficial' places. He said that he himself had interviewed every one of the male witnesses: 'I saw an enormous number of people, all of whom expressed fear.'

Investigators did not find a cache of money, and it appears that the brothers, like so many other criminals, lived from day to day, taking an 'easy come, easy go' attitude towards the profits from their nefarious activities.

Thursday, March 6:

The Kray twins were each gaoled for life yesterday, with recommendations by the judge, Mr Justice Melford Stevenson, that neither should be released for 30 years.

Since the 1965 Act which abolished capital punishment for all murders, a judge has been able to recommend to the Home Secretary a minimum term that a prisoner should serve before being released on licence. The only previous recommendation of a 30-year minimum was made by Mr Justice Glyn-Jones in 1966, when sentencing Harry Roberts, John Duddy and John Witney for the cold-blooded murder of three London policemen at Shepherds Bush. The fact that a 30-year minimum recommendation was imposed on the Kray twins should ensure that they spend longer in prison than criminals such as the Great Train Robbers, seven of whom were sentenced to 30 years, for a person sentenced to a fixed term of imprisonment is entitled to a one-third remission for good behaviour, and can also be considered for parole after serving a third of his sentence.

During Ronald Kray's 10 minutes in the dock yesterday, he created a disturbance when the judge asked Detective Superintendent Read what assets Kray possessed, to see if any order against him for costs could be operative. Superintendent Read said that he had no information on the assets of the twins apart from a house at Bilderstone, Suffolk, worth about £11,000. Ronald yelled, 'No, it don't – it's my mother's.' The judge told him to be quiet. Superintendent Read then added that the house was in fact in the name of the Krays' mother, Violet.

The twins' elder brother, Charles, was jailed for 10 years for being an accessory after the murder of Jack McVitie. John Alexander Barrie was gaoled for life, with a recommendation that he should serve at least 20 years, for his part in the murder of George Cornell. Christopher Lambrianou and his brother Anthony were each gaoled for life, with a recommendation that each should serve at least 15 years, for their parts in the murder of McVitie. Ronald Albert Bender was gaoled for life, with a 20-year recommendation, for his part in the murder of McVitie. Frederick Gerald Foreman was gaoled for 10 years for being an accessory after the murder of McVitie. Cornelius John Whitehead, already serving a two-year sentence passed at the Old Bailey last September for possessing forged American dollar bills, was gaoled for seven years for being an accessory after the murder of McVitie, the new sentence to start at the conclusion of the previous one.

After the sentencing, the jury adjourned to a nearby public house for a farewell drink after their 39 days of working together.

It is expected that the twins will be split up, one going temporarily to Wandsworth Prison and the other to Brixton, as both are soon to face another trial, for the alleged murder of Frank Mitchell, the so-called 'Mad Axeman'.

Leading article:

To say that the fate of the Kray brothers and their associates represents a decisive victory for the forces of law and order in Britain against highly organised crime might well prove premature.

Many gangs no doubt remain in

existence, and their activities are not confined to the metropolis. The Kray brothers are certainly not the first of their kind, nor, unhappily, are they likely to prove to be the last. What can be said is that a number of men who, when at liberty, not only perpetrated squalid crime on a vast scale but also bred criminals, have been effectively neutralised. What is more, the drama which has surrounded this case and the publicity which it has attracted have supplied conclusive evidence – minatory or comforting according to the inclinations of the recipient – that the police are now well able to cope (and cope brilliantly) with a phenomenon to which a few years ago they were wholly unused.

No one should begrudge the vast sums of legal aid which have been expended on this case. They are not an excessive price for the proof that it is possible to defend society against skilled and ruthless malefactors without deviating from the rule of law. Impartial justice is as necessary to the suppression of crime as efficient detection.

Inevitably, the sentences raise questions. A few will ask whether a civilised society can seriously contemplate keeping any man, however unspeakably wicked his behaviour has been, in prison for getting on for half a lifetime. Yet what other course is open to a society which still wishes to protect its existence and has abandoned the death penalty? Many more will wonder whether the judges' recommendation of 30 years ought not to be a mandatory minimum incapable of any degree of remission at the discretion of a future Home Secretary. Few judges, however, would welcome the responsibility of deciding, more or less off the cuff, but irrevocably, for how long a murderer should be confined. It is a responsibility which ought not to be imposed.

* * *

Albert Donaghue, who had pleaded guilty to being an accessory after the murder of Jack McVitie by redecorating the basement flat in Evering Road, was brought up at the Old Bailey yesterday and gaoled for two years. At the same time, he changed his pleas to 'guilty' of conspiring with others to effect the escape of Frank Mitchell from an outside working party at Dartmoor Prison on December 12, 1966, and to harbouring Mitchell in the period until December 24. He did not change his plea of 'not guilty' to the murder of Mitchell on December 23.

Mr Kenneth Jones, QC, prosecuting, said that he would offer no evidence against Donaghue on the murder charge because he intended to call him to give evidence for the Crown in the forthcoming trial, and the judge passed sentence of eighteen months' imprisonment for the conspiracy counts, to run concurrently with the sentence relating to the murder of McVitie.

The Kray twins have already pleaded not guilty to murdering Mitchell. Charles Kray has pleaded not guilty to conspiring to effect Mitchell's escape and knowingly harbouring him at a flat in Barking Road, East Ham. Four other men are also to be tried in connection with the escape.

Mr Jones said that Donaghue had made a 40-page statement in which he had told Superintendent Read: 'You can have the whole lot. I am making this statement because I am sick of the whole lot of them. They talk about being loyal, but I have to be loyal to my kids. They asked me to volunteer for the

Mitchell one' – meaning that he had been asked to plead guilty to murdering Mitchell.

Counsel added that Mitchell, gaoled for life in 1958 for aggravated robbery, was kept in hiding in the East Ham flat for 11 days. He has not been seen since. Donaghue visited the flat from time to time and was one of three men who took a woman there to be Mitchell's companion. Later, he escorted Mitchell from the flat to a van, telling him that he was being moved to another hiding-place; he then heard the sound of shots in the van. In his statement, Donaghue said that he picked Mitchell up because the Kray twins had told him to, and had not known that he was going to be killed.

Under cross-examination by Mr Edward Gardner, QC, defending Donaghue, Superintendent Read said that it was almost entirely due to Donaghue's intervention with the Kray twins that the life of the girl who had acted as Mitchell's companion was spared.

Mr GARDNER: As a result of this man's intervention with the Kray brothers, other people who were on their list were not killed?

Superintendent READ: That is quite true.

Mr GARDNER: And Donaghue himself was on the list?

Superintendent READ: Yes, he was. He expressed the fear that he was one of the future victims of the Kray brothers.

Mr GARDNER: At one of his first meetings with the Kray brothers, he was shot in the ankle by Reginald Kray?

Superintendent READ: He was, sir.

In his mitigation speech for Donaghue, Mr Gardner spoke at some length of the fear created by the Krays' ruthless use of brutality: 'It was revulsion, which ordinary, decent, right-minded people have for such brutality, that provoked Donaghue to turn against his criminal masters, the Kray brothers.'

The Judge, smiling, remarked: 'I hesitate to interrupt you, but I have been here rather longer than you, and I think I should tell you that you seem to be leaning rather heavily on an open door.'

Saturday, May 17:

Reginald Kray and Frederick Foreman were cleared by an all-male jury at the Old Bailey yesterday of murdering Frank 'Mad Axeman' Mitchell. The jury, out for 7 hours and 20 minutes, found Kray guilty of plotting Mitchell's escape from Dartmoor. He was gaoled for five years on that charge and for nine months, concurrent, for harbouring Mitchell. Both of those sentences are to run concurrently with the sentence of life imprisonment that he is already serving.

Earlier in the 23-day trial, on the direction of the judge, Mr Justice Lawton, Ronald and Charles Kray were found not guilty of murdering Mitchell, and the jury cleared them both of plotting Mitchell's escape and harbouring him afterwards.

Wallace Garelick, a 27-year-old minicab proprietor of Sidney Street, Stepney, who had pleaded guilty to plotting Mitchell's escape, was gaoled for 18 months. Superintendent Leonard Read had agreed, when cross-examined, that Garelick was 'one of the least of the fish' connected with the Krays.

The jury returned to the court three times during their deliberations, and as they were leaving their box on the third occasion, Foreman stood up in the dock and shouted: 'I am innocent, my lord. I

can't understand it. I never murdered anybody at all in my life. Honest. I'm a publican, my lord, not a murderer.' The judge, red-faced, told him to 'sit down and stay sat down'.

The prosecution case was that Reginald Kray had arranged with Foreman to shoot Mitchell, who had become a nuisance after being helped to escape. During the trial, Mr Justice Lawton spoke of the 'cloud-cuckoo-land' atmosphere at Dartmoor Prison at the time Mitchell was 'sprung': both inside the gaol and while with outside working parties, he was allowed to do almost as he liked so as to 'keep the peace'; he kept alcohol under the bed in his cell, paid a number of visits to an inn at Peter Tavy, six miles from the prison, and, at least once, took a taxi to the town of Okehampton.

Albert Donaghue, the chief witness for the Crown, told the jury that at about eight o'clock on the night of December 23, 1966, he had taken Mitchell from a flat in Barking Road to a van in nearby Ladysmith Avenue, and that as Mitchell was getting into the van, Foreman and a man named Gerrad had fired a dozen bullets into him. Foreman claimed that at the time of the alleged shooting, he was visiting his sick wife, Maureen, at a nursing home in Weymouth Street, Central London. He called 17 witnesses to support his alibi.

During the trial, a letter purporting to have been written by Mitchell was received by a solicitor. The general opinion that the letter was not authentic was based partly on the fact that it did not bear his deliberately-impressed thumb-print, which he had used to identify himself on letters he wrote to newspapers shortly after his escape, saying that he would give himself up if he was given a definite date for release on parole. At that time, Mr James Cal-laghan, the Home Secretary, stated that no deals could be made with Mitchell while he was an escapee.

The police believe that if Mitchell were still alive, he would have given himself up.

Saturday, March 11, 1995:

The gangland killer Ronald Kray has died from a heart attack, brought on by heavy smoking, at the age of 61. On Thursday, after collapsing at Broadmoor, he was transferred to Wexham Park Hospital, Slough, Berkshire, and was being prepared for further tests when he had the attack at 9 a.m. yesterday. His twin, Reginald, was informed of his death by staff at Maidstone Jail, Kent.

While in Broadmoor, Ronald Kray produced lurid paintings, and published a selection of his poetic meditations and *My Story*, in which he pondered the ethics of murder, concluding that 'we just did what we had to do'. He married twice during his years at Broadmoor. Neither marriage was consummated.

Barbara Windsor, the 57-year-old actress and a friend of the Krays, said: 'It was awful that he died while still in prison. It would have been nice if he had been let out. I think his brother should be let out, especially now. Enough's enough and they have done their time.'

1970

THE WRONG VICTIM

Last night at the Old Bailey, at the end of the 16-day trial of 34-year-old Arthur Hosein and his 22-year-old brother Nizamodeen, both born in Trinidad, the jury of nine men and three women took four hours and nine minutes to find them guilty on all charges against them. Both were jailed for life for the murder of Mrs Muriel McKay, wife of the Deputy Chairman of the *News of the World*. Other sentences – totalling 49 years for Arthur and 39 years for Nizamodeen – were passed for what the judge described as the 'cold-blooded and abominable' kidnapping of Mrs McKay on December 29 last year, for assaulting and detaining her, and for demanding £1 million with menaces. All the sentences will run concurrently.

In an outburst from the dock shortly before being sentenced, Arthur, who was wearing evening dress, repeated his charge of partiality against Mr Justice Shaw, saying: 'From the moment I mentioned Robert Maxwell, I knew you were a Jew.' [During the trial, he had alleged that Mr Maxwell, the publisher who was Labour MP for Buckingham until he lost the seat at this year's General Election, was one of four men whom he had found unexpectedly at his home, Rooks Farm, Stocking Pelham, Hertfordshire, early one morning just before Christmas. Mr Maxwell was a rival bidder against Mr Rupert Murdoch for the ownership of the *Sun* newspaper, which Mr Murdoch, chairman of the *News of the World*, now owns.]

According to the prosecution theory, Arthur's parents in Trinidad were pressing him to provide them with a home in Britain, for they believed his tales that he had become a rich London businessman with a country gentleman's estate in the Home Counties. Had they come, they would have found him still a busy little trouser-maker, saddled with an overdraft, and living with his brother in a heavily mortgaged, dilapidated farmhouse on a smallholding of 12½ acres.

Watching a David Frost TV programme, he saw an interview with Rupert Murdoch in which the descriptions 'tycoon' and 'millionaire' were bandied about, and his fertile brain conjured up a scheme to kidnap Mr Murdoch's wife Anna. His fantasy life spilled over into reality. He would collect ransom of a million pounds from the millionaire. In a simple manoeuvre, all his problems would be solved; all his dreams would come true. He gave no thought at all as to how he would handle such a gigantic sum. For the moment, there was only the planning and the recruiting of his brother as assistant.

Having observed the Murdochs, or just one of them, being driven in a Rolls-Royce, Nizamodeen, using another name, telephoned County Hall and, claiming that he had been involved in a minor accident with the vehicle, requested the owner's address. He was told only that the Rolls-Royce was owned by the News of the World Organisation. The brothers followed the car to a house in Arthur Road, Wimbledon Park, and assumed that they had found the Murdochs' London home. In fact, the house belonged to the McKays, who were using the car while the Murdochs were in Australia.

On Monday, December 29, the brothers kidnapped the wrong victim. Speaking of this, the first of their bungled crimes, the Attorney-General, Sir Peter Rawlinson, QC, asked the jury to imagine 'the horror and terror and shock to that unsuspecting woman. One minute she was beside the fire, waiting for her husband to return, and minutes later she was gagged and trussed and then driven away in the dark.' Sir Peter read one of several letters written by Mrs McKay and sent to her husband; 'Alick darling, I am blindfold and cold. Please do something to get me home. I can't keep going. I've been thinking about my family and friends and I have been calm so far. What did I do to deserve this treatment?'

Before the letters began to arrive, the first of eighteen telephone calls was received at the house. The caller, who sounded Indian or West Indian, referred to himself as 'M3' and said that he was the head of the 'English group of the Mafia'. Though the McKays were far less wealthy than the Murdochs, the caller insisted on a ransom of £1 million; he gave orders regarding the denominations of the notes, insisting that none was to be new, and issued instructions as to how and where the ransom was to be delivered.

Promptly alerted, Detective Chief Superintendent Wilfred Smith, head of the Wimbledon CID, set up a team, operating as a murder squad, which soon grew in strength from 10 to nearly 50 officers; hundreds of other officers were called in from time to time. It was soon established, chiefly by the tracing of telephone calls from 'M3' and from postmarks on the letters, that the kidnappers were operating within a triangular-shaped area spreading north from Wimbledon through north-east London and into Hertfordshire and western parts of Essex. Close liaison was established between Chief Superintendent Smith and Detective Chief Superintendent Ronald Harvey, head of Hertfordshire CID.

The inquiries produced some farcical situations, largely because of a virtually complete lack of police experience in dealing with kidnapping cases (which was only slightly remedied by advice given by the FBI, who have dealt with hundreds of such crimes between the kidnapping of the Lindbergh baby in the early 1930s and the recent kidnapping of Frank Sinatra's son).

Following the first ransom instruction, to leave the money in suitcases between two artificial flowers in a country lane near Ware, in Hertfordshire, Detective Inspector John Minors took lessons in driving the Rolls-Royce used by Alick McKay and obtained a chauffeur's uniform; meanwhile, Detective Sergeant Roger Street had his hair restyled and dyed, and borrowed a suit from the McKays' son Ian. Before they set off, Minors driving, Street sitting in the back, about 40 detectives were briefed;

some were issued with guns and bullet-proof vests, and at least one was told that if the kidnappers appeared with Mrs McKay, he was to grab her, throw her to the ground and shield her with his body. In separate briefings by four commanders, another 140 officers were ordered to use their own cars. Police motor-cyclists were issued with studded leather jackets and instructed to pose as Hell's Angels. Sadly, their training was too thorough to overcome: as a senior officer remarked later, they sat upright, shoulders squared, followed correct driving procedure, and looked exactly like policemen in disguise. As it turned out, there were so many police vehicles in the ransom delivery area that they unwittingly formed a half-mile convoy, travelling slowly past the rendezvous. One of the police cars stopped another, believing it to contain suspicious persons.

Infuriating as it was to the men in charge, it was not an entirely wasted effort. During the muddle, the Flying Squad's Detective Sergeant Arthur Stevens saw the dark-coloured Volvo which was to loom so large in the trial evidence.

Several other attempts at a rendezvous went awry. When 'M3' ordered Mrs McKay's daughter, Mrs Jennifer Burgess, to travel on a specified bus, carrying a suitcase filled with cash, Detective Sergeant 'Chalky' White, in a blond wig, headscarf, miniskirt and tights, boarded the bus in the company of two other sergeants, one disguised as a garage worker, the other as a train driver. The bus was stopped within minutes by a police patrol car, answering a call from the conductress regarding the strange 'woman' passenger with the hairy legs.

Meanwhile, two men were arrested when, separately, they pretended to be the kidnappers and tried to get some ransom money. Telephone calls from cranks poured in, as well as many from people genuinely trying to help. More than 3500 letters were received from spiritualists and clairvoyants.

The final attempted rendezvous with the kidnappers came less than 24 hours before the arrest of the Hosein brothers at Stocking Pelham. On the evening of Friday, February 6, Robert Kelly, the driver of a hire car, received a call to go to Epping Underground Station to pick up a Mr McKay. His drive ended five hours later in a car-park at Theydon Bois Station, only one stop away from Epping Station, leaving him so bewildered and frightened that he was unable to sleep properly for three days.

The fare turned out to be a dapper man wearing a thick camel coat and a fur hat, and carrying two white suitcases, accompanied by an attractive woman. Robert Kelly was asked by the man to wait while he received a telephone call in the public box inside the station, and after a few minutes was told to drive some 15 miles north, to Bishop's Stortford, Hertfordshire. They had travelled only a hundred yards when he was ordered to stop. As he did so, he was surprised to see a bulky, 'villainous-looking' man, wearing a donkey jacket and carrying a pickaxe handle, appear from the shadows. The man got into the back of the car and lay down on the floor, and Kelly was immediately told to drive on. He was further puzzled by odd snippets of conversation he overheard. The man who called himself Mr McKay said to the one on the floor: 'When we get there, John, you'd better crawl out and get behind the hedge. You'll get a good view from there. The others will be waiting.' Kelly's client tried to reassure him by saying: 'Don't worry – it's only a joke. It's someone's birthday.'

The car was stopped again as it approached Bishop's Stortford, and the suitcases, which had been put in the boot, were transferred to the rear compartment. Kelly was then instructed: 'Drive past Gates's Garage slowly, make a circuit, and during the second time around, stop, but get as close to the hedge as you can.' By now extremely puzzled, and more than a little scared, he did as he was told. He watched the man on the floor slide out of the car and, while shielded by the other two, crawl behind the hedge. 'Mr McKay' then placed the suitcases in front of the hedge, got back into the car with the woman, and told Kelly to drive them to Theydon Bois. There, Kelly was paid the £5 fare and given a small tip.

Some weeks later, after he was told that his passengers were police officers and was thanked for his help, he said: 'I thought they were a bunch of hoods. I was particularly worried about what the villainous-looking man in the donkey jacket might do with the pickaxe helve, so though there were times when I thought of leaving the car and running for it, I decided to stick it out.'

The 'hood' in the camel coat was Inspector Minors, who, not for the first time, was posing as Alick McKay; the 'villainous-looking' man was Inspector John Bland, and the woman was an undercover detective from the Flying Squad, Mrs Joyce Armitage, disguised as the missing woman's daughter, Mrs Diane Dyer.

By the time of Robert Kelly's unnerving experience, the indications of the nationality of the kidnappers, the appearances of the Volvo car at rendezvous points, and the geographic pattern of public phones from which the ransom calls had been made pointed towards Rooks Farm and the Hosein brothers. That same evening, as Arthur Hosein sat drinking double whiskies and boasting of his business successes in the small bar of the Raven public house at Berden, a mile and a half from the farm, a detective sat watching him. Next day, many more detectives moved into the area around Stocking Pelham.

As soon as the brothers were arrested, policemen and forensic scientists began searching the farmhouse, outbuildings, the farmyard and adjoining land. Among several items of evidence that were found was a blank sheet of paper bearing impressions from a note sent by the kidnappers to Mr McKay; also a number of paper flowers (made by a nurse, Lily Mohammed, who was a girlfriend of Nizamodeen's) which matched those placed as markers at the ransom-rendezvous points.

The main task was to try to establish whether Mrs McKay had been at the farmhouse. This was done by taking specimens of dust, fibre and hair, to be analysed for any substance identical to specimens taken from the McKays' home; fingerprints were also sought. Earth samples were collected outside the house, and agricultural tools minutely examined. A deep well was cleared, ponds drained, and hedges cut down so that the ground beneath could be searched. Despite difficulties caused by the freezing weather and snow, the search continued, spreading outwards to other areas in the county. More than 200 policemen took part. But no trace of Mrs McKay was found.

During the trial, Nizamodeen's

counsel, Mr Douglas Draycott, QC, spoke of a rumour that Mrs McKay's body was fed to pigs on the farm, and referred to two earlier cases of murder without a body. In the first, a young woman named Eileen ('Gay') Gibson disappeared while on a sea voyage; there was irrefutable evidence that she had been pushed overboard through a port-hole, and a steward, James Camb, was convicted of her murder at Winchester Assizes in 1948 and sentenced to death; subsequently reprieved, he served a term of life imprisonment. The second case concerned Michael Onufrejczyk, a Polish farmer in Carmarthenshire, who was convicted at Swansea Assizes in 1954 of the murder of a fellow Pole, Stanislaw Sykut, and sentenced to death; that sentence was also commuted to life imprisonment. Mr Draycott said that, in the latter case, the local rumour was that the victim had been fed to pigs, and added: 'But though there was no body, there was forensic evidence of murder. The point regarding Mrs McKay is that there is no evidence at all, forensic or otherwise. Although the probability is that she is dead, she may not have been murdered.'

After the brothers were sentenced, Alick McKay left the court in obvious distress. 'I wish to God I knew what has happened to my wife,' he said. 'All I want to know is where she has been put so that I can go and place some flowers.'

The brothers were driven away from the Old Bailey in separate vehicles and taken to separate jails. They have not spoken to each other – and have been kept apart – since Arthur attacked Nizamodeen while they were exercising in Brixton Prison following their arrest.

Friday, June 8, 1973:

Rooks Farm, in Stocking Pelham, Hertfordshire, the scene of two murder hunts, was sold to an unnamed buyer in Bishop's Stortford yesterday for £46,500.

The farm was put up for sale after its owner, 37-year-old Anthony Wyatt, was jailed for three years in March for the manslaughter of John Scott, a tailor's cutter. The case was originally treated as murder.

In February 1990, Nizamodeen Hosein, who had been a well-behaved convict, was released from Verne Prison, Dorset, and immediately deported to Trinidad. His brother Arthur, who is considered to be mentally unstable, remains in a top-security hospital in Liverpool.

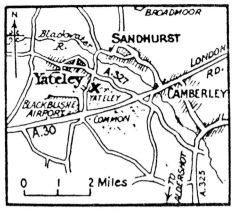

X marks the spot where
the body of Brenda Nash
was found

Arthur Albert Jones

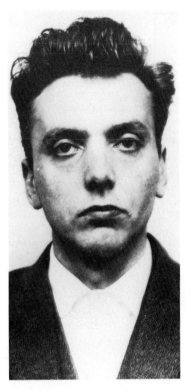

Ian Brady

A recent snap of Myra
Hindley in the grounds of
Cookham Wood Prison
with two of the
Governor's dogs

Brian Tevendale and
Mrs Sheila Garvie at
the East Neuk Bar,
Aberdeen

West Cairnbeg
(X marks the window
of the bedroom in
which Maxwell Garvie
was murdered)

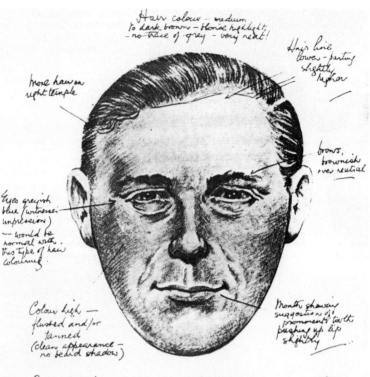

Hair colour — medium to dark brown — blonde highlights, — no trace of grey — very neat!

Hair line lower — parting slightly higher

more hair on right temple

brows, brownish over neutral

Eyes greyish blue (witnesses impression) — would be normal with this type of hair colouring.

Colour high — flushed and/or tanned (clean appearance — no beard shadow)

Mouth showing suggestion of prominent teeth pushing up lip slightly.

Over all appearance one of neatness witnesses say — otherwise this face is very near the man seen.

An artist's impression of the murderer of Christine Darby, which was used on 'wanted' notices sent to every police station in Great Britain

Raymond Leslie Morris

Reginald and Ronald Kray - reunited after they had 'helped' the police with their inquiries into the murder of George Cornell at the Blind Beggar public house (left)

Mrs Muriel McKay

Alick McKay, with members of his family, reading out an appeal to his wife's kidnappers for evidence that she was still alive

METROPOLITAN POLICE
HAVE YOU SEEN THIS WOMAN?

Missing from her home at Wimbledon since evening of 29th December, 1969.

Height 5ft. 9in., medium build, dark brown hair, brownish green eyes, dark complexion. Australian accent.

Wearing black cashmere reversible coat, fawn coloured wool on reverse side, no button. Green jersey suit. Cream patent shoes, square toes, 1¼in. heel, yellow metal chain across instep.

IF YOU HAVE SEEN Mrs. McKay since 5 p.m. on 29th December, 1969, please inform Wimbledon Police Station at 01-946 1113, or your nearest Police Station.

 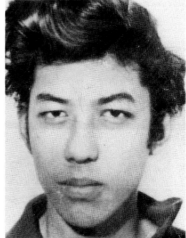

Arthur and Nizamodeen Hosein

Graham Frederick Young

Gary Mark Gilmore

... 1972

Friday, July 6, 1962:

BROADMOOR FOR BOY OBSESSED BY POISON

Poisons fascinated 14-year-old Graham Frederick Young. His deep knowledge of them gave him a sense of power. At last poisons became an obsession and he experimented by giving them to his family and a school-friend in food.

Young, of North Circular Road, Harlesden, London, admitted at the Old Bailey yesterday that he had maliciously administered a poison to his sister, Winifred, 22, his father, Frederick Charles Young, 55, and a friend, Christopher Williams, so as to inflict grievous bodily harm. He was sent to Broadmoor with a restrictive order for fifteen years. He will be the youngest patient there this century.

'I knew the doses I was giving were not fatal, but I knew I was doing wrong,' he told the police. 'It grew on me like a drug-habit, except it was not me who was taking the drug. I knew all along how stupid I have been with these poisons. But I could not stop it.'

Mr E. J. P. Cussen, prosecuting, said that 'Young obtained poisons from chemists, claiming that they were for experiments. In May last year, Williams got stomach pains after eating a sandwich Young gave him. Last September, Young's sister was dizzy and sick. A few weeks later, his father had severe stomach pains after sharing a meal with him.'

Young was the top chemistry pupil at John Kelly Secondary School, Willesden. The science master spotted him bringing poisons to school, and told the headmaster, who got in touch with Young's family doctor. The doctor reconsidered the symptoms of illnesses suffered by the boy's father and sister, and eventually the police were told.

At Young's home they found two books, *Sixty Famous Trials* and *Poisoner in the Dock*. They also found digitalis, atropine, barium chloride, antimony and thallium.

Young made a statement saying: 'I have been interested in poisons, their purposes and effects, since I was about 11. I tried out one of these on Williams. I gave him two or three grains at school. I cannot remember how I caused him to take it. I think it was on a cream biscuit or a cake. He was sick. I gave him a second dose later.

'I started experimenting at home, putting one or three grains on food my stepmother, father and sister ate. I must have eaten some of the poisons occasionally because I became sick as well.

'After eating the foods, my family were all sick. By last September it had become an obsession. I continued to give my family small doses of antimony tartrate on prepared foods.

'One morning I put one-tenth of a grain of belladonna in my sister's milk and left for school. My stepmother told me Winifred had been taken ill. I knew it was the belladonna. I gave some of the remainder to Williams.

'Then I put antimony tartaric solution on foods at home. My stepmother lost weight through it, so I stopped giving it to her. I put poisons on food and in milk and water. As a result, my father became ill.'

Mr Cussen said that Young's stepmother died in April. A postmortem examination had proved that poison was not the cause.

Dr Christopher Fysh, senior medical officer at the remand home at Ashford, Middlesex, said in evidence that Young had a psychopathic disorder but not a mental illness. If the opportunity arose, his behaviour was 'extremely likely' to be repeated. Young had said that poisons gave him a sense of power.

Miss Jean Southworth, defending: 'Would you agree that there is not the killer instinct in him?'

Dr Fysh: 'I would say that he is rather prepared to take the risk of killing.'

The Judge, Mr Justice Melford Stevenson, asked Miss Southworth if, in view of the medical evidence, which was uncontradicted, she could suggest a practical alternative to Broadmoor. She replied that she could not.

Friday, June 30, **1972**:

FREED BROADMOOR MAN POISONS AGAIN

Graham Frederick Young, the 24-year-old storeman sentenced to life imprisonment yesterday for murdering two of his workmates by poisoning them, carried out the crimes while on conditional release from Broadmoor, where he had been sent for giving poison to his father, sister and a school-friend. The judge at that trial, Mr Justice Melford Stevenson, recommended that he should not be released for 15 years without the Home Secretary's consent.

But he was released on medical advice only nine years later, in February 1971. Within four months of his conditional release, Young — who boasted that he would go down in history as a mass-killer — was poisoning again.

His victims were his fellow workers at the John Hadland photographic laboratories at Bovingdon, Hertfordshire — men he used as human guinea pigs to try out the effects of thallium, a rare and deadly poison which, so far as is known, had never before been used by a murderer in Britain.

Throughout the nine-day trial at St Albans Crown Court, Young's past record had to be kept secret from the jury.

Pale and emotionless, as he had been throughout the trial, he stood between two prison officers, his hands gripping the dock, as the foreman of the jury announced the verdicts. The jury had been absent for one and a half hours.

Mrs Dorothy Egle, widow of Mr

Robert Egle, Young's first victim, wept quietly.

Young's hands never left the dock-rail as Mr Justice Eveleigh pronounced sentence without comment. He was immediately hustled out of the dock on his way to Wormwood Scrubs prison, where he will stay while arrangements are made to allocate him to another prison. It is extremely unlikely that he will ever return to Broadmoor, and Young's counsel told the judge after the verdicts: 'He thinks that a prison sentence would be better for his condition than a return to Broadmoor.'

When Young had been sentenced, the foreman of the jury told the judge that he wished to make a recommendation. Reading from a slip of paper, he said: 'The members of the jury in this case consider it to be our duty to draw the attention of the authorities concerned to the apparent failings of the system whereby dangerous poisons may be obtained by members of the public. We ask that the present procedures be reviewed to ensure that the public may be safeguarded in future.'

While at Broadmoor, Young had aspirations of becoming a chemist. In 1963 he wrote, giving his Broadmoor address, to the Pharmaceutical Society of Great Britain, asking if he could become a pharmacist. The society told him that he had not got the entrance requirements of three A-levels and that he needed to have studied at a university for three years. Knowing his record of crime, they said that the disciplinary committee would have to inquire 'into the circumstances of your conviction'.

Young had great admiration for Hitler; he combed his hair across his forehead, wore a swastika armband for a time, and cultivated a Hitler-type moustache which he later shaved.

His obsession for poisons started again not long after he was in Broadmoor. He grew deadly nightshade in the kitchen-garden, extracting the poison belladonna from it.

A former Broadmoor patient has described how Young put sugar soap, which was being used for washing down walls in the dining room, into the tea-urn. One of the inmates engaged on cleaning missed a packet of sugar soap, and found the empty box near the urn, which smelled strongly of soap. He reported the incident to the staff, who dismissed it as a practical joke. According to the ex-Broadmoor patient: 'After that, Young was hated by some of the patients, and we kept clear of him. What was so dreadful was that he didn't appear to have a motive.'

Young did get into trouble with the authorities when he got drunk several times with a group of patients in the common room. It puzzled the staff until they discovered that these inmates were 'fixing' drinks of milk and tea with carbon monoxide from a gas-stove automatic lighter. They blew out the flame and plunged the nozzle into their drinks for a couple of minutes, 'charging' them with the escaping gas. The carbon monoxide remained in the drinks, causing intoxication. Broadmoor has now been converted to natural gas.

Despite his air of innocence, the staff never trusted Young. 'There was something about him which warned us that he could be dangerous,' said one male nurse. 'We knew he had an obsession about poisons, and several times he made the remark that one day he would go into history books as a mass-murderer. We were surprised when he was released.'

The doctor who recommended his release to the Home Office was Edgar Udwin, one of five psychiatrists at Broadmoor working directly under the Medical Superintendent, Dr Patrick McGrath. Dr Udwin, who is South African-born, had held the position for about six years. He was directly responsible for Young, whose release could only have been possible on his recommendation and with the approval of Dr McGrath.

After his release early last year, Young was sent to a Government training centre at Slough, where he took a storeman's course. Only the administrative staff at the centre knew that Young had come from Broadmoor. It was reported that a sailor on another course who had never had an illness in 21 years became ill while Young was at the centre.

In April last year, in the village of Bovingdon, the firm of John Hadland, which employs some 80 people in manufacturing high-speed camera equipment, needed a new assistant storeman. The vacancy was notified to the local employment office, which in turn circulated the job to the Slough centre.

Young, who had satisfactorily passed his course, was recommended for the £20-a-week post. He began working on May 10 with Robert Egle, 60, Frederick Biggs, 56, and Ronald Hewitt.

Within four weeks of Young's arrival, Mr Egle, a happy, healthy married man, became ill with a sickness which baffled doctors. He grew worse, and died within another month.

Towards the end of the summer, illness struck again, particularly among the staff working in the stores. After mid-morning or mid-afternoon breaks, those who worked there would be violently sick and have to be helped home.

Young, the new boy, was always on hand to take the tea to his senior colleagues. A deft movement of his wrist, and deadly poison was dropped into the tea or coffee of the unsuspecting victims.

Young had frequent arguments with his fellow employees, particularly when he turned the conversations to Hitler, saying that England would have been a better place if the Nazis had invaded. His remarks led to heated exchanges, but allowances were made for him because he told his workmates that he had had a mental breakdown caused by a family tragedy.

Eric Baxter, quality control engineer at the firm, has said: 'Young was a compulsive talker. He was impressed by the method Christie used to murder his victims. He knew all the dates and even the number of layers of wallpaper on the kitchen walls at Christie's home in Rillington Place.'

After Mr Egle's death, Young, who was made acting chief storeman, would exclaim: 'I am in charge now.'

Geoffrey Foster, managing director of Hadland's, has described him as a man of above-average intelligence: 'He told me that his mother and sister had died in tragic circumstances, which had led him to going into hospital for treatment and to the Government training centre. He did not say anything about Broadmoor, and I had no idea that he had been an inmate there, much less the reason why. He was given a good reference from Slough.'

Young was finally trapped – but not until he had murdered two people and poisoned others. After Mr Foster was informed by the firm's cost accountant that Young had told him that his hobby was toxicology, the two senior members of the firm voiced their suspicions to the police.

By that time, the mystery illness had become known throughout the factory as the 'Bovingdon bug'. By coincidence, the following day Chief Detective Superintendent Ronald Harvey, head of Hertfordshire CID, was at a lunch in London with forensic science officers. He mentioned the mystery, and one of the experts told him: 'It looks as if you have a case of thallium poisoning on your hands.'

Superintendent Harvey, having no idea what thallium was, had to send out for a copy of a foreign medical textbook which gave its history.

Discovered in 1861 by Sir William Crookes, thallium is a poisonous metal, most of the world production of which is converted into thallium sulphate, used to kill rats and insects. The effects of the poison are cumulative, usually appearing within one to five days. It is both tasteless and odourless.

Senior police officers held a conference that same night and decided to question Young immediately. A mass of medicines and poisons was found in his room. Even more horrific was a diary, recording the progress until death of two of his victims, and the sickness of the remainder. All were referred to by their initials. There was also a drawing of two hands pouring out a bottle bearing the word 'poison' and a skull and crossbones; a genie was coming out of the bottle, and beside it was graveyard equipment and a headstone.

Young, the man who showed a macabre interest in his experiments, and who defined his victims as guinea-pigs, made 'sympathetic' inquiries about their health from their relatives and friends. These inquiries were a smoke-screen, simply to see how his experiments were working, and how much more poison some of them could take without dying. He had no grudge against Fred Biggs – 'dear old Fred,' he said to people at the factory on learning of his death. He was even chosen to represent the stores at the funeral of his first victim, Robert Egle. He expressed regrets to his widow and sympathised with other relatives before Mr Egle was cremated, knowing full well that it was by his hand that the man had died in agony.

After he was arrested, Young brazened it out with the police, but his ego led him to admit the poisonings. He even lectured Superintendent Harvey on the effects of thallium on the human body, and explained that he had given Mr Egle and Mr Biggs 18 grains, with lesser doses to Jethro Batt and David Tilson. He nonchalantly described how he measured the doses against a crushed aspirin, but would not say how he selected his victims and why he gave some of them antimony, from which they recovered.

Young's mother died when he was a baby, and from an early age he was brought up by his aunt, Mrs Winifred Juvenat, returning to his home when his father re-married. He continued seeing his aunt regularly, and she visited him in Broadmoor. She has said: 'He was intelligent, but the family never trusted him after the first poison affair. I would never let him brew me a cup of tea if I could help.'

Young claimed to the police that he had poisoned his stepmother, although her death was recorded as being due to shock and injury to the spine caused in a bus accident. One of the effects of the poison administered by Young is that it weakens the bone-structure.

At his Old Bailey trial, Young admitted giving poison to his stepmother, but said that when she began losing weight he stopped giving it to her. Mrs Juvenat believes that Young did kill his stepmother: 'He gave different poisons to his father and stepmother. When I later asked him the reason for the difference, he said "I am not silly. Father was supposed to die from a broken heart because of her death."'

Mrs Juvenat recalls that Mrs Young visited her on the day she died. 'She was crying and said she had been to see the doctor and he wanted to call an ambulance to take her to hospital immediately. She refused and said she had Graham with her and they would go by bus. She died a few hours later. Graham had a great affection for her.'

Asked about Young's release from Broadmoor, Mrs Juvenat said: 'I can't understand why the authorities didn't get in touch with myself or his father before releasing him. I'm sure his father would have said he should not be let out.

'As a schoolboy he was always interested in little bottles, and kept them in his pickets. My mother used to find them and throw them out. He and a school-friend used to experiment on mice, caterpillars and frogs.

'When we used to visit him in Broadmoor, we heard that he took a great interest in sick patients. One doctor told me, "He had all the patients diagnosed before I even got to the ward to examine them. I had to brush up on my medical knowledge before I talked to Young".'

Leading article:

Certain people, some mentioned in the Graham Young case, some not, must be wondering in their hearts whether any part of blame for the crimes can be laid at their door. For in 1962, at the age of 14, this man was found guilty of poisoning his father, his sister and a schoolfriend, and was consigned to Broadmoor. His release from there was described by his counsel yesterday as 'a serious error of judgment'. With the benefit of hindsight, we can all agree.

Among those with no cause for heartsearching are the two psychiatrists who, at Young's first trial, predicted that he would poison again and whose predictions have been so tragically fulfilled. Another who can bear no blame is Mr Justice Melford Stevenson, who set a 15-year minimum on the time Young should spend in Broadmoor. Yet these warnings, this stipulation, were subsequently brushed aside; and, on the authority of two Broadmoor psychiatrists, endorsed by the Home Office, Young was discharged six years early. Doubtless, those concerned acted in good faith. But they must be anxiously wondering, and not for the first time, whether the present state of psychiatric science enables anyone to pronounce with confidence who is mentally ill and who is not, who is cured, who not, who is safe, who not. Those who have to take such decisions, who have to steer between the twin rocks of needless harshness to the patient and needless danger to society, are not to be envied.

We do not know whether to blame the system or human fallibility for what followed after Young's release. He went first to a Government training centre, then to a private firm, the chief of which seems to have acted with some acumen. At neither place was anyone told of his previous record. The reason for this silence – not to give a dog a bad name – is clear and honourable. Even so, it is good to know from the Home Secretary that this knowledge will in future be more freely available.

The jury at Young's second trial was also kept in total ignorance of his record. The reasons here – to avoid prejudice – are also clear and honourable. But in trying certain types of crime, where no rational motive can be adduced but where there is a proven history of psychopathy, might this not, at the judge's discretion, be disclosed to the jury? Lives as well as liberty are at stake here.

POSTSCRIPT

From an article entitled 'Murder Most Sophisticated' by Dr James Le Fanu, which appeared in the Sunday Telegraph *of January 29, 1995*:

Trends in the forensic-pathology service have reduced the thoroughness of investigations into sudden or unexpected death, thus increasing the chances that death by poisoning will be overlooked. The number of autopsies is certainly falling – and, according to Michael Green, Professor of Forensic Medicine at Sheffield University, so is their quality. As a result of financial constraints, it is now more difficult to persuade hospital laboratories to screen for drugs and other toxic substances. 'Poisoning,' Professor Green urges, 'should always cross the minds of those dealing with an unusual case of sudden illness or death.'

There could be no better illustration of the importance of this advice than the following very unusual case of a mystery illness, described by Victor Dubowitz, Professor of Paediatrics at the Hammersmith Hospital, London.

Early one Sunday morning, Professor Dubowitz was phoned by a doctor in the sheikhdom of Qatar and asked if he would admit a 19-month-old girl who, over a period of 10 days, had become increasingly drowsy and lethargic and was unable to sit upright or walk. By the time the girl arrived at the Hammersmith, she was semi-conscious and unresponsive to commands. She made continuous restless movements when disturbed, had a hoarse cry, and was sweating excessively, even though her temperature was normal.

Professor Dubowitz suspected a viral infection of the brain, or encephalitis, and was disconcerted when his investigations failed to support such a diagnosis. However, the girl's condition deteriorated to a point where it was thought that she would have to be put on a ventilator. While this was being discussed on a ward-round, a nurse sitting by the child's bedside interrupted to say that she thought the diagnosis was thallium poisoning.

In response to the somewhat surprised reaction of the medical staff, she pointed out that the Agatha Christie novel she was reading, *The Pale Horse* [1962], described several cases of thallium poisoning, in which the victims' symptoms were remarkably similar to those of the girl. In addition, the one consistent feature stressed in the book – loss of hair – had just become apparent that morning.

Professor Dubowitz ordered an urgent toxicological analysis, which revealed very high urine levels of thallium – a domestic poison widely used in the Middle East to eliminate cockroaches and rodents, with which she may have been deliberately poisoned. Luckily, the girl responded to treatment, although even four months later she still needed support when standing or walking.

'We are indebted to the late Agatha Christie for her excellent and perceptive clinical description,' Professor Dubowitz concludes in his report. And to the nurse's powers of observation, it would be fair to add.

1976

Thursday, July 22:

DONALD NEILSON,
THE DIM RECRUIT WHO BECAME
A ONE-MAN CRIMINAL ARMY

To all appearances, Donald Neilson was a quiet and colourless family man. He was known to his few acquaintances as a born trier – and a born loser.

Seeking to make something of his life, he put his hand to diverse jobs – door-to-door brush-selling, running a taxi business, training security dogs, joinery and building. But success always eluded him.

So he turned to the 'trade' he had learned as a National Serviceman in the infantry, putting his military skills of stealth, concealment and killing to criminal ends. He ultimately failed in this, too. But before he was caught, he left a trail of terror through the Midlands as his violence and ruthlessness increased with his criminal ambitions. Dubbed the Black Panther, he became the most infamous mass-murderer of the decade.

The foray that was to be his 'golden handshake' to crime shocked and sickened the nation to an extent which no atrocity had done since the Moors murders of the 1960s. He kidnapped 17-year-old Lesley Whittle, a science student, from her home in the remote village of Highley, Shropshire, between 1.30 and 7 a.m. on Tuesday, January 14, 1975. On Friday,

March 8, her naked body was found, hanging from a wire noose, in a 60ft-deep drain-shaft in Bathpool Park, Kidsgrove, Staffordshire. A post-mortem examination showed that she had died from vagal inhibition (over-stimulation, due to fear or shock, of the vagal nerve which runs from the brain to the heart); that she had died before the noose tightened as she fell – or was pushed – from a ledge in the shaft.

The girl's elder brother had tried to pay the £50,000 ransom that was demanded, but mishaps along the 'ransom trail' had prevented him from doing so. Neilson had intended to use the money to enable him to revert to a softer, easier domesticity. Instead, he now faces a lifetime in prison.

Home Office psychiatrists who interviewed him after his capture last December found in the 5ft 4in Yorkshireman a complex and twisted character, fuelling his aggression with the frustrations and bitterness of failure. The insignificant jobbing builder from a working-class suburb of Bradford had become a one-man guerilla unit, meticulous in his planning, cunning, and supremely confident until the very end of his ability to outwit the authorities. He revelled in his tactical successes, basked quietly in the 'glamour' of the Panther tag, and held the police in utter contempt. 'They ought to have used the SAS [Special Air Service] against me,' he told the judge at his trial.

As the police admitted grimly during the man-hunt, Neilson had the devil's own luck. He helped it along with careful preparation, regarding his crimes as military field exercises. But when his luck ran out, the one contingency that he had not prepared for was capture. The Panther had no bolt-hole and no alibi; the locked attic at his home was a criminal 'black museum', a treasure-trove of clues for the grateful police. Such was his disdain for his hunters.

He was born Donald Nappey on August 1, 1936, at the maternity hospital in the coal-mining town of Morley, Yorkshire. His father, Gilbert Nappey, was a textile worker, and the family lived in a two-bedroomed terrace house in Henry Street, which has long since been demolished.

The name Nappey was, of course, a gift to the boy's cruel school-fellows. At Hill Street Junior School, and later at Victoria Road Secondary School, he was known as 'Nappey-rash'. Ridicule at such a formative age, together with his lack of physical stature, may well have played some part in the development of his character. He was considered quiet and introverted – 'a bit of a loner' – by teenage acquaintances, Army contemporaries, and relatives. He was articulate enough if he wished to be, as he often demonstrated in the witness-box, but usually he was taciturn and sullen.

On leaving school in 1951, Nappey started work as a joiner. His mother had died of cancer a year before, when he was 14, so shortly after setting out in the world, he left home to live as a lodger with another family in Morley. He worked hard and learned his trade; but this was the time of National Service, and on January 6, 1955, Nappey, then 18, was conscripted into the Army. Joining the King's Own Yorkshire Light Infantry at Pontefract, he actually enjoyed the rigorous 10 weeks of training, during which he learnt how to fight with rifle, light machine-gun and sten, bayonet and grenade. This business of being turned into a disciplined killing machine was something that most of the young conscripts forgot when they were discharged. Nappey remembered.

The training had not come that easily at first. A man who was in the same intake recalls: 'At the end of the course, Nappey was "back-squadded" to do part of it again. He wasn't very bright.'

Before being called up, he had met a local girl, Irene Tate, who was 20, two years older than himself. She was the daughter of a building labourer and worked in a textile mill. The couple got engaged when he received his papers, and when his prolonged military training was finally over, the wedding took place at St Paul's Church, Morley. That was on April 13, 1955. Behind the conventionally joyful wedding pictures was an unhappy background, for the bride's mother, now living in a council flat in Bradford, did not approve of the groom – 'he was so unfriendly.'

Four months later, Private Nappey kissed Irene goodbye and sailed with his unit for Kenya, where the Mau Mau crisis was raging. There, he was drafted into a tracker team, hunting down the rebel bands in the East African bush – living rough, practising stealth, and learning to match the devious tactics of the guerillas. His grounding in the martial arts continued in Aden and Cyprus, the other trouble-spots of the time, before he returned to England for discharge in 1957, and rejoined his wife.

After living in Morley for a time, the couple moved to a house in Undercliffe, Bradford, and again, a few months later, to their present home in Grangefield Avenue, in the Thornbury district of Bradford. By then, their only child, Kathryn, was born. She had her 16th birthday on January 12, 1976.

Back in civvie street, Nappey began his misery-go-round of jobs. He tried selling brushes door-to-door, but was unable to master the vital skill of appearing to be genial. He did odd jobs, obtained by advertising in local shop windows. And he briefly tried training security dogs in his postage-stamp backyard. When he took over a small taxi business, he decided to change his name from Nappey to that of the firm: Neilson. His main reason for making the change seems to have been to protect his daughter from the barbs and quips he himself had endured as a schoolchild. He displayed a deep affection for the girl, neighbours have recalled, and at his trial the mere mention of her was enough to reduce him to tears.

The taxi business suited Neilson, who enjoyed driving over long distances. It also gave him considerable knowledge of the geography of the Northern counties and the Midlands.

But the jinx returned: custom diminished and the business folded. Neilson went back to joinery, temporary building work and odd jobs to pay the household bills. According to a neighbour: 'He was a very good and eager worker, but everything he did seemed to end in failure. It was pathetic really.'

He took to making garden sheds, offering them for sale on the forecourt of the Westgate Filling Station near his home. (At his trial, he said that he had considered making a sound-proof shed in which to hide his kidnap victim, but had rejected the idea because of ventilation problems.) In return for the space on the forecourt, he did weekend shifts on the petrol pumps. One of the full-time attendants has said that he was meticulous and reliable: 'A lot of money was taken at weekends, but at the end of the day, when he handed over, it was always absolutely correct.' Petty dishonesty was not for Neilson. He would probably have been offended at the very suggestion – just as, while having cold-bloodedly murdered Lesley Whittle, he showed outrage at any suggestion that he had interfered with her sexually.

To make some extra money at this time, the family let out part of their tiny house as flatlets, Neilson having done the conversion work himself. One of their former tenants has said that 'it was all a bit cramped. The owners slept in the attic, and there were two women living in rooms in the house as well as myself and my wife.' Neilson was not a sociable landlord: 'Everyone used the same sitting room, but there was no small talk from him. He was a sullen sort of man.'

It was about now that the seed of the idea of turning to crime began to germinate in Neilson's deeply depressed mind. In addition to all his other troubles, he had a stomach ulcer (from which he still suffers), and it seemed to him that the whole of society was against him. So why not declare war on society?

Displaying a kind of nostalgia for

the time of his life when he had not entirely failed – during National Service – he brushed up on his physical fitness and combat-readiness. It became almost a fetish. He did exercises, walked long distances as though on route-marches, and often swam at the nearby Undercliffe Baths. He did not smoke and was never seen at his local public house, the Junction. Acquaintances noted, with some amusement, that Army mannerisms returned: not only the brisk stride and ramrod back, but also the brusque way of speaking (in court, it was all 'Yes, Sir' and 'With respect, Sir'). He took to wearing paramilitary denim clothes, boots, and even webbing. And he bought himself an ex-government Austin Champ, the British version of the American Jeep.

A neighbour has said: 'I used to call him Castro for fun. He wasn't a bad bloke really, and I only had one argument with him, when I called him a callous bugger for the way he treated his dogs. But he didn't seem to hold a grudge about it.'

When the lodgers left, Neilson turned the attic into his 'operations room', using maps and a stop-watch to plan his crimes. At first, it was all rather like Walter Mitty with his day-dreams. But the dreams soon became real.

Neilson roamed wide in his search for burglary 'targets' while keeping up appearances as the conscientious self-employed artisan. His usual method of entry was true to his trade: with brace and bit, he drilled through window frames, slipping the catch inside with a piece of bent wire. It became a hallmark of his activities to several police forces.

This was the method he used when, in November 1970, he broke into a house at Thornhill, a district of the Yorkshire town of Dewsbury, and stole an automatic shotgun, a 12-bore shotgun, and a number of cartridges. It was a haul that turned him from a petty burglar into a potential armed killer.

Early in the following year, he augmented his private armoury by getting the name of an arms dealer from a shooting magazine, breaking into his home at Cheadle Hulme, Cheshire, and stealing two ·22 pistols, two ·22 automatic rifles, a ·177 air-rifle, a leather shoulder-holster, a pair of shooting spectacles and 300 rounds of ammunition.

The one-man combat unit was now ready for action. Armed, ruthless and guileful, Donald Neilson, formerly Nappey, was about to show the world, which had seemingly spurned all his earlier efforts, just what he was made of.

He stole from houses and business premises, but preferred small sub-post offices because hard cash was to be found in them. He did not want to kill. As a professional criminal, his aim was to remain undetected – and it was to this end that he cautiously reconnoitred the 'target premises', weighed up the occupants, and carefully plotted his getaway route. He habitually wore a black mask which left – as one witness recalled it – 'only his small, pink eyes visible'.

But with his cold, military logic, anyone who caught him during a crime, and any victim who resisted, had to be eliminated. Without compunction, Neilson murdered three sub-postmasters, savagely beat the wife of one of them, and tried to shoot his way out of being arrested.

His attention to detail enabled him to defeat, for nearly two years, the massive police operation mounted to catch him. That operation cost nearly £2 million and involved hundreds of officers. But

Neilson's reign of terror was eventually ended by two police constables in a patrol-car who were carrying out a routine check.

According to the police, Neilson would have been caught within the following six weeks by the signature on the application form for his driving licence. An example of the Panther's handwriting had been found in a car abandoned by Lesley Whittle's kidnapper, and a pilot-scheme for checking the signatures of 500,000 men in Staffordshire had been completed by the time of Neilson's arrest, and other checks were under way in the West Midlands and Yorkshire. Plans had been drawn up to search records from the Bradford area, and the police claim that these would have found Neilson: 'His writing was so distinctive that he could not have escaped,' a senior detective has said. The enormous search of driving-licence records was instigated by Commander John Morrison, then head of Scotland Yard's Murder Squad, who was called in to co-ordinate the inquiries by various police forces.

The hunt for the Black Panther had started in February 1974, after the murder of Donald Skepper, a sub-postmaster at Harrogate, Yorkshire, although country-wide inquiries into a series of raids on post offices in towns and villages many miles apart had been in progress for two years: the police suspected that one man was responsible for all of those relatively minor raids. When the raider could not find the keys to the Harrogate post office, he went into Donald Skepper's bedroom, but the sub-postmaster shouted to his son, 'Let's get him,' and tried to arrest the man – who shot him at point-blank range and fled empty-handed. He eluded road-blocks set up after a 999 call from the son and

made his way home to Bradford, about 20 miles away.

Seven months passed before Neilson killed his next victim, 43-year-old Derek Astin, sub-postmaster at Higher Baxenden, near Accrington, in Lancashire. Detective Chief Superintendent Joe Mounsey, head of the Lancashire CID, took charge of this inquiry, and set up an incident room to correlate information on post office raids. Before long, a map was peppered with red pins marking a seven-year trail of unsolved raids, ranging south from Newcastle-upon-Tyne to Mansfield in Nottinghamshire.

Eight weeks after the murder at Higher Baxenden, the raider killed again, his third victim being 54-year-old Sidney Greyland, who ran a sub-post office at Langley, near Birmingham. Mr Greyland died from stomach wounds caused by a ·22 rifle, and his wife Frances, who was in the shop with him, had her hands tied and was left for dead after she had been so savagely beaten with the butt of a pistol that her skull was crushed. Miraculously, she survived.

Eventually, various clues collected in the hunt for Lesley Whittle's kidnapper pointed to the fact that the Black Panther and the kidnapper were the same man. Detectives at last grasped the extraordinary extent of the activities of the man they were seeking.

Inquiries into the post office murders were now controlled from the small brick-built police station at Kidsgrove, where Commander Morrison had set up his headquarters, and the massive task began of tracing the source of the Whittle case exhibits which the Panther had abandoned in and around the drainage shaft in Bathpool Park. Some 250,000 people were interviewed, 60,000 statements were taken,

32,000 telephone messages were noted, one and a half million cards for the reference index were hand-written by 35 policewomen and were then typed and filed by 20 girls working daily until 2 a.m. One of the detectives said that he had learned so much about the man that 'I could make a suit to measure for him. All that is missing is the name.'

But Neilson was eventually caught, not by the extensive investigative operation, but by the vigilance and courage of two police constables patrolling in a car at Rainsworth, near Mansfield. They were Anthony White, who was 25, and Stuart Mackenzie, three years older. They saw a man carrying a hold-all near a sub-post office: 'He was walking quickly, almost running,' PC Mackenzie has said. 'He turned his face away from us as we passed the mouth of the street.' When they stopped the man, he produced a sawn-off shotgun and, having forced them back into the car, tried to hijack the vehicle with them in it. They tackled him, braving the blast of the gun which had already claimed three lives, and he tried to flee – but, with help from several men who had been in a fish and chip shop, the two constables caught and subdued him. Injuries to his face on photographs taken of him at the local police station bore witness to the fact that he had fought like a tiger, or a panther, in trying to escape, and that some of the men from the fish and chip shop had not pulled their punches.

A call was put through to the murder team at Kidsgrove. Chief Superintendent Eric Buckley, the Mansfield divisional commander, subsequently commented: 'It was routine police work which led to Neilson's arrest – and it shows the importance of checks, to which people sometimes object.'

In the attic of Neilson's home in Bradford – locked when the first detectives mounted the stairs to it – was found, concealed behind false walls and under floorboards, a number of firearms, ammunition, an array of hoods and masks, crowbars, 799 car-ignition keys, and enough heavy-weather clothing and equipment to stock a small quartermaster's stores. Forensic and ballistic tests linked some items to the post office killings. One small item found in the house convinced detectives – if they needed convincing – that they had caught the right man. It was a porcelain figure of a black panther.

Yesterday, at the end of the proceedings in Oxford Crown Court (held there rather than in a court in the North or the Midlands, where prejudice against Neilson might have swayed jurors), he stood in the dock, with his head erect but eyes damp, as Mr Justice Mars-Jones sentenced him to five terms of life imprisonment together with other concurrent but lesser terms, telling him that 'in your case, life must mean life. If you are ever released, it should only be on account of your age or infirmity. In my judgment, the enormity of the crimes of which you have been convicted puts you in a class apart from almost all murderers in recent years.'

As the judge piled sentence upon sentence, Neilson's brow creased almost into a wince. A nervous tic, which had afflicted the right side of his face at moments of stress throughout the proceedings, had become very noticeable.

As soon as the sentencing was over, he quickly turned and almost ran down the stairs to the corridor leading to his cell in the nearby Oxford Prison.

Before dismissing the jury, Mr Justice Mars-Jones paid tribute to Police Constables Stuart Mackenzie and Anthony White, saying: 'You showed outstanding courage, tenacity and initiative in dealing with a situation which would have reduced lesser men to timorous inaction. By reason of your swift, decisive actions, you can claim credit for having brought to justice one of the most dangerous criminals who have been abroad in this land. I direct that these observations be brought to the attention of your superiors.' The judge also commended two members of the public – Keith Wood, an engineer, and Roy Morris, a miner – who had helped the constables, and instructed that they should each receive a reward of £50 from public funds.

During his summing-up, the judge had rebuked Detective Chief Superintendent Robert Booth, who, while giving evidence, had made no secret of his dismay at the part played in the investigation by officers from Scotland Yard, referring in particular to an 'embarrassing' incident in the early hours of January 17, 1975, when a Staffordshire policeman in a Panda patrol-car had innocently driven into the middle of a Scotland Yard stake-out at a proposed ransom drop in Bathpool Park, Kidsgrove, and started taking the numbers of the unmarked surveillance cars. Mr Booth had also spoken disparagingly – and somewhat emotionally – of a Scotland Yard search-team which had combed the area of the abortive ransom drop on the following day. According to Mr Booth, though the team had found 'not a scrap of evidence', local children had later picked up several useful clues. Mr Booth's remarks had been followed by a comment from Mr Gilbert Gray, QC, for the defence,

speaking of the police operation in the Whittle case: 'You have heard of the Black Panther and Donald Neilson – this was more like the Pink Panther and Peter Sellers.'

Mr Booth, a portly, balding man with a small moustache, sat stonefaced on the police benches as Mr Justice Mars-Jones, peering at him over his half-moon spectacles, rebuked him for using the privilege of the court to deliver 'a bitter attack on fellow officers who could not answer back'. Turning to the jury, the judge went on: 'I had no warning of what [Mr Booth] was going to say, but if I had, I would not have allowed it. Be that as it may, his views are of no help to you in arriving at your verdict. They were irrelevant.'

Tuesday, September 28:

Donald Neilson, who had been brought from Leicester Jail under an armed escort, yesterday stood handcuffed between two prison warders at Stafford Court while giving evidence on behalf of his wife Irene, who was appealing against the sentence of 12 months' imprisonment that was imposed upon her on September 3 by magistrates at Eccleshall, Staffordshire, after she had admitted seven charges involving postal orders stolen by her husband in raids on sub-post offices and had asked for another 76 such offences to be considered. The grounds of Mrs Neilson's appeal were that the sentence was oversevere, that she had no previous convictions, and that the offences were committed at the behest of her husband.

When Neilson was asked by Mr Gilbert Gray, QC, for Mrs Neilson, how he had treated her, he broke down. After a pause, he said that he had always put his work first and his family and home second. He had told his wife to mind her own business when she questioned him and he took her with him to cash the stolen postal orders. 'I was the boss in my home. There was no doubt about that. If this involved knocking her about, it had to be done.'

After giving evidence for 30 minutes, he left the dock without looking across at his wife, who, with her head lowered, had sobbed throughout the time that he was questioned.

Judge Toyne, who sat with two of the Eccleshall magistrates, rejected Neilson's evidence, saying: 'What has been alleged about his domination over his wife has a vagueness about it which we find unconvincing and uncompelling – particularly in the manner in which he gave his evidence. We dismiss the appeal, feeling that the sentence was neither wrong in principle nor excessive in degree.'

While Neilson was escorted back to Leicester Jail, where he has been kept almost continually in solitary confinement since the end of his trial, Mrs Neilson was taken back to a different prison.

Thursday, June 10, 1977:

A DEADLY DREAM

Nineteen-year-old Mark Rowntree, who had passed four A-level and five O-level examinations, and had qualified for university entrance, was possessed of a dream. He wanted to be locked in a cell with the Black Panther, and hear a warder tell the murderer of four people: 'This man has killed *five* people. You'd better watch out. He's good with a knife.'

In the twisted grip of schizophrenia, Rowntree, the adopted son of a wealthy and doting couple, set out to make his dream come true. Within eight days, he stabbed four people to death. All of them lived within a 10-mile radius of his home at Tranmere Park, Guiseley, Yorkshire.

His first victim, on New Year's Day, was Mrs Grace Adamson, an 85-year-old widow living in Bingley. He knocked at her door and, after saying that he was from the police, stabbed her seven times with a commando-knife which he had bought as a collector's piece but later decided that he 'wanted to use for the purpose it was manufactured for – to kill'. After the killing, he hid the knife in a cemetery.

Two days later, carrying another knife, he walked up to 16-year-old Stephen Wilson of Keighley, who was standing at a bus-stop, and stabbed him three times. Before the boy died in hospital, he was able to give police a description of his attacker.

On Wednesday, January 7, Rowntree went to the home of Barbara Booth in Green How Crescent, Leeds. He had met her through a 'contact magazine', and about a year earlier had visited her and paid her for sex. Now he stabbed her 18 times. Fearing that her three-year-old son Alan, cowering in a corner, could identify him, he stabbed the child 15 times.

When a detective questioned him, suspecting him only of the first murder, he suddenly announced: 'I will just tell you a little story before I go to sleep. It will interest you. I did all those killings.'

At Leeds Crown Court yesterday, his answer to each of four charges of murder was: 'Not guilty, but guilty to manslaughter on the grounds of diminished responsibility.' His plea was accepted by the Crown, and he was committed to Broadmoor for an unlimited period.

Mr Franz Muller, prosecuting, said that it was clear from Rowntree's voluntary statement to the police that he was driven by an insatiable desire to kill. 'After each killing, he had a sense of elation; but it was only short-lived – the desire to kill soon returned. He has stated that his original ambition was to execute girls between 15 and 20 years of age – those he despised. He felt hurt and let down by girls. This motivated him to seek revenge on anyone or anything. He began by smashing cars and shop windows, but this did not relieve his frus-trations, and he felt that he had to resort to human targets.'

Mr Muller added that Rowntree's adoptive parents had given him everything they could. His father, a managing director, had paid for him to be educated at private schools; he always had ample pocket-money, and he was sent on holidays abroad. He was a keen sportsman, but at one time was banned from the local swimming baths for frightening small children with an air-gun.

Generally thought to be a quiet and reserved boy, he was destined to become what Detective Chief Superintendent Jack Dibb, the head of the Bradford CID, has described as 'the most dangerous man ever, so far as mass-murder is concerned'. Mr Dibb believes that he would have carried out a threat to kill others. In his statement, Rowntree had mentioned the names of two girl students. And he had confessed that his intention was to beat the Black Panther's tally of killings.

1976

KILLER FIGHTS TO BE SHOT

Gary Mark Gilmore, a convicted murderer who is due to face a firing squad in Salt Lake City, Utah, on November 15, has tried to dismiss two court-appointed lawyers who are trying to prevent the execution. Though Gilmore has said that he would rather die than spend the rest of his life in prison, the lawyers believe that he does not have the legal right to go to his execution without proper appeals. One of them, Craig Snyder, said: 'There is a question, and a substantial one, as to whether he has the right personally to die on November 15 or at any other time that might be set.' There is no automatic appeal against a death sentence in Utah.

No executions have been carried out in the United States since 1967,* and many feel that those now scheduled will not take place, even though some of the condemned men, not only Gilmore, insist that they deserve to die.

Gilmore has been given the choice of a firing squad or death by hanging. He has chosen the former. Utah is the only state that offers such a choice. Of the 44 men executed in Utah's history, 39 chose the bullet rather than the noose.

Gilmore, the son of a hard-drinking building worker, has spent 18 of his 35 years in prison for rape, armed assault, and robbery. Last summer, while on parole, he flew into a 'murder rage' because his 20-year-old fiancée, Nicole Barrett, a divorced mother of two, had fled into hiding to escape his boozy, drugged tantrums. On consecutive nights, he pitilessly robbed and killed two unresisting victims, a motel clerk and a petrol station attendant. Both men were in their mid-twenties, working their way through college. They left young widows and children. Gilmore was found guilty of the motel murder, but has not been tried for the second crime.

* In 1968, two decisions by the US Supreme Court had the effect of creating a virtual moratorium on capital punishment: the decisions were (1) that the section of the Lindbergh kidnapping law which authorised the death penalty should be excised; and (2) that the exclusion from juries in murder trials of persons who expressed ambiguous scruples regarding capital punishment was unconstitutional, since it could result in 'hanging juries'. In 1972, the Court decided that the death penalty offended against the Eighth Amendment to the Constitution, which prohibits 'cruel and unusual punishment'. In 1976, Utah was one of a number of states which revised death penalty laws so as to meet the new standards set by the Supreme Court.

Friday, November 12:

MOVES TO STOP
'DIE-LIKE-A-MAN' EXECUTION

Last-minute legal moves were under way in Utah and Washington, DC, yesterday to stop next Monday's scheduled execution of Gary Mark Gilmore.

Utah's Governor, Calvin Rampton, yesterday gave opponents of capital punishment two additional days to mount their case by issuing a stay of execution until next Wednesday. The delay allows the State Board of Pardons, which has the power to commute sentences or issue pardons, whereas the Governor does not, to consider any action in Gilmore's case. The Board has three options: it can commute the sentence to life imprisonment against Gilmore's wishes, order a complete review of the case, or refuse to take any action and ask the trial judge to set a new execution date.

Between now and next Wednesday, two groups which have led the opposition to capital punishment, the American Civil Liberties Union and the National Association for the Advancement of Coloured People, intend to explore every legal avenue to get the US Supreme Court to intervene in the case and stop the execution. In doing so, they will clearly be acting against the condemned man's wishes.

In a hand-written letter to the Utah Supreme Court, Gilmore has declared: 'Any and all efforts made by any group of people, including particularly the ACLU or any other organisation, should be considered null and void. These people do not represent me.

'Don't the people of Utah have the courage of their convictions? You sentenced a man to die – me – and when I accept the extreme punishment with all grace and dignity, the people of Utah want to back down and argue with me about it. You are silly.'

Monday, November 15:

LINE-UP OF VOLUNTEERS
TO JOIN FIRING SQUAD

A 'long line of volunteers' have come forward to join a firing squad for the execution of Gary Mark Gilmore, if it is eventually needed, Samuel Smith, Warden of Utah State Prison, Salt Lake City, said yesterday. Mr Smith did not identify the volunteers, but it is reported that one is a former employer of Gilmore.

Warden Smith was angry that prison regulations were broken when a newspaper reporter had a telephone interview with Gilmore in which the possibility of a 'Death Row marriage' was discussed. The interview was arranged by Gilmore's lawyer, Dennis Boaz, who said that the newspaper had offered him 250 dollars cash. Gilmore reportedly wishes to marry Mrs Nicole Barrett, who jilted him last summer. Mr Smith said that Gilmore had not discussed the matter with him – and 'without any deep review, I can see no value in it.'

Mrs Barrett tearfully told a television interviewer last week that she felt some responsibility for Gilmore's murderous actions after they separated. She said that she left him because she wanted to return to her former husband. Since Gilmore's conviction, she has been visiting him regularly in jail.

Wednesday, November 17:

CONDEMNED MAN TAKES DRUGS OVERDOSE

Gary Mark Gilmore tried unsuccessfully yesterday to cheat his executioners by swallowing an overdose of drugs smuggled into his cell.

At about the same time, his girlfriend, Nicole Barrett, who became engaged to him during a prison visit on Monday, was found unconscious in her flat in Springville, Utah, also apparently the victim of a drug overdose. It is believed that Gilmore and Mrs Barrett managed to discuss a suicide pact before or after he proposed to her.

Wednesday, December 1:

DEATH SENTENCE IS CONFIRMED FOR KILLER WHO WANTS TO DIE

Gary Gilmore was told by the Utah Board of Pardons in Salt Lake City yesterday that it would not commute his death sentence, and thereby cleared the way for his expressed wish to die before a firing squad. He sat calmly and thanked the Board for its decision. George Latimer, the chairman, said that he and Thomas Harrison had voted that the sentence 'will not be commuted or lessened'. The third member of the Board, Harriett Marcus, had dissented, saying that she wanted the Utah Supreme Court to decide whether the State's death penalty was constitutional. Mr Latimer ordered the case to be returned to the trial judge for a new execution date to be set. But the execution still faces legal challenges from the Civil Liberties Union and lawyers representing other prisoners on Death Row.

Before the hearing, Gilmore had sent the Board a defiant, obscenely-worded letter, saying: 'Let's do it, you cowards.' He has been on a hunger strike for nearly two weeks following his abortive suicide pact with his girlfriend, Mrs Nicole Barrett, who is now in a mental hospital.

Saturday, December 4:

GILMORE EXECUTION DELAYED

Gary Gilmore, who was due to face a firing squad at dawn on Monday, received an unwanted stay of execution yesterday from the US Supreme Court, which ordered Utah officials to file by Tuesday a response to a request for clemency from Gilmore's mother, Mrs Bessie Gilmore, who, bed-ridden with arthritis at her caravan home in Oregon, has belatedly, and to her son's surprise, entered the controversy surrounding his execution. About an hour earlier, the Utah Supreme Court had denied the mother's petition.

Utah State expense vouchers for $725 (about £453) were processed yesterday to pay the five-man firing squad, one reserve, and the squad captain.

The Federal Aviation Administration had imposed a restriction on air-space for a mile around the State prison, so as to forestall reporters and television cameramen who had hired helicopters to view the death.

Friday, December 17:

'EXECUTE ME' KILLER TRIES SUICIDE AGAIN

Gary Gilmore, the condemned murderer whose demands to be executed without delay have three times been thwarted by appeal courts, yesterday tried for a second time to commit suicide. He was taken to a hospital from Utah State Prison after apparently swallowing drugs, but later his condition was said to be 'good'.

His latest attempt came one day after a judge had set a new execution date of January 17. Gilmore had asked to be shot next Monday, but later said he would attempt to gain his freedom on a legal technicality – that his execution should have taken place within 60 days of sentence.

Saturday, January 15, 1977:

JAIL READY FOR GILMORE'S LONELY WALK TO DEATH

Five people have received verbal invitations to attend Gary Gilmore's dawn execution by firing squad, due on Monday. They are his girlfriend, an uncle, two lawyers, and the agent for the publishers who have bought his life story. The four men were thought likely to accept, but the girlfriend, Mrs Nicole Barrett, is still in a mental institution in Provo, Utah. Gilmore's lawyer, Ronald Stanger, said yesterday that his client realised that hospital authorities were unlikely to allow Mrs Barrett to see the execution. He thought that Gilmore would consider it 'appropriate' to place an empty chair at the execution site should she not be able to attend.

If the execution takes place, Gilmore will not leave his 7ft by 9ft windowless cell on the ground floor of the maximum-security wing of the Utah State Prison until about 7 a.m. on Monday. At that time, guards will lead him to the secret indoor execution site. He will not be taken past any other cells.

For his last meal he will be offered the standard Sunday night prison dinner – tossed salad with dressing, rib steaks with mushroom gravy, baked potatoes and peas, cherry pie and coffee – or a special meal if he wishes. 'We'll get him most anything he wants,' said Assistant Warden Leon Hatch. 'If he should say he wanted pheasant, we would make every attempt to get it.' Gilmore has said several times that his only 'last meal' request is for a six-pack of a particular brand of beer brewed in Denver.

At his request, his vital organs will be removed immediately after the execution for use in transplant operations and in medical research.

Desperate last-ditch suits to stop the execution were being brought yesterday in state and federal courts by opponents of capital punishment. Yet American public opinion seems opposed to these efforts. A national poll found that 71 per cent of those questioned believed that Gilmore should die on Monday. But 86 per cent disagreed with a recent Texas court decision permitting television coverage of executions pending in that state.

Monday, January 17:

11TH-HOUR APPEAL TO SAVE GILMORE FAILS

After the failure of a further legal move yesterday, Gary Gilmore appeared certain to go before a firing squad today, getting his wish to become the first person to be executed in America for a decade. The 36-year-old homicidal maniac is due to die at sunrise, 7.49 a.m. (2.49 p.m. British time).

Justice Byron White of the US

Supreme Court yesterday refused to block the execution after an application was filed by the Civil Liberties Union, which contended that Gilmore's death would prejudice the appeals of two other men on Utah's death row. The judge announced his decision after telephoning other members of the Court. Lawyers immediately resubmitted the application to Justice Thurgood Marshall, but the Clerk of the Court said that he was unavailable.

There will be vociferous demonstrations against Gilmore's execution from groups opposed to the death penalty. But locally there is no overwhelming sense of outrage. A belief in blood atonement is buried deep in the traditions of the Mormons who founded Utah.

Last week, Gilmore was reported to be 'looking forward to getting it over with'. But at the weekend his mood was more edgy; he was talking quickly and resenting the stares of two warders guarding him. He is an evil, complex man with a good IQ (117), a considerable talent for drawing, and a lesser one for poetry. He is quite tall, but his body has been wasted down to 10 stone by hunger strikes.

Unlike the proposed execution of another prisoner in Texas, Gilmore's death will not be televised. Instead, elaborate arrangements have been made for reporters and television crews to camp all night in the prison car-park to get what are described as hourly 'human interest' bulletins and see the scene of the execution soon after the shooting. These details were worked out during a rowdy meeting with Samuel Smith, warden of the prison. He said that the 'activity' would start promptly at 7.05 a.m. but refused to give the precise time of the shooting.

A reporter from the television show *Good Morning, America* complained: 'Can't you give even an approximate time? We've got a network to worry about.' All three networks will interrupt their breakfast shows and commercials to carry news of the death direct from mobile transmitters in the car-park. By a gentleman's agreement, they will not jostle Warden Smith for details in the corridor, but will wait until he is seated at a press conference. This, he promised, would be after some legal 'chores', probably ten minutes after the shots ring out. In his view, none of this amounts to a macabre circus, although he feels that the press has made a hero out of Gilmore – 'and I personally resent that'. Gilmore will be shot indoors, thwarting a plan to take television pictures from a helicopter. Details of the execution, including whether Gilmore will wear a hood, are still being worked out. He does not want to wear a hood. 'His views will be considered,' says Warden Smith.

Several psychiatrists have declared that the very existence of the death penalty, confirmed by the US Supreme Court last summer, could have prompted a death-wish in Gilmore and spurred him to commit the murders. 'He's been reading his obituary for months – and loving it,' said one psychiatrist.

WILD RUSH FOR RIGHTS
AS GILMORE BECOMES BIG BUSINESS

The merchandising of Gary Gilmore has developed into an intense business involving big money and depending for its profits on his determined drive towards self-destruction. There was a wild scramble for rights to his life story for films, books and the press when he first announced his intention not to appeal against his death sentence for murder. The singer Paul Anka was reported to have offered £45,000, but dropped out as the bidding rose. The contract eventually went to Larry Schiller, who calls himself a 'communicator'. He specialises in deals with people whose lives have been affected by tragedy and sensation. His clients have included Susan Atkins of the Charles Manson 'family', Lee Harvey Oswald's widow, and Jack Ruby, the killer of Oswald.

He flew into Salt Lake City and decided that he was dealing with amateurs when he discovered that Gilmore's lawyer had sold a telephone chat with the doomed man to a British newspaper for £225. He made contact with Gilmore's uncle, Vern Damico, and struck a deal for around £54,000 for film, book and other rights. Of this, about £27,500 will go to Gilmore, £9000 to his fiancée, Nicole Barrett, who is still in a mental home, and £18,000 to the widows of Gilmore's two murder victims. Gilmore must pay his two new lawyers and Uncle Vern out of his money, which he is otherwise unable to spend.

Meanwhile, the *National Enquirer*, a weekly tabloid published in Florida, has entered into a secretive deal with Uncle Vern and, apparently, Nicole's family. The *Enquirer* has also been running comments from Gilmore under Uncle Vern's copyright. The latest comments have the headline: 'Gilmore's death-cell letters reveal shrieking, hideous ghosts are tormenting him.' Mr Schiller said that the *Enquirer* initially offered around £25,250.

Tuesday, January 18:

'LET'S DO IT,' GILMORE SHOUTS
– AND DIES

With a defiant cry of 'Let's do it,' Gary Gilmore met the death he had so earnestly pursued, in front of a firing squad in an old tannery at Utah State Prison yesterday, eighteen minutes after an icy sunrise.

He died strapped in an oak chair, with a black corduroy hood covering his head and a white target pinned over his heart. From a black canvas cubicle eight yards away, the barrels of five ·30-calibre rifles protuded from tiny slits. One gun fired a blank in the execution volley. The other four bullets tore through Gilmore and punched a small cluster of blood-stained holes into the chair's black upholstery. All four hit the heart, said State Medical Examiner Dr Serge Moore, although Gilmore did not die clinically for a further two minutes.

Within ten minutes, his body was speeding in a blue Ford station wagon to a Salt Lake City hospital, where it was to be used for transplants and research. A nurse was putting drops into the eyes to preserve the corneas as the car slipped through the prison gates.

The execution, at 3.07 p.m. British time, ended a 10-year moratorium on the death penalty in America.

The state of Utah was as eager and determined to kill Gilmore as he was to be killed. To that end, officials thwarted a maverick judge who in the early hours of the morning had issued a restraining order, by rousing three other judges from their beds, flying one of them to another state on a special plane, and getting the order reversed in a pre-dawn session. In the process, the American judicial system was exposed for all its cumbersome complexity, in this case bordering on the macabre. The law was stretched to the limit, and Gilmore died – with dignity, by all accounts.

In the space of seven hours, Gilmore was told that he would be shot at sunrise, then that he would not, and finally, four minutes before sunrise, that he would. He reacted to the reported postponement with fury, screaming obscenities at the TV set in his cell when the news was broadcast.

The drama began on Sunday evening, when Judge Willis Ritter, the crusty old chief Federal judge for this district, contacted lawyers for the Civil Liberties Union. He told them that he had heard on the radio that they had been trying to get in touch with him all day to enter a new plea to stay the execution, and

that he was prepared to open his court in the Salt Lake City Federal Building at 10 p.m.

Although the retirement age for Federal judges is now 70, the 77-year-old Judge Ritter, who has a reputation for being erratic, was appointed before the age limit was set, and is retained under what is known as the 'grandfather clause'.

The civil liberties suit was complex – and, perhaps, slender. At its simplest, it argued that taxpayers' money should not be used for executing Gilmore because Utah's revised death penalty has never been reviewed by the Utah Supreme Court. This was unconstitutional, the suit contended, because Utah does not have a mandatory review of each death sentence.

At 1.05 a.m., after a recess, Judge Ritter said that he agreed sufficiently with the argument to issue a temporary restraining order on the execution. Utah's Attorney-General, Robert Hansen, immediately responded by going to the Federal Court of Appeal for this part of the United States. He woke Federal appeal judge David Lewis in Salt Lake City and offered him a Utah National Guard plane to take him 500 miles to Denver, Colorado, to confer with two other Federal appeal judges on Utah's counter-suit.

As the plane flew south in the small hours, Gilmore vented his rage, denouncing Judge Ritter and the opponents of capital punishment, and telling his lawyers angrily: 'I wish these people would keep out of my life.'

Despite Judge Ritter's legally-binding order, which he himself took to the prison, the State of Utah did nothing to stop the execution schedule. The firing squad of five plus one reserve arrived, as did the doctor. Gilmore remained in a visiting room in the maximum-security wing, chatting with his Uncle Vern and some cousins.

As dawn approached, the appeal court was still sitting in Denver. This raised a new legal problem. The judge who sentenced Gilmore had specified that he must die at sunrise, 7.49 a.m. local time. He was telephoned at home by one of the Utah Attorney-General's staff in Denver, and agreed to alter his order verbally so that Gilmore could die at any time during yesterday.

By now, tension was running high in the prison – and all over America via network television. A packed press room waited for one of Warden Smith's staff to be called on a special 'hot-line' phone set up for the cameras. The call would say either that Gilmore was spared or that he was to die.

Behind the scenes, at 7.45 a.m., word came from Denver that the appeal court had dismissed Judge Ritter's order – and told him not to intervene further.

Gilmore, who had eaten a breakfast of hamburger and eggs, was told of the decision, and taken manacled from the visiting room. He was led to a van parked on the frozen ground in the shadow of the Rockies, and then driven around the prison perimeter to the tannery, a low building made of concrete blocks. He was strapped to the chair, and a Roman Catholic priest said the last rites.

And then he was shot.

In the aftermath, graphic details emerged. Gilmore had wanted to die standing, with no hood, but his request was declined by Warden Smith, who thought a flinching target would be impossible for the volunteers on the firing squad. There were 35 witnesses, a large number that was not explained. Among them was Larry Schiller, who has bought the rights to Gilmore's troubled life story. He afterwards described, with no apparent emotion, how blood oozed around the target-patch over Gilmore's heart and on to his black T-shirt and white trousers. 'It seemed to me the body had movement in it for approximately 15 to 20 seconds,' he said.

Gilmore spent his last night talking to lawyers and relatives, and dancing a little with a girl cousin. He telephoned his arthritic mother in Oregon. He also phoned a country-and-Western radio station with two record requests, one for a ballad about the suicide pact he had made with his fiancée.

In spite of all blocking attempts, the State of Utah had exacted its revenge for two pitiless killings – and made history as the first state to act on the new death penalty guidelines handed down by the US Supreme Court last July.

Wednesday, January 19:

GILMORE EXECUTION OUTCRY

The debate on the death penalty was reopened in the United States with a new urgency yesterday as the nation read detailed and grisly accounts of Gary Gilmore's last moments. With the legal battle to spare his life at an end, opponents of capital punishment are mobilising for what is expected to be a bitter struggle.

A total of 421 condemned prisoners – 416 men and five women – are in death cells throughout the country, and the judicial fate of many of them is likely to be influenced by Utah's determination to carry out the Gilmore execution.

1977

'SON OF SAM' ARRESTED

The biggest manhunt in New York since the 'Mad Bomber' terrorised the city in the 1950s* ended last night, when a 24-year-old postal worker seized by police as he stepped into his car outside his flat in Yonkers, just north of New York, confessed to being 'Son of Sam', the gunman who has killed six young people and wounded seven others in the past year.

It was a $35 parking ticket that led to his arrest. Twelve nights ago, a woman was out walking her dog in the Brooklyn waterfront area when she apparently came face-to-face with the killer. A few minutes earlier, she had seen a policeman slipping a parking ticket under the windscreen-wiper of a cream-coloured sedan that had been parked too close to a fire hydrant. Then a young man approached her, stopped a few feet away, 'saw that I was middle-aged', and hurried off. He carried 'a dark object' in his hand. The frightened woman ran home. She had just reached the front steps of her house when she heard the shots that caused the death of 20-year-old Stacy Moskowitz, a pretty, blonde secretary, and the blinding of her boyfriend, Robert Violante. They had been sitting in a car on the waterfront, admiring the full moon over New York Bay. The woman went to the police, and a computer-search of all parking tickets issued in the area that night produced the registration details of the car, including the name of its owner – David Berkowitz – and his address.

Soon after he was captured, the Police Commissioner, Michael Codd, made the startling disclosure that between 1970 and 1973 Berkowitz was an unpaid auxiliary New York policeman; he received training in 'law and unarmed defence' but not in the use of firearms.

Late last night, he was ordered to be held under heavy guard in a mental ward while it was determined whether or not he was com-

---

* George Metesky, who bore a grudge against his former employers, Consolidated Edison, planted more than 30 bombs in public places, two during the early 1940s, the rest during the early 1950s; several people were injured – one critically, none fatally. Eventually arrested (after someone had come up with the good idea of scouring the electricity company's records for details of perhaps-resentful ex-employees), Metesky was pronounced insane, and in April 1957, when he was 54, was ordered to be kept in a mental institution – where he remained until, psychiatrists having decided that he had recovered his wits and lost his antipathy towards ConEd, a release order was signed in December 1973.

petent to plead. Meanwhile, he was being kept in a special cell – referred to by policemen as 'the Black Hole of Calcutta' – in the Brooklyn Criminal Court building. 'We want to be sure he gets to court,' said an official, 'so we've put him in isolation because other prisoners might try to kill him.' The official made no reference to a crowd of people gathered outside the building, glaring up at the barred window of the cell and chanting: 'Kill – Kill – Kill the bastard!'

Berkowitz's arrest may have prevented a bloodbath in one of the crowded discotheques in the Hamptons, the fashionable string of resorts near the eastern tip of Long Island. The police there recently received a letter, together with some lines of demented verse, suggesting that 'Son of Sam' was planning to go out in a blaze of horror – switching from his 'trademark weapon', a .44-calibre revolver, to a .45-calibre submachine gun, which could wreak unimaginable carnage on a crowded dance-floor.

A loaded submachine gun, recklessly stowed in a gunny sack, with the butt protruding, was found in Berkowitz's 1977-model Ford by the police who arrested him. He was carrying the Bulldog revolver that has struck fear into the hearts of New Yorkers and caused young people to change their life-styles by avoiding late-night places of entertainment and romantic parking spots. Two dozen extra bullets were contained in a brown paper bag in one of his pockets. He also had several clips, each bearing 30 bullets, for the submachine gun.

A chilling letter addressed to police in Suffolk County, the part of Long Island which includes Southampton and East Hampton, was lying on the front seat of the car. Unstamped, it may have been writ-

ten by Berkowitz with the intention of leaving it at the scene of his 'last' crime. The letter read, in part: '. . . because Craig is Craig, so must the streets be filled with Craig (death) and huge drops of lead poured down upon her head until she was dead – yet the cats still come out at night to mate and the sparrows still sing in the morning'. 'Craig' is believed to be Craig Glassman, a deputy sheriff in Westchester County, north of the city, who lives in the flat below Berkowitz's. Glassman says that for the past couple of months he has been receiving threatening messages, and that last Saturday a fire was started outside his flat and live ·22-calibre bullets tossed into it. 'I figured it was just some nut who took a dislike to me. The letters were all in block letters and signed, "Your brother".'

'Son of Sam' has turned out to be a pleasant-looking, rather pudgy young bachelor. His night-shift job in a post office involved the monotonous work of punching buttons on the keyboard of a machine that channelled a river of letters into Zip-code areas.

Some of his neighbours describe him as a 'weirdo'; others speak of him as 'a quiet, nice guy'. The boy who delivered his newspapers says that Berkowitz tipped him lavishly – $30 at Christmas – but often acted furtively when he came to the door.

Hung on the walls of his sparsely-furnished flat were confused writings similar to the letters received by the police and newspapers during the killings. Stacks of newspapers and clippings dealing with the crimes and the manhunt were found in the flat. Empty liquor bottles were scattered about. The living-room, unfurnished except for a sleeping bag, was strewn with books and records. There were also two shotguns, one of which Berkowitz evidently bought a few months ago.

Who was 'Sam'? The first name of Berkowitz's father, now living in Miami, is Nat. In one of the mysterious communications received by the police, 'Sam' was identified as a man who lived 6,000 years ago but still loomed as an omnipotent force in the killer's mind; there were hints that messages – orders to kill – were transmitted through a dog.

But now a different explanation has emerged. During police interviews, as Berkowitz's madness was reflected both in his words and in his demeanour – a half-smile flickering around his mouth, a vacant cast to his eyes, a compulsive licking of his lips – he contended that 'Sam' was a meek-looking man from this century rather than from the mists of time: Sam Carr, a 64-year-old neighbour who runs a small telephone answering service. This slight, bespectacled man has said that Berkowitz launched a hate-mail campaign against him earlier this year. His black retriever, Harvey, who had sometimes howled late into the night, was the target of the young man's fury.

'That crazy guy, Berkowitz – he shot my dog in the leg on April 27,' the suddenly notorious Sam Carr said yesterday. 'He blasted off three or four shots in quick succession, hitting my dog in the hind leg. We found another of the slugs in the back yard. It was a brass-ringed slug.'

Amazingly, Carr went to the police three weeks ago, insisting that Berkowitz was the '·44-calibre killer' who was being hunted not only by a special force of 300 detectives and patrolmen and a team of FBI agents, but also by 5000-odd Mafia 'soldiers' acting on the orders of their new 'Godfather', Carmine Galante, who apparently feared for the safety of his four daughters. Carr says: 'A detective told me he would put my information on the hopper and see how it all came out. I understand that the police received a lot of calls like mine.'

In one of the hate-mail letters sent to Carr, the writer said that his life had been 'torn apart because of this dog' and threatened retribution. 'You wicked, evil man – child of the devil – I curse you and your family for ever. I pray to God that he takes your whole family off the face of the earth. People like you should not be allowed to live on this planet.'

The police case against Berkowitz would appear to be iron-clad. In the small hours of this morning, ballistics tests showed that his ·44-calibre revolver was the weapon used in the murder of Stacy Moskowitz and the wounding of Robert Violante.

Saturday, August 13:

Two formerly close friends of David Berkowitz say that while he was serving as a soldier in South Korea in 1972, he took mind-bending LSD trips, and that he returned home with a totally transformed personality. In one of a number of increasingly incoherent letters from him at that time he referred to 'a great bargain . . . a 12 gauge, pump action short barrel riot control PDNY shotgun for 78 dollars. I will probably get one by next pay check'. At the end of the letter, after writing 'Love, Dave', he crossed out his name and wrote in its place, 'Master of Reality'.

According to one of the men, whose earliest memory of Berkowitz is as an unremarkable teenager in the Bronx: 'When he came back from Korea, he scared so many people with his new beliefs, his sudden changes, that they just started turning off him and trying not to be with him.' The other former friend says that 'it was while he was in Korea that the change was tremendous: there was LSD and then there was everything else, be it revolution, Jesus, or total incoherence'. When he returned home he renounced his Judaism, was baptised by a Baptist Minister in Kentucky, and for a time 'carried a Bible wherever he went – he tried to convince everybody, and he was really very persistent'.

Yesterday, Berkowitz reiterated his confession to being 'Son of Sam' during eight hours of almost non-stop interrogation by a roomful of senior detectives. Afterwards, the detectives and other members of the task-force went back to their precincts for a night of celebration. For the first time in the history of the New York Police Department – on orders from Mayor Abraham Beame – whisky was allowed to be served in the station houses.

Berkowitz was co-operative during the interrogation, and showed that he has a phenomenal memory by recalling every detail of each of his thirteen strikes. 'He's amazing,' said one detective. 'He seems to have total recall – he corrected us on minor facts here and there.' Though the questioners tried to catch him out as to his motivation, he insisted that he had received his 'orders to kill' from the black retriever named Harvey. He said that he had been 'out driving every night since July 1976, looking for a sign to kill. The situation would be perfect. I would find a parking place for my car right away. It was things like that which convinced me it was commanded.' At one point, he put a question to the detectives, and then, by answering it himself, confirmed that he was setting out for a night of 'real' slaughter when he was arrested. 'Do you know why I had a machine-gun with me?. . . I'll tell you. I wanted to get into a shoot-out. I wanted to get killed, but I wanted to take some cops with me.'

'After I'd started him off,' one of the interrogators remarked, 'I said to him, "I'll bet you could do pretty good with girls. Do you go with girls?" and he said, "No."' For a time during his rampage, his victims were all young women with shoulder-length brown hair – a fact which caused thousands of women to wear their hair pinned up when they went out at night – but Berkowitz insists that he simply went after 'pretty girls', irrespective of the colour or style of their hair.

Though he said that he made 'sentimental journeys' to the graves of some of his victims, when he was asked if he felt any remorse, he put on his unnerving smile and answered: 'No – why should I?'

Wednesday, August 17:

Unsmiling, and with his hands manacled in front of him, David Berkowitz stood in a Brooklyn court yesterday while his lawyer entered a plea of 'not guilty by reason of insanity'. Wearing faded blue jeans and a blue-and-white pin-striped shirt with a white T-shirt underneath, the almost cherubic-faced young man displayed no emotion as he was arraigned for the murder of Stacy Moskowitz and the attempted murder of her boyfriend, Robert Violante. He was also charged with illegal possession of the ·44-revolver which ballistics experts say was used in all 13 attacks ascribed to 'Son of Sam'. (Berkowitz has confessed to another attack, not included in the official count: the wounding, early this year, of an elderly Yonkers woman, whom he claims to have shot with the ·45 submachine-gun that was found in his car after his arrest – and which, it has emerged, he bought in a New York gun store upon production of his $3 firearms licence.)

Berkowitz had been brought to court with the sort of security measures that might be put into force around a president under threat of assassination. He rode in a large van with barred windows, escorted by three marked and four unmarked police cars, while a police helicopter whirled low overhead. Police in the van and the escort cars carried shotguns as well as revolvers. Some 40 patrolmen formed a cordon around the court, and as many more officers were on security duty inside the building. It appears that 'Son of Sam', who has already cost New York about a million dollars in police overtime, will continue to be the city's most expensive individual criminal nuisance for some time to come.

According to police sources, a diary of the murders, hand-written in a folder of forty loose-leaf sheets, was found in Berkowitz's flat; it reveals, among other things, that he was in the habit of driving to a diner for a leisurely early-morning breakfast after each of his crimes.

Berkowitz's natural mother, traced by his lawyers, bore him by a Tony Falco to whom she was not married. The woman, who works as a cleaner, is said to have seen Berkowitz only once since she put him up for adoption when he was an infant. That was three years ago, when he located her, at the same time learning that she had also given birth to an illegitimate daughter but had not had her adopted.

Saturday, August 20:

New York's Criminal Justice Agency, which screens defendants and gives advice to judges, has recommended that David Berkowitz should be released on his own recognisance. By referring to him as 'aka [also known as] "Son of Sam",' the agency, which is financed by the Federal Government and the city, showed that it was aware of the accusations against him. But it pointed out that he was a first offender and had a permanent residence and a steady job with the Post Office – criteria routinely applied in determining that a defendant is unlikely to skip bail.

The recommendation, which most New Yorkers are inclined to put in the same category of madness as the explanations given by 'Son of Sam' for his killings, was disclosed – and denounced – by Mayor Beame at a hastily called Press conference. 'It defies belief,' he said, clearly infuriated. 'Obviously, no judge would accept such a recommendation, but it does make us wonder whether judges on other occasions, confronted with busy court calendars, are accepting recommendations that could permit dangerous criminals to walk the streets on little or no bail.'

Nicholas Scoppetta, Deputy Mayor of Criminal Justice, and therefore in charge of the agency, told the Mayor on Thursday that it had stamped its Berkowitz file 'recommended for ROR [release on own recognisance] on non-verified community ties' – but hastened to explain that this was 'the result of a mechanical and literal interpretation by the agency for recommending bail'.

Wednesday, August 31:   A book-length psychiatric report released yesterday asserts that David Berkowitz is not mentally competent to stand trial because he 'lacks the capacity to understand the proceedings against him'.

Saturday, October 22:   David Berkowitz is mentally competent to stand trial, a judge ruled yesterday.

Monday, October 31 (Hallowe'en):

Thousands of Americans, many with young children, are descending on a rickety house called 'Blood Manor', not far from Washington, DC, in the hope of being scared out of their wits.

The highlight – if that is the right word – of the programme is a re-enactment of the 'Son of Sam' killings. Having shot his seventh victim through the eye, the 'killer' turns on his terrified but ecstatic audience, yelling: 'Get outa here before I blow your brains out!'

Mr Ed Atkins, who created 'Blood Manor' seven years ago and has so far terrorised 82,000 visitors paying $2·50 (£1·40) a time, feels he has his finger on the reason for its popularity. 'It either means there's a lack of sophistication, a pretty bored society or a pretty sick society', he says, with no apparent regret.

By the time the patrons, who have queued for up to four hours, reach the creaking front door, some of them are already so scared that they have to be pushed inside. For the next ten minutes, they scream, grovel, cling to friends or strangers, sob, become incontinent or pass out.

Each room of the house contains a grisly tableau brought to 'full reality' by actors and actresses.

In one room, Lizzie Borden cuts off her father's hand and then offers to do the same for her guests. In another, a small girl is hanged and the hangman then advances on the visitors with his noose. Dracula appears, moving to push his cash-paying prey into a giant spider's web; a boa constrictor slithers from a coffin, and a maniac chases the audience with a chain-saw, catching one of them and applying it, buzzing, to his leg.

At this point, the show ends and the guests come running from the house, some shrieking, others laughing. The only ones genuinely terrified are the young children, some barely of school-age.

Psychologists in the area see no great harm in 'Blood Manor'. Dr James Mosel of George Washington University, says that it gives 'the benefit of arousal without threat,' and his colleague, Dr Roland Tanck, adds: 'A place like this provides an outlet for anger. It doesn't mean a person is sick.'

Tuesday, May 9, 1978:

Against the wishes of his lawyers, who wanted him to plead not guilty because of his insanity, David Berkowitz yesterday pleaded guilty to the six murder charges against him. All the pleas were to second degree (unpremeditated) murder, and were entered successively before three State Supreme Court judges from the boroughs of New York City in which the killings were committed. The unusual arrangement to bring the judges together in the same court was made so as to reduce security and other costs. The judges said that they would pass sentences on May 22.

An unexpected disclosure at the hearing was that Berkowitz has also confessed to starting more than 2000 fires in the city since 1974. Mario Merola, the Bronx District Attorney, said that a spot-check on the claims, made in Berkowitz's diaries, confirmed that the fires had occurred.

Tuesday, June 13:

David Berkowitz was jailed yesterday for a total of 315 years for murdering six young people and wounding seven others. The three judges, between them, passed sentences of 25 years to life for each of the murders and additional sentences for the woundings.

At the start of the proceedings, Justice William Kapelman asked Berkowitz whether the 'demons' which, so he insists, commanded him to kill had anything to do with his guilty pleas, and he replied: 'They had some influence. That's what the demons want.'

Berkowitz, who was manacled, was sombre and docile, in contrast to his behaviour in the court on May 22, when, his eyes rolling and his face flushed, he had shouted: 'Stacy [Moskowitz] was a whore!' – and, while relatives and friends of the victims screamed abuse at him, had needed to be restrained by guards. Earlier, he had tried to leap from a seventh-floor window, and in the ensuing struggle with police escorts, had bitten one on the arm, sufficiently deeply for the man to require hospital treatment. As a result of these disturbances, the judges had postponed the hearing until a further psychiatric examination had been carried out.

Before the sentencing yesterday, Justice Joseph Corso announced that the examination had found that Berkowitz was mentally competent to be sentenced.

Under New York State law, Berkowitz could be eligible for parole in 30 years, but Justice Kapelman said that it was his 'earnest desire that this defendant remain in jail for life, until the very day of his death'.

1980

Thursday, December 11:

THE DEATH OF A BEATLE

Just as The Beatles were at the forefront of the turbulent social revolution in the Sixties, so the brilliant, erratic John Lennon was at the forefront of the pop group.

He was born during an air-raid on Liverpool in 1940. Soon after his birth, his mother, Julia, left her husband Fred Lennon for another man, and John was looked after by his Aunt Mimi.

When he became famous, his father turned up – and had the door slammed in his face. 'I don't feel that I owe him anything,' John explained. 'He never helped me. I got there by myself.' But Aunt Mimi – a Mrs Smith – now lives in a luxury bungalow at Poole, which he bought for her in 1965.

At primary school, he was quick to learn but resentful of routine work. He began writing verse when he was seven. At Quarry Bank secondary school, he became interested in rock music, and after teaching himself to play the mouth-organ, learned simple chords on a £10 guitar. When Elvis Presley became a star in 1956, Lennon was captivated; he soon joined the host of Elvis-imitators and helped to form several local rock groups, including the Quarrymen. In 1958, Lennon formed The Beatles with Paul McCartney and George Harrison. The Cavern in Liverpool (£7 a night) and the Star Club in Hamburg (£30 a week) gave them bookings that enabled them to concentrate full-time on their music. But it was not until three years later, when drummer Ringo Starr joined them and Brian Epstein, a former public schoolboy, took over as manager, that the group became well known.

In September 1962, The Beatles cut the record, 'Love Me Do', which was to start their meteoric rise. Within a year, their flat Liverpool accents and collarless suits, and McCartney's violin-shaped bass guitar, were the ingredients of a craze that swept from Southend to San Francisco. Their music, dress and thoughts influenced a whole generation. Lennon and McCartney co-wrote more than 200 songs in a partnership that was not always harmonious but which attained heights that neither achieved in later years during solo careers. Their best ballads became modern classics. 'Yesterday' has been recorded more than a thousand times by various artists. More than 250 million Beatles records have been sold. Lennon once claimed that The Beatles were 'more popular than Jesus Christ'.

Themes of drug-influenced psychedelia, anti-Vietnam protest, and Indian mysticism moved through The Beatles' work. In 1965 – the heyday of Beatlemania – the four were made MBEs, but Lennon later returned his award as a protest against Britain's policy in Biafra and Nigeria and its support of America in Vietnam.

Before the break-up of the group in 1971, through disagreement over the control of the business, Lennon's marriage to his first wife, Cynthia, whom he had met at a Liverpool art college, was dissolved; they had a son, Julian, who is now 17 and wants to be a rock musician. After moving to America with his new wife, Yoko Ono, a Japanese artist, Lennon dropped out of the high-pressure world of pop, saying that he was devoting his energies to bringing up their son Sean. In 1974, he faced deportation because, six years before, in England, he had been convicted of possessing marijuana; but he finally won his battle to stay.

Death came to him just as his musical career seemed to be taking off again. A long-playing album, 'Double Fantasy', which he recorded in August with Yoko Ono, is now in the American Top-20 chart. He was composing again and was about to start a series of recording sessions.

Eerily, on Monday afternoon, only hours before he was shot, Lennon talked of death in a radio interview, saying that he hoped to die before his wife – 'because if Yoko died, I wouldn't know how to survive. I couldn't carry on.' Describing his new album as a greeting to long-time fans, he said: 'I hope the young kids like it as well, but I'm really talking to the people who grew up with me. I'm saying, "Here I am now. How are you? How's your relationship going? Did you get through it all? Wasn't the seventies a drag, you know? Well, here we are. Let's make the eighties great, because it's up to us to make what we can of it." You have to give

thanks to God, or whatever is up there, for the fact that we all survived. We all survived Vietnam – Watergate – the tremendous upheaval of the whole world. I feel secure here in New York. I can walk out of the door and go to movies and the restaurant. People might ask for an autograph, but they don't bug you. They might shout "I like your record" or "How's the baby?" but there's no harassment. I'm going into an unknown future, but I'm still all here, and while there's life there's hope.'

In recent years, Lennon had bought five flats in the famous Dakota building, and was creating a spacious private domain overlooking Central Park.

During the weekend, 25-year-old Mark David Chapman was seen loitering outside the stately, chateau-type building, and on Monday afternoon he accosted Lennon and Yoko Ono as they were setting off for a recording studio, and persuaded the ex-Beatle to autograph a record album for him.

Some six hours later, at about 11 p.m., he was crouching by the entrance to the Dakota courtyard when the Lennons returned in a Cadillac. Instead of driving into the courtyard, as many of the public figures who live at the Dakota are in the habit of doing, the couple got out of the limousine in the street. According to Chief of Detectives James Sullivan, Chapman approached them as they were walking under the high, arched entrance. He was holding a small, snub-nosed ·38 revolver.

'Mr Lennon?' he asked. Then, without waiting for a reply, he took what Chapman has described as a 'combat stance' and emptied the revolver into Lennon, hitting him in an arm, in the back, and three times in the chest, severing arteries to the heart. Lennon staggered up half a dozen steps to an office area before he fell to the ground.

Chapman, still standing just inside the courtyard, dropped the revolver.

The message, 'Man shot – 1 West 72nd Street', was soon crackling over police radios. The crew of the first patrol car at the scene – the men who arrested Chapman – were two officers who had been Beatle fans in their youth. One of them, Tony Palma, lifted the dying man from a pool of blood and placed him in the back of another patrol-car for a futile dash to Roosevelt Hospital, a few hundred yards away, where desperate resuscitation methods were used. 'We opened his chest and massaged his heart,' said Dr Stephen Lynn, the Director of Emergency Services. 'They worked on him like crazy,' said a hospital worker. 'There was blood all over the place.'

Another police-car had taken Lennon's wife to the hospital. She was not injured in the shooting but was on the point of collapse and had to be supported by friends. 'Tell me it isn't true,' she sobbed repeatedly when told that her husband was dead.

At the Dakota building, several people who heard the shots and saw Chapman before he was taken away said that he seemed pleased with what he had done. 'He was smirking,' said one witness.

The feelings of the crowd that soon gathered outside the building, some playing songs by Lennon on tape-recorders, some threading flowers through the wrought-iron gates, could be gauged from their comments: 'For every momentous occasion in my life, there was a Beatles song – for all my romances, there was a different Beatles tune' ... 'They were a part of my life,

whether I wanted them to be or not' ... 'I guess this truly is the end of the sixties' ... 'He took us places where we had never been before' ...

A surprising number of Beatles-lovers were affected so intensely by the murder that they talked of revenge. According to a high-ranking New York policeman, 'The switchboard was lit up all night with threats.' He added that this was one reason why extraordinary security precautions had been ordered to protect Chapman. 'We don't want another Jack Ruby,' he said, referring to the Texan who shot and killed Lee Harvey Oswald in the police headquarters in Dallas before the latter could be brought to trial for the assassination of President Kennedy.

Curiously, in comments made by mourners standing in the rain outside the Dakota building as well as those in similar gatherings in other American cities, and in more philosophical words from newspaper and television commentators, an attempt has been made to draw a parallel between Lennon's violent death and that of John Kennedy seventeen years ago. To some extent, this explains the highly charged atmosphere which has enveloped the handling of the case – an atmosphere in which the New York District Attorney's office yesterday made an extraordinary and embarrassing mistake over the defendant's arrest record: at Chapman's first appearance in the Manhattan Criminal Court, the prosecutor submitted a record of twelve arrests and four convictions prior to 1972, but was soon contradicted by the police, who said that the record was that of another man named Chapman and that Mark David Chapman had no criminal record whatsoever.

America's mourning for John

Winston Lennon is impressive in its scope and sincerity. On the morning after the murder, some radio stations dropped all advertising so as to play as many requests as possible for Beatles favourites; many stations broadcast phone-in expressions of grief in breaks between records made by 'the fab four', and there were countless enquiries from fans as to where they could send flowers. (Meanwhile, a simple posy placed on the site of the Cavern Club in a rubble-strewn back-street of Liverpool is the only apparent memorial to Lennon in his home town.) In music shops across America, there has been a rush to buy Beatles' records and Lennon's new album. (And shops throughout Britain have reported a sell-out of such records. Workers at the EMI factory have been put on overtime to cope with the sudden demand. Sales of Lennon's new single, 'Starting Over', which had been slipping down the chart, are now outstripping supply, and it appears that, ironically, Lennon's death will give him his first No. 1 hit as a solo performer.) President Carter said in Washington that he was saddened by the killing and 'distressed by the senseless manner of it', adding that Lennon had 'helped create the music and mood of our time'. President-elect Reagan, on a brief visit to New York before returning to the capital to continue the work of assembling his Cabinet, spoke of 'a great tragedy', but said that his opposition to tougher gun-control laws had not changed.

As with previous 'celebrity killings' in America, the ease with which Mark Chapman was able to buy a weapon has unleashed a barrage of calls for stricter sanctions; but that, in turn, has prompted cries of protest from the pro-guns

lobby, led by the powerful National Rifle Association.

It has emerged that on October 27, two days before Chapman left his home in Hawaii and flew to Newark Airport, one of the three major airports serving the New York City area, he purchased the ·38 revolver at a gunshop close to the Honolulu police station. The owner of the shop said yesterday that the gun had cost $169 (£70.40). He did not think that publicity over the Lennon murder would harm his business: 'Any kind of publicity is good. The fact that we sell guns to people who shoot people can't be blamed on us.' He said that if there had been anything unusual in Chapman's manner, he would have been turned away: 'If a guy starts staring weird, saying he is going to shoot someone, we won't sell him a gun. There have been times when a guy comes in here with police clearance, but then he starts cracking his neck and rolling his eyes, and we say the sale is off.'

Chapman is tall, 5 feet 11 inches, and hefty, nearly 14 stone, with dark brown hair that is neatly cut. He has never drunk or smoked, is religious, and has always spurned having a television set. Born in a white, middle-class suburb of Fort Worth, Texas, he grew up in Decatur, Georgia, ran away for a while when he was 14, had a few minor skirmishes with the law, played in a rock band, and assembled a large record collection with an emphasis on the Beatles. In his late teens, school friends detected a change in him; one of them has recalled that he became a 'Jesus freak' after going through a fairly typical teenage period – 'long hair, old Army jackets, that kind of thing'. In the mid-1970s, he went to Lebanon on a YMCA exchange and then did excellent work with the same organisation in Arkansas, teaching English to refugees from Vietnam and running the library and the recreation programme.

Chapman's yearning for travel took him to Hawaii in 1977. Soon after his arrival, he was admitted to hospital with mental problems; he wrote to a friend that he had 'completely fallen apart'. But he recovered sufficiently to hold down jobs at the hospital, first as a caretaker and later in the print shop. In 1978, he borrowed money from the hospital's credit union so as to take a trip around the world. At the travel agency, he met Gloria Abe, a Japanese-American, and upon his return from the six-week trip, he courted her, and they were married in a big formal cermony at a Methodist church in July last year. He came to dominate his shy wife, who is now 29, cutting her off from her social life, her friends, and even her family, who to this day live in a traditional Japanese house where shoes are left at the door. He persuaded her to leave the travel agency, where she had been both successful and happy, for a job in the office of the hospital where he worked. Soon afterwards, he himself gave up working at the hospital and became a guard at a vacation complex in Waikiki, close to Honolulu.

People with whom he worked, both at the hospital and at the complex, say that he was by turns engaging or mean-spirited and bullying; several remember him as being conscientious to a fault, with small infractions of procedures bothering him out of all proportion, and one describes him as 'a jerk, a creep – just a negative, secret, insensitive, cold person'.

On October 23 this year – four days before he bought the gun, six days before he flew to the mainland – he gave up his job. After making his final entry in the logbook, he signed out as 'John Lennon', but then crossed out the name with a double line. At the same time, he also wrote that name on a piece of paper which he then stuck over the name-tag on his shirt, and calmly assured his replacement that he was indeed John Lennon.

Given those facts, a Honolulu psychiatrist has now suggested that Chapman may have come to see himself as the real John Lennon and believed that 'he might find his rightful place if he got rid of the "impostor"'. To others who have tried to discern a motive for his cold-blooded act, three intertwined themes appear to have emerged:

First, Chapman's admiration for The Beatles and for Lennon in particular – he smiled appreciatively when the ex-Beatle autographed a record album for him on Monday, only about six hours before he shot him down. Second, his religious fervour – he is said to have complained about Lennon's most famous remark: 'Who the hell are they to compare themselves with Jesus?' Third, his obviously troubled mind, manifested in his fixation on Lennon and in two suicide attempts: he has told his legal-aid lawyer in New York that, three years ago, he ran a rubber tube from the exhaust to the inside of his car, and sat in the vehicle with the windows closed, and has given a confused account of another attempt recently, using the gun with which he later killed Lennon.

Chapman, who is subject to a court-ordered 'suicide watch', has been talkative ever since his arrest, discussing his background in Texas, Georgia and Hawaii, his wife, and his love of music, photography and painting. But when asked why he shot Lennon, he has almost invariably simply stared at the ceiling and refused to answer. He has, however, said: 'I heard voices. I just kept hearing them' – Satanic instructions to execute a man he greatly admired.

Leading article:

MUSIC AND MORTALITY

The Beatles' music was – still is – a prerogative of the young, and the murder of John Lennon shocks both today's teenagers and those who were teenagers in the Britain that created The Beatles. Lennon was a child of the swinging sixties. It was in many ways an age of innocence. We *had* never had it so good. It was a time when consciences could be worn on sleeves – consciences about Vietnam, Biafra and much else. It was a time ripe for protest movements, and The Beatles were troubadours of those movements. Technically they created, with skill and indeed charm, a new kind of pop music. Socially they symbolised protest against authority and convention.

If it was a revolution, it was – to begin with, anyhow – a benign one. (Apart from anything else, The Beatles had a shrewd manager who realised that respectability was a more marketable commodity than militancy.) But all revolutions tend to have sinister trainbearers. Kicking over the traces of parental stuffiness somehow got transformed into the need to try out drugs. An agreeable, if rather woolly, philosophy that the world's problems could be solved if only everyone would love one another became, for Lennon, a stepping-stone to involvement with outlandish and potentially disastrous political activity. The silly but mainly harmless mob-hysteria which followed The Beatles round the world in the 1960s has now, in the streets of New York, a sequel in which some kind of perverted autograph-hunting has turned into murder. A man who lived with the philosophy of peace has perished by the gun. In the sixties, The Beatles were a symbol of the culture of the times. Lennon's death has some grim meaning, if we know where to look for it, for the eighties.

Tuesday, August 25, 1981:

Mark Chapman, who had pleaded guilty to the murder of John Lennon – and who, while in jail, has constantly listened to tapes of Beatles music – was yesterday sentenced at the Manhattan Supreme Court to from twenty years to life imprisonment.

He now looks markedly different from when he committed the crime. His hair is close-cropped and he has lost a good deal of weight, the result of sporadic hunger strikes that he has staged.

When asked if he had anything to say, he opened a copy of J. D. Salinger's novel *The Catcher in the Rye*, which he had with him when he was arrested, and, apparently trying to explain the motive for his crime, read a passage towards the end of the book in which the narrator, Holden Caulfield, visualises thousands of children in a field of rye, oblivious to danger:

'I have to come out from somewhere and *catch* them. That's all I'd do all day. I'd just be the catcher in the rye and all.'

Chapman's lawyer said that the significance of the passage – so far as his client was concerned – was that the hero felt that the world was 'phoney' and that 'children should be saved from adulthood'. But that does not seem to have left anyone any the wiser as to why Mark Chapman killed John Lennon.

1980

Monday, December 29:

MURDER WILL OUT – EVENTUALLY
(*From Ian Ball, New York Correspondent*)

Since criminology became a science in Victorian times, popular wisdom has tended to maintain that the British, and Europeans generally, went in for bizarre murders, while the Americans, as befits the size of their land, went in for quantity.

The two Rippers, Jack and Yorkshire, almost a century apart, are among the exceptions held up to reinforce the general rule. In a sense, the killings in West Yorkshire fit very neatly into the American pattern: a deranged individual seeking out a particular type of victim; vast police manpower apparently making little headway; the hunt prolonged while the killer finds ways of taunting his pursuers; the headlines proliferating while a whole community lives in fear.

Can we perhaps learn something from the American experience? The answer in Yorkshire is no. While the American police have wrapped up all but about three of the celebrated recent cases of mass-murder, none was cracked with dispatch, none revealed especially creative sleuthing, and most dragged on until the toll of victims reached 'the double-digit area,' as a New York lawman coolly summed it up for me.

'Basically, you do your plodding police work,' he added. 'But you wait for your killer to make a mistake –

and all the time you're hoping for that lucky break which is part of so many of our success stories. Remember that it was a parking ticket that helped lead us to "Son of Sam".' He went on to say that he had been following the Yorkshire case closely and wished 'the boys in Leeds just that bit of luck'.

Against the grim backdrop of Leeds, it is perhaps worth reviewing America's recent mass-killers and how they were brought to justice. They fall into three broad categories: the psychotic or sex deviate who preys on women; the racist killer who selects his victims purely on skin-colour; and the homosexual who murders with chilling sadism.

It is the last category which holds all the records for mass-slaughter, American-style. Two men, one in California, the other in Chicago, are each serving life terms for killing 32 times. A third homosexual killer, a Texan who was eventually slain by the youths who procured his victims, snuffed out 27 lives, the eldest 28, the youngest 13.

Whereas the looniness of David Berkowitz was apparent to a few who came in contact with him, these three killers succeeded in masking their inner vileness. The two who lived were certainly sane enough to stand trial. To neighbours and *workmates, it was incomprehensible that they were operating their private charnel-houses.*

The homosexual mass-murderer in California became known as the 'Trashbag Killer'. He left his 32 young victims, each hideously mutilated to delay identification, in plastic dustbin liners beside highways south of Los Angeles. Most of his victims were runaways whose disappearances were not immediately reported.

But the body of the thirty-second victim, a 17-year-old boy, was traced promptly after a disappearance which linked him to the man who eventually confessed to this and the other killings – Patrick Kearney, a mechanic at an aircraft factory. Kearney had hacked off the head, hands and feet before disposing of the body by the road-side. However, a birthmark on the torso and freckles across the back enabled police to match the remains with information on a missing-person sheet.

In Chicago's 'House of Bodies' case last year, the police found most of the young victims under the floorboards in a cottage owned by John Gacy, a small-time building contractor. There were so many bodies, in fact, that police had only to use their noses once a search warrant had been obtained. Gacy was caught for reasons similar to those which had led to Kearney's capture three years earlier – he had departed from his practice of preying on runaway youths. His final victim, a 15-year-old boy, provided a link to Gacy through the murderer's known offer of part-time employment to the boy. When a police check showed that Gacy had a conviction for sodomy in Iowa, a search of his house was the obvious next step.

A similarly deranged homosexual, Dean Corll, an electrician in Houston, had been unmasked in 1973 as the man behind a series of killings which became known as the 'Texas Mass-Murders'. Only 18 of the 27 bodies were ever identified. Some were found stacked in layers in a small warehouse Corll owned, and others were in graves dug in sand-dunes. His two helpmates, high-school dropouts who procured teenage victims for payments ranging from five to ten dollars, were convicted of his murder. They, not the police, cracked the Texas Mass-Murders.

Common-or-garden human greed lurks behind most modern-day crime, but it was not a factor in these assembly-line slayings. Nor is it present in other American multiple killings.

If California is the 'laboratory for social change' for the country as a whole, it is a particularly busy lab when it comes to police work. In the past few years, eight different mass-murderers in Los Angeles were being hunted at roughly the same time.

There were two cold-blooded killers preying on the city's derelicts. The 'Skid Row Slasher' claimed 10 victims in what police said were 'predominantly homosexual' crimes. The 'Skid Row Stabber' simply went after the blood of hapless tramps, and also struck 10 times. The successful police tactic in both cases was to send out officers posing as transients.

The 'Hillside Strangler,' perpetrator of a rash of 13 sex-related killings of young women, turned out to be two men who happened to be cousins. The 'Freeway Killer,' it transpired, was four separate murderers using similar methods. Their collective tally was 43 victims over seven years. All four were run to ground through slogging detective work.

The Hillside Strangler case offers

the closest parallels to the killings in Yorkshire. As an example of police organisation, it has been widely studied in America. The Los Angeles Police Department had the resources to establish an 80-man Strangler Task Force. So many clues were being generated by eight different police agencies in the area that a computerised 'clue-control system' was established. And yet there were still blunders by the men in blue. They had overlooked the fact that one of the men eventually charged lived across the road from two of his victims. And when this man was arrested in the State of Washington for two similar stranglings, the local police there almost had to beg the big-city task-force men to fly north to take a look at their catch.

In the 'Peach Orchard Murders,' so called because the 25 bodies were found in shallow graves under peach trees near Yuba City in northern California, the victims were migrant farm-workers from Mexico. The obvious suspect was the labour contractor, Juan Corona, who had brought them across the border. He is now serving 25 consecutive life sentences.

The 'Chicago Nurse Killer' was trapped after he had killed eight women living in flats near hospitals. Police got 'that lucky break' and pursued it diligently. At a time when detectives had a hunch that their suspect might be a seaman, the killer, Richard Speck, signed on at a maritime union office for work aboard a ship. When his name wasn't called, he got impatient and tossed his application form into a wastepaper basket. A policeman found it there. Speck's name was checked in the FBI's fingerprint files, and his prints matched those left at the murder scenes.

After killing 13 women, the 'Boston Strangler,' Albert DeSalvo, tripped himself up in a simple assault and robbery. With the confessions he volunteered after that arrest, he solved one of the country's most baffling mass-murder cases.

1981

Saturday, May 23:

THE RIPPER'S NINE LETHAL LIVES

Peter Sutcliffe was questioned nine times by the police during the long hunt for the Yorkshire Ripper, but on every occasion coincidence or luck helped him to slip through their fingers. Throughout the investigation, the West Yorkshire police maintained that they knew virtually everything about the Ripper except his name and address. They did, in fact, have those details, but many of their other assumptions were ill-founded.

Detectives were misled by a number of plausible but false clues which were followed up during the five-year hunt involving five county forces and, finally, a small team of Scotland Yard specialists.

Sutcliffe, a native Yorkshireman living in Bradford, was initially interviewed after his sixth murder. In the course of committing that crime, he made his first blunder – by luring the victim, a prostitute, into his car with an unused five-pound note from his wage-packet. Days later, before the body was discovered, he realised the importance of the clue he had left behind and went back to make a hurried search for it. The note, which he had failed to find, became the focal point of the investigation. Newly issued to a bank at Shipley, Yorkshire, it was part of a batch of £25,000 circulated among a handful of firms in the area, including T. & W. R. Clark (Holdings) Ltd of Bradford, for whom Sutcliffe worked. Each of the firm's employees was interviewed, and Sutcliffe was one of those taken to the police station for closer scrutiny. But he was only one of 8,300 people who could have received the note. And the alibi he gave for the night of the murder was supported by his wife Sonia. (During further inquiries, it was believed that she had confused the date.)

Three months later, having drawn a blank in the search for the recipient of the note, detectives re-checked the 8300 report-forms. Again, Sutcliffe was one of those interviewed. Away from the glare of publicity, some men, including Sutcliffe, were questioned for a third time.

There were other pointers towards Sutcliffe. For instance, his car – one of several he used over five years – was noticed in the red-light district of Chapeltown, Leeds, where some of the murders occurred. Sutcliffe and his wife, when interviewed separately at their home, explained that they, together in the car, had simply passed through Chapeltown on their way to or from a nearby night-club.

The final interview with Sutcliffe before he was unmasked followed a positive breath-test near Bradford's red-light area in June last year. It seems unlikely that prosecution for that offence, still pending, will be proceeded with.

George Oldfield, an Assistant Chief Constable of West Yorkshire, was in charge of the investigation for most of the time. His successor, Jim Hobson (also an Assistant Chief Constable of West Yorkshire), who took over after the thirteenth and final murder in November last year, has defended the efforts of the police by saying: 'It is all too easy to put [indications of guilt] together once a man has been arrested. But thousands of men could have fitted the descriptions we had been given. Not only West Yorkshire, but the reputation of the whole force throughout the country was at stake. We had to catch this man – and we did. It was the longest murder inquiry in the history of the British police. I hope no other senior officer in any force is ever again faced with such a series of murders. I always maintained that the Ripper would be caught with the co-operation of every policeman, and it was a routine inquiry which ended the series.' [On Friday, January 2, 1981, a police patrol, suspicious about a car parked in a dimly-lit driveway, took the driver in for questioning, and the man, who had said that his name was Peter Williams, admitted that he was Peter Sutcliffe, and subsequently confessed to being the Yorkshire Ripper.]

Asked to explain reports that Trevor Birdsall, a close friend of Sutcliffe's, had sent the police an anonymous letter naming him as the culprit, Mr Hobson said: 'The letter arrived at headquarters about two weeks after the final murder, of Jacqueline Hill. Because it was anonymous, it was given low priority. It was processed into the system, but before it could be acted upon, Sutcliffe was arrested. At the time of its receipt, we were receiving between 500 and 1000 letters every day from the public. In all, we interviewed 21,000 people, checked on 5 million car numbers, and dealt with many thousands of letters and calls.'

The letters given the highest priority – and most publicity – were three posted in Sunderland, franked with the dates of March 8 and 13, 1978, and March 22, 1979. A tape-recording arrived on June 18, 1979, again with a Sunderland postmark. The letters and the tape, purportedly from the Ripper, were regarded as crucial, and a major part of the hunt was diverted to north-east England. The advertising campaign conceived by George Oldfield was unprecedented in criminal history, with enlarged samples of the handwriting of the letters emblazoned on billboards, as well as being reproduced in a specially printed four-page 'newspaper' issued by the West Yorkshire police. Mr Oldfield called a dramatic press conference, during which he played the taped message to the world. Speaking with a pronounced Geordie accent, the man who had made the recording began: 'I'm Jack. I see you are still having no luck catching me. I have the greatest respect for you, George – but, Lord, you are no nearer to catching me now than four years ago when I started.' The mocking voice was broadcast nationally and in public houses and night-clubs in the north; it could be heard by anyone telephoning a special Leeds number.

Before the letters and the tape were ascribed to a hoaxer, Sutcliffe was interviewed yet again – and was dismissed because he had no trace of a Geordie accent.

It appears that the sinister and evil side of his nature was largely hidden from most, if not all, of his family and friends.

He was born on June 2, 1946, when his parents – John, a baker, and Irish-born Kathleen – lived in a tiny, stone-built terraced cottage in Heaton Row in the market-town of Bingley.

He attended St Joseph's Roman Catholic primary school, where he was regarded as a bright pupil; but his work at Cottingley Manor secondary school was only average. By the time he was 15, the family, now consisting of three boys and three girls, had moved to a larger house on a council estate. His upbringing was typical of the working-class neighbourhood.

As he grew older, Sutcliffe took an interest in motor-cycles and cars, and so it was natural that when he left school he became an apprentice at a local engineering firm. His decision not to complete the apprenticeship was to be reflected in the way he failed to hold down several jobs in later years. For the next 18 months, he worked at a fibre-products factory, but left in 1964 to work as a grave-digger at Bingley cemetery – where, he claimed later, he first heard 'a call from God' to rid the streets of prostitutes. Certainly, it was during this period that the stranger side of his nature began to surface. A fellow grave-digger has recalled that Sutcliffe once asked him to return to the mortuary adjoining the cemetery to examine two bodies. 'Another time, while re-opening a grave, he brought out a skull and chased some girls from the local girls' grammar school. He seemed to think it was a great joke.' Sutcliffe appeared to enjoy working with corpses. He would secrete himself among coffins in the cemetery chapel, and when his workmates appeared, would moan and move the cloths covering the coffins. A Bingley window-cleaner says that Sutcliffe removed rings from corpses: 'He told one of his sisters that she could have one for her wedding, but when he said where it had come from, she jumped back in horror. He thought it was a big laugh.' About this time, he began drinking in public houses, and would tell flesh-creeping tall stories in an effort to impress people. The visits to pubs ended when he was dismissed from the grave-digging job for poor time-keeping.

He was a keep-fit fanatic who liked to prove that he was stronger and fitter than his brothers and friends.

By this time, he was going out with girls. They found him to be a smart, good-looking young man who, in the words of one girlfriend, 'followed the old-fashioned courtesies of courtship'. According to another of them, his most ardent approach was 'a kiss and cuddle' at a bus-stop. 'There was no sexual side to our relationship, which lasted for about four years.'

The girls were unaware that, in the company of young male friends, Sutcliffe drove around red-light districts of Leeds, Bradford and Halifax, following prostitutes and shouting at them.

During one of his wife's visits to him while he was on remand, he said that if he could convince doctors that he was mad, he would only do '10 years in a loony-bin'. A full-scale trial would not have taken place had not Mr Justice Boreham expressed 'grave anxieties' about the prosecution's offer to accept Sutcliffe's plea of guilty to the lesser charge of manslaughter when the case began. There have been instances of 'plea-bargaining' in far less serious cases, but Mr Justice Boreham ordered

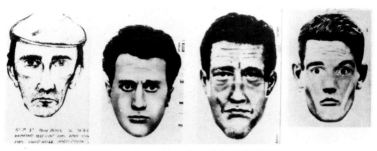

A sketch and three Photofits of the 'Black Panther'

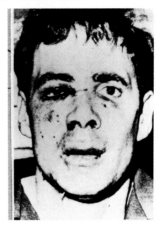

centre left
Donald Neilson

centre right
Neilson, soon after his
fight with bystanders
and his arrest by
policemen

left
The 'Black Panther'
outfit and accessories

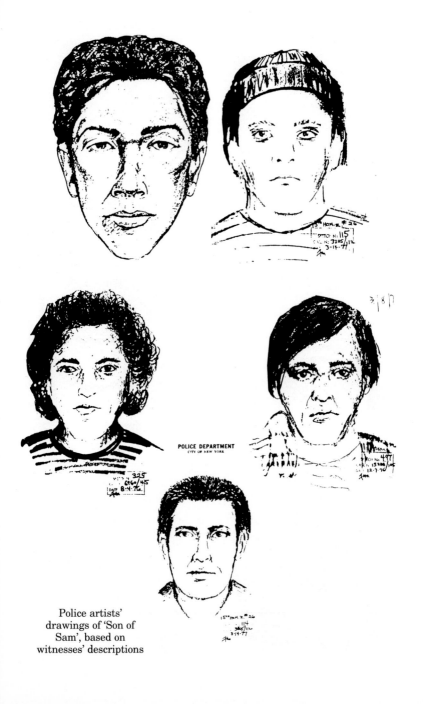

Police artists'
drawings of 'Son of
Sam', based on
witnesses' descriptions

David
Berkowitz

I am so glad I've been apprehended but I wish that someone would help me.

final desperation

I am not well   Not at all

A doodle by Berkowitz

The crossed-out 'John Lennon'
name written by Mark Chapman
when he signed off at the end
of his last day's work in Honolulu

VICTIM 1
Wilma McCann, 28,
Leeds prostitute

VICTIM 2
Joan Harrison, 26,
Preston prostitute

VICTIM 3
Emily Jackson, 42,
Leeds prostitute

VICTIM 4
Irene Richardson, 28,
Leeds prostitute

VICTIM 5
Pat Atkinson, 33,
Bradford prostitute

VICTIM 6
Jayne McDonald, 16,
Leeds shopgirl

VICTIM 7
Jean Royle,
prostitute, 21

VICTIM 8
Helen Rytka,
prostitute, 18

VICTIM 9
Yvonne Pearson, 21,
Bradford prostitute

VICTIM 10
Vera Millward,
prostitute, 40

VICTIM 11
Josie Whitaker, 19,
Halifax clerk

VICTIM 12
Barbara Leach, 20,
Bradford student

Jacqui, the last victim

HILL

opposite page
Victims of the
'Yorkshire Ripper'

above
Police officers struggling
to hold back a little old
lady and other persons
keen to catch a glimpse
of Peter Sutcliffe upon
his escorted arrival at
Dewsbury Magistrates'
Court; January 1981

right
Peter Sutcliffe

The Sutcliffes' house
in Garden Lane,
Heaton, Bradford

23 Cranley Gardens,
Muswell Hill: the last
private residence of
Dennis Nilsen

Dennis Nilsen

Michael Ryan

Michael
Benneman Sams

Joyce and
Syd Dernley

that a jury should be empanelled to decide whether Sutcliffe was guilty of murder or of manslaughter on the grounds of diminished responsibility. Paradoxically, when the prosecution presented its case, much emphasis was laid on the fact that Sutcliffe had feigned madness in order to deceive the psychiatrists who examined him.

Yesterday, at the end of a 14-day trial at the Old Bailey, and after the jury, composed equally of men and women, had deliberated for five hours and 58 minutes, the bearded foreman announced the verdict – by a majority of 10 to 2 – that Sutcliffe was guilty of murder on each of the 13 counts. The victims were Wilma McCann, aged 28, who was killed in Leeds on October 30, 1975; Emily Jackson, 42, Leeds, January 20, 1976; Irene Richardson, 28, Leeds, February 5, 1977; Patricia Atkinson, 32, Bradford, April 23, 1977; Jayne MacDonald, 16, Leeds, June 26, 1977; Jean Jordan, 21, Manchester, October 1, 1977; Yvonne Pearson, 22, Bradford, January 21, 1978; Helen Rytka, 18, Huddersfield, January 31, 1978; Vera Millward, 41, Manchester, May 16, 1978; Josephine Whitaker, 19, Halifax, April 4, 1979; Barbara Leach, 20, Bradford, September 2, 1979; Marguerite Walls, 47, Leeds, August 18, 1980; Jacqueline Hill, 20, Leeds, November 17, 1980.

Prior to the sentencing, Dr Terence Kay, a psychiatrist who had given evidence about Sutcliffe's mental state, was recalled to the witness-box by the Attorney-General, Sir Michael Havers, and told the judge that with the present knowledge of the illness of schizophrenia, doctors believed that Sutcliffe should remain in custody 'for the rest of his natural life'.

Sutcliffe, who was wearing the grey suit that he had worn since the trial began, with an open-necked blue shirt, was ordered to stand. Flanked by five prison officers, he listened impassively as the judge told him that he had committed 13 murders 'of a very cowardly quality, for each was the murder of a woman. It was murder by getting behind the woman and beating her on the head with a hammer before inflicting other injuries. It is difficult to find words that are adequate to describe the brutality and gravity of these offences. I am not going to pause to seek those words. I am prepared to let the catalogue of crime speak for itself.'

Referring to the 'depth of human terror' that Sutcliffe had caused over a wide area of West Yorkshire, the judge commented: 'It is a population which, to my knowledge, does not lack fortitude. But I am left in no doubt that many women were in the deepest fear – and I have no doubt that fear spilled over to their menfolk on their account.'

Saying that he had to assess the danger that Sutcliffe would represent if he was at large, the judge said that because he could not, in law, order that he should remain in jail for the rest of his life, he could only recommend to the Home Secretary that he should be imprisoned for a minimum of 30 years. The judge then completed the sentencing by stipulating that seven charges of attempted murder, to which Sutcliffe had pleaded guilty, should also carry sentences of life imprisonment.

Sutcliffe, who had not said a word since the jury's return to court, turned briskly in the dock and was led away to the cells. After a short time in Wormwood Scrubs, he will be moved to a dispersal prison where 'category A' men – those considered to be 'most dangerous' – are kept.

In a newspaper interview, Mrs Sonia Sutcliffe has said that she first learned that her husband was the Ripper when he told her, 'It's me, love,' while he was in custody at a Dewsbury police station, and has added: 'I shall go on seeing him, wherever he is.'

Leading article:

MAD OR WICKED?

British criminal justice is overworked, expensive, and not the place for arguing over moral niceties. Yet its cause was surely well served by Mr Justice Boreham's decision that the case of Peter Sutcliffe must be held in full, despite the readiness of the prosecution to accept a plea of diminished responsibility. The judge's action and the jury's verdict, that Sutcliffe was guilty of murder, go against the growing trend of 'plea-bargaining,' and reaffirm the belief that people who do the most revolting and pointless things may yet be responsible for their actions. That belief is essential for the strength and sanity of society.

In popular usage, madness seems to be a word to describe something we do not like and cannot understand. To say that someone is mad is somehow reassuring – he is quite different and can be left to the experts. The unbeliever often thinks the religious man mad, and the same is true of the political moderate who refers to terrorists as 'psychopaths,' believing that anyone who commits political acts of extreme violence cannot be acting rationally. Yet history is full of men who have killed and maimed far more freely even than the modern urban guerrilla, and been regarded as fathers of their countries. And people before Peter Sutcliffe have acted on what they took to be voices from God, and been thought saints, not lunatics. Madness may be only what we choose it to be.

If, however, someone is said to be responsible for his actions, even if they are utterly horrible and quite unlike those of most people, then the reality of his deeds confronts everyone. He is not an animal, or a robot gone wrong, but a fellow-citizen who chose to do what he did, whose attitudes and motives can be examined. He felt hatred and anger, as does almost everyone, but he acted as if there was no moral law restraining or criticising his feeling. If Society faces this moral reality, it becomes harder to forget that every human institution designed to make life worth living needs to be watched and guarded, and is always threatened by breakdown. The explanation of madness allows society to put its evil outside itself, instead of facing its ever-present reality. The example of the Soviet Union is worth pondering. There, the men who understand what evil is spend their lives in psychiatric hospitals.

1983

HEAD OFFICE: ISOPAD LTD Stirling Way, Borehamwood,
Herts, WD6 2AF, England. Tel: 01-953 6242 Telex: 261761

KEEPS FLUIDS FLOWING

Saturday, November 5:

THE MAN WHO TALKED TO CORPSES

In February this year, 23 Cranley Gardens, a semi-detached house in a quiet street in Muswell Hill, north London, was divided into flats, which were occupied by five people in all. A self-contained flat on the upper floor was occupied by a 37-year-old, bespectacled civil servant named Dennis Nilsen, who lived there alone with his dog, a mongrel called Blip.

During the first week of the month, the lavatory on the first floor became blocked. After a Dyno-Rod man had called but failed to deal with the trouble, the disgruntled occupants telephoned the landlord's agents, and on Monday the 8th Nilsen wrote them an indignant letter: 'When I flush my toilet, the lavatory pan overflows. Obviously the drains are blocked. An unpleasant odour permeates the building.' Later that day, another man from Dyno-Rod called at the house. As soon as he lifted the man-hole-cover, he noticed the smell of rotting flesh. Arming himself with a torch, he went down into the man-hole and found 30 or 40 small bones and pieces of flesh, some mere strips, others the size of a fist. Nilsen, who was standing nearby, said that it looked as if someone had flushed away their Kentucky Fried Chicken.

The Dyno-Rod man went into the house and, with the tenants clustering around, telephoned his manager to suggest that the police should be called. He was told that nothing was to be done until a further inspection had been made on the following morning.

Late that night, a young couple who lived on the ground floor of the house heard the manhole cover being raised and, after some minutes, replaced. They came out and saw Nilsen going up to his flat.

On the Tuesday morning, soon after Nilsen had left for work, the Dyno-Rod engineer and his manager arrived. The engineer opened the manhole cover – and was most surprised to find that nearly all of the flesh that had been there the previous evening had disappeared. He extracted the few remaining pieces, together with four small

/

bones. One of the tenants phoned the police, who soon afterwards collected the flesh and bones and took them to Charing Cross Hospital, where they were examined by a Home Office pathologist, Dr David Bowen. He concluded that the bones were from a male hand or hands and that the flesh was from a human neck.

The police continued their inquiries and were waiting at Cranley Gardens that evening when Nilsen returned from work. After accompanying him up to his flat, Detective Chief Inspector Peter Jay explained: 'It's about some human remains inside your drains.' Nilsen, feigning shock, said: 'How horrible.' On impulse, Jay asked: 'Where are the rest of them?' and Nilsen, pointing to the wardrobe, said: 'Over there.'

Inside the wardrobe were two plastic bags. Each of the bags contained a badly decomposed human head.

'Is there anything else?' Jay asked.

'It's a long story,' Nilsen replied. 'It goes back a long time. I'll tell you everything. I want to get it off my chest – not here but at the police station.'

After being cautioned, he was taken down to a police car. On the way to the station, he was asked how many bodies he was talking about. 'Fifteen or 16, since 1978,' he said. In the charge room at Hornsey police station, Chief Inspector Jay said to him: 'Let's get this straight. Are you telling us that since 1978 you have killed 16 people?'

'Yes,' was the reply: 'Three at Cranley Gardens and about 13 at my previous address, 195 Melrose Avenue, Cricklewood [just over three miles south-west of Cranley Gardens].'

The remains of three bodies were found in the flat at Cranley Gardens, and at the back of the house were some piles of flesh which Nilsen admitted that he had removed from the manhole. The ground floor flat of 195 Melrose Avenue had been decorated since Nilsen had moved out in September 1980, but he showed the police places under the floorboards where he had temporarily kept bodies; he also pointed out the sites of bonfires in the garden, upon which he had incinerated parts of bodies. During an intensive search of the garden and a patch of ground at the back of the house, the police were told by neighbours that they had complained to Nilsen about his bonfires – particularly the smell from them, caused by old tyres piled on the material he was burning. It occurred to the police that he had burnt the tyres to disguise the smell of burning flesh, even though the pungent smell from the tyres might have drawn more attention. The hundreds of bones, both whole and fragmented, found near the house were taken to Hornsey Mortuary, where Dr Bowen and his team of specialists examined them, sorted them – and eventually ascertained that at least eight bodies had been disposed of in the vicinity of 195 Melrose Avenue.

Meanwhile, detectives were delving into Nilsen's background. He was born on November 23, 1945, in the close-knit fishing community of Fraserburgh, on the east coast of Scotland, the second of three children his mother Betty had by her first husband, a dashing Norwegian Army officer whom she had met while he was stationed in the town during the war. His older brother, Olav, now 39, still lives and works in Fraserburgh; his 35-year-old sister Sylvia is a housewife in Canada. His mother has four children by her second marriage.

Childhood acquaintances of Nilsen in the picturesque town remember him as a quiet, likeable boy who loved painting and little else. In such an isolated area, there was not much to cause young people to stay once their school-days were over, and so there was nothing out of the ordinary about young Nilsen's decision to join the Army at the age of 16. His one regret, it seems, was that it meant abandoning his painting, at which he had shown considerable aptitude.

His Army career lasted for 12 years, during which time he spent a period in the Catering Corps, learning certain butchering skills which he was to put to use in some of his killings. Though he often returned home when he was on leave, he gradually lost contact with all of his friends and acquaintances, most of whom had themselves moved away. Thus, when he left the Army, there was nothing to draw him back to his home-town. At the time of his arrest, his mother, now Mrs Betty Scott, a kindly and well-preserved 63-year-old who had never been out of Scotland in her life, had not seen him for about nine years. She recalls: 'When Dennis joined the Army, he used to come home whenever he could, and would spend his days playing with his younger stepbrothers and step-sisters, cooking them treats like toffee, biscuits and cakes. They used to love him coming home because he made such a fuss of them. He spent a few weeks here just having a rest after all that time in the Army; he had become very fond of poetry. But from then, although I wrote to him regularly, he only replied occasionally. I have always taken the view that my children should be left to lead their own lives when they grew up, and as long as I knew where he was, I didn't mind.'

He was in London. Immediately after his final visit to his mother, he joined the Metropolitan Police, first attending the Hendon training school and then becoming a probationary constable in the Willesden district, just south of Cricklewood, but left the force within a year, saying that the pay was not good enough. He became a security officer with the Manpower Services Commission in 1974, and was then promoted to the post of executive officer at the Kentish Town Job Centre, eventually receiving a salary of £7000 a year.

He moved into 195 Melrose Avenue in November 1975. Various young men shared his flat with him until the late summer of 1978, when he began to live there alone. As a branch officer of the Civil and Public Services Association, he was away for a week at a union conference in September 1978, and when he returned to the flat he found that some of his property had been stolen. This, he has told the police, made him feel lonely and miserable. He invited young men to the flat; some were homosexuals, some were 'rent boys' (male prostitutes). According to one of his statements, he 'supposes that he is emotionally homosexual'. However, he has denied that he killed any of his visitors because he had made sexual advances which they rejected.

Many of the men he killed were homeless down-and-outs whose disappearance, he knew, would not be noticed. Usually meeting his victims in pubs, he invited them back to his flat to continue drinking, talking about politics and society, and listening to records. The combination of audio and alcohol had a profound effect on him, and he has said that drink made him two or three times as strong, adding that the murders were 'like taking candy from a baby'.

Yet by no means all of his young male guests died at his hands. Scores are known to have visited one or other of his flats without coming to any harm.

Nilsen's first strangling was at the end of December 1978. The victim, still unidentified, was an Irishman whom he had met in a Cricklewood pub.

The second victim was British-born Kenneth Ockendon, aged 21, in London on holiday from Canada, and the only one of the victims who was not homeless. He was killed in November 1979.

Victim No. 3 was the youngest: 16-year-old Martyn Duffey, who had left his home on the Wirral, Cheshire, to look for work, and was doing a catering course. He was murdered in May 1980. Nilsen used the boy's own kitchen knives to dissect the body.

Nilsen's dog Blip became excited and had to be calmed down after the fourth killing, some time between the beginning of July and the end of October, 1980. The victim was a 25-year-old Scotsman, Billy Sutherland, a heavy drinker with two failed marriages behind him, who had shuttled between Edinburgh and London.

The fifth and sixth victims have not been identified.

Victim No. 7 was a pathetic young vagrant. Nilsen felt that he had done him a favour, as his life had been one long fight for survival: 'I wound a tie around his neck and slowly pulled it tight. There was a weak struggle, but no sound. Then his legs lifted and separated in slow motion like a bicycle rider's. . . . I remember thinking, "You have no more troubles now, squire."'

Nilsen's horrifying matter-of-factness about the killings is exempli-fied by comments in his statements: his first victim, the Irishman, was 'just another ship in the night', and a murder after a night's drinking was 'end of the day, end of the drink, end of the person'. The sickening dismemberment of bodies was rationalised thus: 'The victim is the dirty platter after the feast, and the washing-up is the clinically ordinary task.'

His eighth victim was a 'hippy type', still unidentified, and No. 9 was a young Scot picked up in a Soho pub; he remains unidentified, as do the tenth and the eleventh, an East London skinhead, boastful of his toughness and of how much he could drink, who, according to Nilsen, had the words 'cut here' tattooed around his neck.

Victim No. 12, in September 1980, was Malcolm Barlow, a 26-year-old epileptic vagrant from Rotherham, whom Nilsen had 'rescued' after finding him having a fit in Melrose Avenue. While Nilsen was watching television, Barlow became unconscious: '[As I was unable to rouse him,] I decided what to do. I put my hands around his throat and held my position for two to three minutes. Not feeling much like prising up the floorboards, I dragged him into the kitchen and put him under the sink.'

Before leaving Melrose Avenue for Cranley Gardens, he had a final bonfire upon which he piled Barlow's body and the remains of four earlier victims from under the floorboards in his flat: 'Kids gathered round and started prodding the fire with bits of stick. I told them to keep away as it was dangerous. They stood some way off and soon lost interest. . . . When I spotted a skull, I would crush it with a rake so the casual observer would not notice it.'

His next victim, John Howlett – nicknamed 'John the Guardsman' – was a fairground worker from High Wycombe, Buckinghamshire. Nilsen used an upholstery strap to throttle him. That was some time in March 1982. Later in that year, a 28-year-old Glaswegian, Archibald Allen, was strangled as he was settling down to eat an omelette that Nilsen had cooked for him.

The final murder, about a week before the Dyno-Rod men arrived at 23 Cranley Gardens, was of 20-year-old Stephen Sinclair, a native of Perthshire, Scotland, who as well as being a heavy drinker was a drug-addict.

It can be seen from the selection of Nilsen's comments quoted above that he has ostensibly been most co-operative with the police. Four days after his arrest, he passed a letter to Chief Inspector Jay. Under the heading, 'Unscrambling Behaviour (Sexual Depression)', the letter read:

'I guess I may be a creative psychopath who, when in a loss of reality situation, lapses temporarily into a destructive psychopath, a condition induced by rapid and heavy ingestion of alcohol.

'At the subconscious root lies a sense of total social isolation and a desperate search for a sexual identity.

'I experienced transitory sexual relationships with both males and females before my first killing. After this event I was incapable of any intercourse. I felt repelled by myself and as stated I have had no experience of sexual penetration for some years.

'In a society of labels, it's convenient for me to let others believe that I am homosexual. I enjoy the company of both men and women. But I prefer to drink specially with men. I'm not in sympathy with the state of women who are the worse for drink.

'God only knows what thoughts go through my mind when it's captive within a destruction binge. Maybe the cunning, stalking killer instinct is the only single concentration released from a mind which in that state knows no morality.

'It may be the perverted overkill of my need to help people – victims who I decide to release quickly from the slings and arrows of their outrageous fortune, pain and suffering.

'There is no disputing the fact that I am a violent killer under certain circumstances. ... It would be better if my reason for killing could be clinically defined, i.e. robbery, jealousy, hate, revenge, sex, blood-lust or sadism.

'But it's none of these. Or it could be the subconscious outpouring of all the primitive instincts of primeval man.

'Could it be the case of individual exaltation at beating the system and the need to beat and confound it time and time again?

'It amazes me that I have no tears for the victims. I have no tears for myself or those bereaved by my actions.

'Am I a wicked person, constantly under pressure, who just cannot cope with it, who escapes to reap revenge against society through a haze of a bottle of spirits?

'But maybe it's because I was just born an evil man. Living with so much violence and death, I've not been haunted by the souls and ghosts of the dead, leading me to believe that no such fictional phenomena has, does, or ever will exist.

'Memories of man's best friend, i.e. my dog, are already a little faded.'

Later, Nilsen gave Chief Inspector Jay a summary of his victims as best he could and stated: 'In the normal course of my life, I feel I had normal powers of mental rationality and morality. When under pressure of work and extreme pain of social loneliness and utter misery, I am drawn compulsively to a means of temporary escape from reality. This is achieved by taking increasing draughts of alcohol and plugging into stereo music, which mentally removes me to a higher plane of ecstasy, joy and tears. That is a totally emotional experience. This glorious experience and feeling is conjured up in this manner. I relive experiences from childhood to the point where I am taking out the bad bits.'

Nilsen added a further summary: 'In order to enlarge on Melrose Avenue and Cranley Gardens, I have made several attempts to strangle men. In some cases the attempts were foiled by the struggle or escape of the subject. In others, I did not have the heart or desire to carry through the task. In all of the latter cases, the subject was already unconscious, although heavily confused. The next day, they were aware of painful throats and noticed their bloodshot eyes. There are at least three such men at large from the Cranley Gardens experience.'

In another letter to Peter Jay, Nilsen said that he did not maliciously plan any of his activities: 'I could never contemplate any assault against any living person or creature. My remorse is deep and personal and will eat away inside me for the rest of my life. I am tragically a private person not given to public tears.

'The enormity of the act has left me in permanent shock. The trouble was that, as my activity increased, so did the unbearable pressures which could only be escaped from by taking the best routes to oblivion via the bottle.

'I have slain my own dragon as surely as the press and public will slay me. They all need to see the forces of law and order slay a dragon or monster occasionally, even if the dragon is only a myth.'

In the letter, he remarked that writers, photographers and sociologists would have a field-day – but the Nilsens, Sinclairs and Duffeys (two of his victims) would have to stagger along their own weary way, unnoticed and alone.

In interviews conducted by Detective Chief Superintendent Geoffrey Chambers, who was in charge of the investigation, Nilsen said that he cut up the bodies on plastic sheeting in the front room. He kept a pot in which to boil the pieces. Asked why he had killed, he replied: 'I don't know. I have been trying to work it out. I am not a head-shrinker. Everyone keeps walking out on me. I drink to relieve the pressure. I think I'm a chronic alcoholic. Even after drinking a bottle of Bacardi, I can still talk rationally. I may not remember afterwards, but at the time I'm OK.'

Speaking of the chores following the murder of Stephen Sinclair, he said he had taken the body from the cupboard where he had originally put it, laid it on a plastic sheet on the carpet, and cut off the head with a long kitchen knife: 'I put the head into the pot, put the lid on it, and lit the stove. When the head was coming to the boil, I turned the pot down to simmer.

'Then I took the dog out for a walk.'

He said that it was easier for him to dispose of the pieces of bodies when he was living in the ground-floor flat in Melrose Avenue. He took them out into the garden and buried them, and when the garden became 'full', used the nearby waste ground. He moved to the third-floor flat in Cranley Gardens in an effort to stop the killings – to give himself a new chance.

That decision rebounded on him. As it was less easy to get rid of the dismembered bodies, he was forced to boil the pieces until they were soft enough to force down the sink. The larger pieces, such as heads, he had to put into black plastic bags which he kept in a wardrobe. The remains forced down the sink eventually blocked the drains of the Victorian house.

Nilsen displayed an icy, dead-pan humour that was chillingly at odds with the bestiality of his crimes. When, soon after his arrest, an animal-lover wrote to the police, offering to look after his dog and to return it as soon as he was free, he commented: 'Well, who'd want an 80-year-old dog back?' On another occasion, after a long session with detectives, during which he had confessed to at least 15 killings, he was being taken back to his cell when he stopped on the stairs and said: 'All right, I'd better tell you the lot,' and as the detectives stared at him, expecting to hear of further horrors, went on to say; 'I've no television licence or a licence for my dog.' Nor had he. Another time, when he was with a detective con-stable in an interview room and had nowhere to stub out his cigarette, the officer suggested that he should drop the butt down the plug-hole of the sink – but he questioned the idea, saying: 'The last time I put something down a drain, I got myself into an awful lot of trouble.'

One of the psychiatrists who examined Nilsen, Dr James McKeith, a former consultant at Broadmoor, concluded that he was an 'extreme egocentric, grandiose in the way he talks about himself, with a craving for attention'. During the course of ten hours of interviews, Nilsen told the doctor that he had become furious with men he had invited to his home who would not listen to him: 'They would sit down. I would talk incessantly, like an auditor – outbursts about music, politics, and Maggie Thatcher. If they entered into it, it would be OK. If sleeping, they would be dead already, if you like. I would think they didn't care about anything, were only struggling from day to day. I was giving them a chance to live. You have got to listen to me, I thought; I am a valuable member of society. I used to get very intense. Once they were dead, it would stop me thinking at fever-pitch. It was part of the message. It was the ultimate to pay for apathy – so many things mixed up together.'

Dr McKeith based his diagnosis that Nilsen was suffering from a 'severe personality disorder' upon, among other points, his loneliness, his perverted sex-life and paranoid tendencies. In the doctor's opinion, Nilsen's maladjusted patterns of behaviour, starting in childhood, were the result of 'constitutional factors'. His father, who had left the family home when Nilsen was aged three, was an unreliable person who drank heavily and who contracted four marriages before his death in 1977. The doctor believed that Nil-sen's insecurity could be traced back to the death of his maternal grandfather, with whom he was very close, when he was six: unable to understand the fact that the grandfather was dead, Nilsen, dis-traught, had tried to find him. Nilsen said that he had resented his mother's remarriage when he was 10, and described himself in child-hood as someone who always felt quite alone, often lost in fantasies.

During the interviews, he often said that his loneliness was an extreme problem for him. 'He said that he tried to meet the problem by becoming involved with others, but potential relationships broke down. He looked back upon his decision to leave the Army as impulsive and self-destructive; at that time he had been attracted to a young fellow soldier, and he was disappointed that the relationship had not developed.

Dr McKeith concluded that Nilsen had a markedly abnormal sexual development, having noted, for instance, that from the age of 10 he had been aroused by pornographic material involving both males and females. The doctor believed that two stories Nilsen had told him indicated that he was unusually preoccupied with nakedness and unconsciousness in the sexual context.

The first story was of when, as a child, he walked fully-clothed into the sea near his home, lost his footing, and was drowning. Recovering consciousness, he found that he was lying naked among sand-dunes, with his wet clothes neatly folded beside him. He noticed a substance on his abdomen, thought it was semen, and believed then and now that he had been rescued by an unknown boy of 16 whom he had seen nearby and who had masturbated over him.

The second story related to when he was serving in the Army in the Middle East. Sleeping from the effects of drink while returning to his base in a taxi, he was awoken by the driver coshing him. He was bundled into the boot, and then became aware that he was naked and that his clothes were beside him. Fearing that his throat would be cut, he scrambled out of the boot, hit the driver on the head with a jack, killing him, and returned to the depot. He never reported the incident.

Dr McKeith considered that, for the purposes of diagnosis, it was not important whether the stories were fact or fantasy.

Nilsen told him that he had sometimes dusted his body with powder so that it had the appearance of a corpse and then masturbated in front of a mirror. He also said that he had washed and powdered the bodies of men he had murdered before examining them and himself in a mirror. On occasions, he had 'felt obliged' to masturbate near a body before he could cut it up.

He said that, from 1972, he had frequently experienced blackouts after solitary drinking bouts, and had been unable to recall everything he had done. The blackouts had increased, and once in 1977 he was alarmed to find himself in a strange part of London, with no knowledge of how he had got there, and having 'lost' about five hours. He had become so concerned about his drinking that he had asked a colleague at the Job Centre whether he was going mad. Workmates characterised him as being extremely opinionated, rather aggressive in manner, and desperate for company.

Nilsen talked about his trial as if it were more a case of fame than of notoriety, and Dr McKeith was firm in his belief that 'he is concerned about being mad or being thought of as being mad; it is his principal preoccupation not to be sent off to a hospital and be subdued by needles.'

Even so, at the trial, which began at the Old Bailey on October 24, Dr McKeith was one of two psychiatrists called by the defence to say that Nilsen was mentally ill throughout his four-year campaign of killing.

Detectives involved in the investigation have contended that Nilsen's motive was shockingly simple: loneliness. They believe that he talked to the bodies kept in his home until they decomposed, and looked forward to returning at night to the company of a corpse. Chief Superintendent Chambers describes him as 'an evil man with no moral conscience', while his deputy, Peter Jay, says that he is 'a cold, intelligent man with a sense of humour – a different person to different people'.

The trial ended yesterday afternoon when, after a retirement of nearly 12½ hours, the jury of eight men and four women returned 10-to-2 majority verdicts that Nilsen was guilty of the six murders and one of the attempted murders with which he was charged, and a unanimous verdict that he was guilty of the other attempted murder. (The murder charges related to Kenneth Ockenden, Martyn Duffey, Billy Sutherland, Malcolm Barlow, John Howlett and Stephen Sinclair; the charges of attempted murder arose from information given by two men, Douglas Stewart and Paul Nobbs, who had each managed to escape.)

The judge, Mr Justice Croom-Johnson, sentenced Nilsen to life imprisonment, with a recommendation that he should serve at least 25 years.

Now that Nilsen's murderous career has ended in the blaze of publicity that he craved, his dearest wish is to be reunited with another man high on the list of public enemies, the 37-year-old transvestite gunman David Martin, with whom he established a close relationship when they were both in Brixton Prison awaiting their respective trials.

Though it appears that Nilsen is now denying that he is homosexual, he is known to have taken the dominant role in numerous male relationships. During his spell as a probationary policeman, he joined the Campaign for Homosexual Equality, and Dr Paul Bowden, the first psychiatrist to study him following his arrest, came to the conclusion that he was driven to kill so as to compensate for his feelings of criminality over his homosexual life.

According to prison sources, Nilsen and David Martin were so disruptive in Brixton that there is little likelihood that his dearest wish will be fulfilled.*

* But it was. Martin, a busy burglar who had been imprisoned several times since his teens, and who had escaped from custody almost as often, is probably best remembered because, in January 1983, soon after his escape while awaiting trial on a number of serious charges, including the attempted murder of a police constable, a posse of armed Metropolitan detectives ambushed a car which they believed Martin was driving, unaccountably opened fire, and seriously wounded the actual driver, a young film editor named Stephen Waldorf. Martin was arrested a fortnight later, though not until a large number of Flying Squad officers had chased him through Underground tunnels, and in October, after a 14-day trial at the Old Bailey at which he had refused to plead, was convicted of 15 major offences and sentenced to 25 years' imprisonment. His trial ended just before Nilsen's began. Both men were sent to Parkhurst Prison on the Isle of Wight, but they were separated permanently on March 13, 1984, when the sexually ambivalent Martin, depressed by the unfaithfulness of a woman-friend, concocted a noose from bits of wire and a boot-lace, and hanged himself.

Saturday, April 27, 1991: Lord Longford visited mass-murderer Dennis Nilsen yesterday at Albany Prison, Isle of Wight, despite Nilsen's reported comment that a visit from the prison reformer [and campaigner for the release of Myra Hindley] 'adds 20 years to your sentence'.

1985

Saturday, March 9:

THE LADY IN THE LAKE

After seven and a half years of wondering whether he had got away with killing his wife, Peter Hogg, a 57-year-old pilot for Air Europe, was last night found guilty of manslaughter, for which he was sentenced to three years' imprisonment, with a further consecutive 12 months for obstructing a coroner and committing perjury in divorce proceedings begun after his wife's death. He had been brought to justice at the Old Bailey by a stroke of fate as outrageous as any in an Agatha Christie plot.

Exactly a year ago this weekend, police divers searching for a French student who had disappeared into secluded Wast Water, the deepest and blackest lake in England. They found no trace of 21-year-old Veronique Marre. Indeed, no trace of her has ever been found.

What they did find, trussed in plastic sheeting and weighted with a block of concrete, was the mummified body of Hogg's faithless wife Margaret, resting where he had dumped it on an October night in 1976.

Nobody had known that she was dead. Nobody had ever looked for her since Hogg reported that she had left him.

But for the divers' freak discovery, the lady in the lake might have lain for all time on the underwater ledge. And in the ultimate irony for Hogg, his secret would have been absolutely safe had he rowed his inflatable dinghy another 50 yards out into the lake to where the bottom drops away beyond the reach of skin-divers.

He had neglected to remove his wife's wedding ring, inscribed 'Margaret 15.11.64 Peter', and had bundled her in plastic sheeting marked with the name and address of a firm at Guildford, near his home. A second macabre parcel, also tied to the concrete block, contained blood-stained clothing and a book called *Flyers' World*.

The evidence led straight to him.

When Chief Inspector Stephen Read of Cumbria police arrived on his doorstep in Mead Road, Cranleigh, Surrey, and told him of the discovery, Hogg eventually said, with weary resignation, 'That was unlucky, wasn't it?' After telling the story that he had stuck to for 7½ years – that his wife had walked out on him – he admitted that he had strangled her following a row about her affair with a banker, Graham Ryan. He told the officer that his wife had had 'the cheek' to ask him to wash the bedclothes that she and Mr Ryan had taken with them for a week in the country. The comment about his bad luck served as a fitting epitaph to his conviction – and to his 13-year marriage to the tempestuous former air-hostess, 11 years his junior.

Hogg, the son of an author, was divorced, with twin sons from his previous marriage, when he met the vivacious Margaret Hawkins. Their relationship seemed doomed from the start. Friends have told how Margaret loved to throw lively parties, whereas Hogg was 'quiet and mild-mannered'.

In 1973, at a cocktail party in Los Angeles, she met Graham Ryan – like her husband, in his late forties – and began the adulterous affair which was to end in her death. Back in England, she relentlessly pursued the successful international businessman who lived nearby, in the heart of the Surrey stockbroker belt. She invited him to lunch, entertained him to free meals at the restaurant she ran in Cranleigh, and even followed him when he took his wife and two children on holiday. One of her friends said recently: 'Margaret thought he was going to be a very, very good catch. She had marriage in mind from the very beginning.'

Mr Ryan, who is living with his family in Fir Tree Road, Banstead, Surrey, told the jury at Hogg's trial that after the cocktail party in Los Angeles, Mrs Hogg, then 34, telephoned him in England: 'It is fair to say that she was chasing me. I don't know if I was flattered by it, but it affected me, it's true.' He said that their three-year affair had developed into a serious loving relationship.

But he admitted that Mrs Hogg was emotional and impulsive: 'She would always react emotionally when she didn't think she was going to get her own way. She made scenes. I sometimes found them distressing.' He said that she was 'in the driving seat' of their affair: 'In a sense, I was the passenger.' She was given to hysteria and 'indulged in fantasy', said Mr Ryan, who described two incidents when he had fought with her. He said that she once punched him as they sat in his car. On another occasion, she bent his thumb back, and he reacted by hitting her across the wrist with his umbrella.

Mr Ryan said that his wife knew about his long-running relationship with Mrs Hogg, who flaunted the affair in public while Hogg kept his marital difficulties to himself.

Although one friend said that Margaret Hogg was 'certainly no sex-pot', she managed to weave a captive shell around her husband and her lover. She was fickle to both. One minute she announced that she was going to stay with her husband and the next that she wanted to live with her lover. Early on during her affair with Mr Ryan, she agreed to her husband's having a vasectomy so that they would not have any more children. But she said that she was determined to go ahead with a pregnancy when she found that she was to have Mr Ryan's baby, which she called her 'love-child'; soon afterwards, she had a miscarriage. She boasted to her husband that she was sleeping with Mr Ryan: 'It was marvellous – three times on one night,' she taunted him.

Hogg told the court that she made numerous promises to end the affair, but broke them within days, meeting Mr Ryan secretly. She stayed the night with him in hotels while Hogg was on flying duty abroad, often getting acquaintances to look after their sons, David, now 19, and Geoffrey, now 15. Hogg explained: 'One has to think of the younger parties – our boys. It is best not to have a break-up if it can be avoided.'

The climax came when, despite

his protests, she went for a week's holiday with Mr Ryan at a cottage in the New Forest. When she returned on Sunday, October 17, 1976, she and her lover had their usual lunchtime drink before she went home. They had arranged to meet again, later that day, at a car-park near Guildford. Mr Ryan waited there for four hours, then left, 'feeling sad and rejected' because he believed that he had been jilted.

By that time, his mistress – described by defence counsel at the trial as 'a piece of erring humanity' – was dead. He said that when she failed to contact him over the next few days, 'I thought she had had enough of our relationship. That made me very unhappy, of course.' Later, he telephoned Hogg and was told: 'I thought she was with you.'

In evidence, Hogg described what happened when his wife returned on the Sunday afternoon. 'She went upstairs to lie down. I followed her, bringing up the subject of her going away the previous week with Ryan – to remonstrate with her. I was very cross about many things. Her reaction to my criticism was fury. She came at me violently. She was shouting. She struck my face and she kicked me in the crotch, in the testicles. It was extraordinarily painful.'

He said that she backed away when he raised his fist at her, but he followed her towards the bedroom window. 'I hit her on the forehead with a closed fist.' He added that he had only ever hit her once before, when she had broken his finger with a wooden sandal. 'When I struck her, I was angry, very angry. When we were both by the window, she started punching, kicking, shouting and screaming at me. I attacked her again and she climbed on to the bed and I fol-

lowed. Well, I think we had a tussle for a short time, and then at that point I got hold of her around the neck. I think I can only describe that as a loss of any sort of control. I just wanted to stop the noise and the shouting. Suddenly she stopped any form of movement and the look in her eyes didn't appear normal. I realised that I had killed her. I was horrified by what had happened. I had destroyed a life – unintentionally, but I had destroyed a life, and I felt pity and remorse.'

But, within minutes, his 30 years' experience as a pilot came to his rescue, and he understood 'surprisingly quickly' that he would have to put his mind to the 'current emergency'. He found some flex and rope, and trussed her up, parcelled in plastic sheeting, then locked the bedroom door until it was safe to move her body into the boot of his car, after his seven-year-old son Geoffrey – who had returned from visiting a friend – was asleep, and the au-pair had also gone to bed. He dragged the body downstairs and put it in the boot with a second parcel containing bloodstained clothing and books.

The next day, Hogg arranged an appointment with his 11-year-old son David's headmaster at a boarding school at Taunton, Somerset, and drove the 130 miles to the school with his wife's body in the boot. Also in the car was an inflatable dinghy and a concrete block which he had picked up at Gatwick Airport.

Assuming that everyone would think that he was spending the night at Taunton, he drove 325 miles north from Somerset to the Lake District, arriving at Wast Water shortly before midnight.

He inflated the dinghy, put in the body, the other parcel and the concrete block, and rowed out to the middle of the lake, where he tied the two parcels to the block and tipped them into the dark water.

He drove back through the night to Taunton, collected David for his half-term holiday, and returned to Cranleigh.

He told anyone who asked that his wife had left him, and reported her as a missing person at the local police station. Subsequently, he began divorce proceedings, citing Mr Ryan, and swore an affidavit that his wife had left him and that he had no idea where she was.

He said in court that all he needed was a few more years to set Geoffrey on his feet. The boy, who has learning problems due to dyslexia, is still at school.

Speaking recently to friends, he said that he had 'the most awful shock' when the police came to his house. He had not seen any reports of a body being found or police notices asking for information about the wedding ring. And he said that there was no relief that his dark secret was out; he felt only regret that it had been discovered after so many years.

At his trial, Hogg denied prosecution suggestions that he had kept his long silence to hide murder. He said that he had never meant to kill his wife. 'I have had recurring nightmares and have woken up sweating about this for several years – usually around the anniversary of the events. The thoughts were ever-present; they have never been wholly extinguished. Even now they are there.'

As for the faithless lady in the lake, her long-dead body has now been cremated. At the request of her son David, her ashes were scattered over the part of Wast Water which had hidden her for so long that Peter Hogg must have been sure that she would never be found.

THE NEW WOMAN IN HIS LIFE SAYS: 'I WILL WAIT FOR HIM'

The woman who has been Peter Hogg's companion for two years buried her face in her hands as he was sentenced. Mrs Rosemary Steele, who had walked hand-in-hand with him to court every day of the trial – he was free on bail – said: 'I will stand by him. A relationship doesn't sink just because someone goes away for some time.'

Following the trial, members of Hogg's family and friends went to the Waldorf Hotel for a small get-together. One of the guests was Detective Chief Inspector Tim Blake, who had headed the inquiry.

Wednesday, May 8, 1985:

STUDENT'S BODY FOUND

The body of Veronique Marre, a French student who disappeared during a walking trip nearly two years ago, has been found near Wast Water in the Lake District. Miss Marre, 21 at the time of her disappearance in July 1983, was last seen when she left Wasdale youth hostel, near the lake.

A walker found her body on Monday on screes overlooking the lake. Cumbria police said that foul play was not suspected.

The disappearance of Miss Marre, an agriculture student from Paris, set off one of the biggest searches of the lake. It was during the search that police found the body of Mrs Margaret Hogg.

Friday, June 27, 1986:

NEW LOVE FOR 'LAKE' KILLER

Peter Hogg, 58, was released on parole yesterday from Northeye Prison, Bexhill, Kent, after serving 15 months of a four-year sentence. Waiting for him was French-born Miss Marie Christine Pinoul, who was his pen-friend during his time in jail.

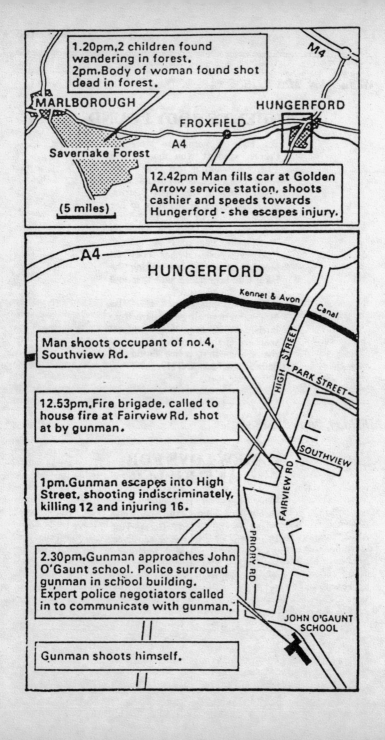

1.20pm, 2 children found wandering in forest.
2pm. Body of woman found shot dead in forest.

MARLBOROUGH

FROXFIELD

HUNGERFORD

M4

A4

Savernake Forest

(5 miles)

12.42pm Man fills car at Golden Arrow service station, shoots cashier and speeds towards Hungerford - she escapes injury.

A4

HUNGERFORD

Kennet & Avon Canal

HIGH STREET

PARK STREET

Man shoots occupant of no.4, Southview Rd.

SOUTHVIEW

12.53pm. Fire brigade, called to house fire at Fairview Rd, shot at by gunman.

FAIRVIEW RD

1pm. Gunman escapes into High Street, shooting indiscrimnately, killing 12 and injuring 16.

PRIORY RD

2.30pm. Gunman approaches John O'Gaunt school. Police surround gunman in school building. Expert police negotiators called in to communicate with gunman.

JOHN O'GAUNT SCHOOL

Gunman shoots himself.

1987

Thursday, August 20:

MICHAEL RYAN:
'I WISH I'D STAYED IN BED'

Could it really have happened here? There is the scent of mown grass in the Berkshire market town of Hungerford; a Union Jack flies above the parish church, and tractors chug along the main street.

Yesterday, during six hours of fear, Michael Ryan, a 27-year-old gun fanatic, went through Hungerford, his home town, dressed in black combat fatigues, and firing from both hands at anyone and anything that moved with a Kalashnikov AK47 assault rifle and a pistol, reloading from an ammunition-belt slung across his chest.

His murderous journey began ten miles away in Savernake Forest, just across the county boundary with Wiltshire, where Mrs Susan Godfrey, from Reading, had brought her children, a boy of four and his two-year-old sister, for a picnic. After forcing Susan Godfrey to leave her children, he fired 14 shots into her. Minutes later, the children, James and Hannah, approached an elderly woman walking in the forest, and James said to her: 'A man in black has shot our Mummy.'

Ryan was by then driving his D-registered Vauxhall Astra towards Hungerford. He stopped at the Golden Arrow filling station in the village of Froxfield, about three miles from the town, and fired through a glass partition at a woman cashier, showering her with fragments but not injuring her.

After arriving at Hungerford, he set off on foot through the streets. He shot at his mother and their black labrador in the house they shared, in South View, and set it on fire. Then he collected more weapons and ammunition from the garden shed and went out to murder again ... and again ... and again.

A young man, Christopher Bowsher, saw Ryan 'running down the street with what looked like a Russian gun and a pump-action shotgun held at the hip like Rambo. I ran into a building and then saw him shoot a man driving a Norlands Nursery van. The shots went through the windscreen, and the driver got it badly in the throat and face. Then a father and his son came out of a side-road with two little girls. Ryan let the little girls run away, and as they legged it, screaming, he shot at the two men. A minute later, his mother came running after him, shouting out and begging him to stop all of this. Then there was another shot, and someone said he had killed her.'

Shortly before, at 12.47 p.m., the Thames Valley police had received the first 999 call from South View – a lane adjoining Hungerford Common – that someone had been shot, and the usual warning had been broadcast to all officers that a firearm had been used and that caution should be exercised. Almost immediately afterwards, a call was received from Police Constable Roger Brereton, a 41-year-old traffic policeman who had driven to the vicinity of South View in a patrol-car. He gave his call-sign, '18', and the message 'ten-nine, ten-nine', meaning that assistance was needed urgently; then he was heard crying out: 'I have been shot.' He had been killed by a bullet in the back.

Next, an 84-year-old pensioner, Abdur Khan, who had come to England from India when he was a boy and had established a chain of restaurants in London, was cut down in the garden of his bungalow in Priory Avenue, dying in his wife's arms. Then Marcus Barnard was shot dead through the window of his taxi-cab; his wife, who had recently given birth to a baby boy, heard the shots from their house just 50 yards away. Another resident of Priory Avenue, Ken Clements, who was unemployed, had just set out for a walk with his grown-up son Robert, when he was killed by a rain of bullets; Robert escaped by leaping over a wall.

Another victim was Douglas Wainwright who, recently retired, had driven from Kent with his wife, intending to look for a house in Hungerford so that they could be close to their son, a policeman in the town. Ryan pumped eight bullets into the car, wounding Mrs Wainwright in the chest and taking off the tips of two of her fingers. Even before the car crashed, her husband, slumped over the steering wheel, was dead. Among others who

were killed was Francis Butler, an accounts clerk in his mid-twenties: he had a day off from work, and had just left his wife and two children at their home in Coldharbour Road to take the dog for a walk – a walk that bisected Ryan's murderous route. His dog stayed, whimpering, by his side.

The full tally of the carnage appears to be: 16 dead, 14 injured.

Police helicopters and armoured vehicles were drafted in, the town was sealed off, and gradually the net tightened around Ryan, who eventually dashed into the John O'Gaunt School, empty because of the holidays.

Thirty-five-year-old Police Sergeant Paul Brightwell and other officers of the Thames Valley Tactical Firearms Unit were undergoing training at Kidlington, Oxfordshire, when they heard of the events at Hungerford. They made their way to the town separately. At about 5.15 p.m., Sergeant Brightwell heard on his radio that a shot had been fired from the front of the John O'Gaunt School, and he went through the back gardens of houses in Priory Road to join Police Constable Anthony Bates, who was already in position, with his gun aimed at an upstairs window of the school.

Constable Bates shouted: 'You in the building. Can you hear me?' He repeated the question several times before Ryan shouted: 'Yes.'

Both officers shouted to him a number of times: 'You are surrounded by armed police. Do as you're told and no harm will come to you.'

Ryan shouted a reply that neither could make out. They moved closer. Sergeant Brightwell asked the gunman his first name. Ryan replied: 'That is nothing to do with you – mind your own business.'

The sergeant told him: 'That's OK, Mr Ryan. I just want to talk to you and get you out safely. Do you understand?'

RYAN: Yes. I have nothing against you.

BRIGHTWELL: What weapons do you have with you?

RYAN: One 9 mm pistol and ammunition.

BRIGHTWELL: This is very important. Do not come to the window holding any weapon. Do you understand?

RYAN: I understand. I also have a grenade.

BRIGHTWELL: Do not come to the window with the grenade. Do you understand?

RYAN: Yes.

BRIGHTWELL: I want to get you out of the building safely. Do you understand?

RYAN: Yes. . . . I want to know how my mother is. Tell me about my mother.

BRIGHTWELL: I'll try to find out about her. Just bear with me.

RYAN: I must know about my mother. . . . Tell me or I'll throw the grenade out of the window.

BRIGHTWELL: Don't do that. I'm trying to find out about your mother, believe me.

RYAN: That's ridiculous. I want to know. I must know.

The officer instructed Ryan to look at a large rubbish bin with a green lid so as to identify a nearby staircase from which to leave the school.

RYAN: I'm not standing up. Have you found out about my mother yet?

BRIGHTWELL: Not yet. I'm still trying.

RYAN: I'm not coming out until I know.

BRIGHTWELL: I want you to leave all your weapons in that room. Do you understand?

RYAN: Yes. My pistol is tied to my wrist with a lanyard. I have one round of ammunition.

BRIGHTWELL: Can you undo the lanyard?

RYAN: No.

BRIGHTWELL: Do not come out with any weapon whatsoever.

RYAN: I had an M1 carbine which I left in the park. It was on a gravel path near the body of a man I shot near the swimming pool. There should be a 30-round magazine with it.

BRIGHTWELL: Thank you for that, Mr Ryan.

RYAN: Also, there's my dog. Has anybody found that? It's a black labrador. I shot it. I had my eyes shut the first time, and I just winged it.

BRIGHTWELL: I'll find out about your dog.

RYAN: I've undone the lanyard. I also have body armour.

BRIGHTWELL: Thank you. Will you come out?

RYAN: I'm not coming out until I know about my mother.

BRIGHTWELL: I'm trying to find out. But I want you to come out, leaving all your weapons in the room.

RYAN: Where shall I leave them? On the window-sill?

BRIGHTWELL: Don't come to the window holding any weapon. Just leave them on the floor. Do you understand?

RYAN: Yes. . . . I'll come down the stairs outside.

The officer told Ryan to walk down the stairs very slowly, with his hands in the air, and then unlock and open the outside doors.

BRIGHTWELL: When you come outside, look to your left and you'll see me. . . . I want you to leave your body-armour in the room as well, Mr Ryan.

RYAN: Why is that? What for?

BRIGHTWELL: I need to be able to

see that you have nothing concealed. You understand my position?

RYAN: Yes, I understand. But I'm not going to come out until I know about my mother.

BRIGHTWELL: I'm doing my best, Mr Ryan – I'm still trying to find out about your mother. If you come out, we'll be able to sort it out much quicker.

RYAN: What are the casualty figures?

BRIGHTWELL: I don't know. Obviously, you know you shot a lot of people.

RYAN: Hungerford must be a bit of a mess.

BRIGHTWELL: You're right. They know you've been through. How many do you think you've shot?

RYAN: I don't know. It's like a bad dream. My mother – she's dead, isn't she? That's why you won't tell me. I'm throwing the magazine of the pistol out. [*The magazine was thrown from the window.*] I still have one round left.

BRIGHTWELL: Why do you have that?

RYAN: It's obvious, isn't it?

BRIGHTWELL: Don't do anything silly.

RYAN: Don't worry. I've nothing against you. You've got your job to do.

The officer then repeated his instruction to Ryan to leave his weapons in the building, said that he wanted him to get out safely, and added that he was still trying to find out about his mother.

RYAN: You must have a radio. Get on that and find out. How many people are with you?

BRIGHTWELL: Just a couple.

RYAN: Well, get *them* to do it. Have you found the M1 carbine yet?

BRIGHTWELL: They're still looking, Mr Ryan. I've passed on all the details.

RYAN: It's just that there were some kids nearby. I don't want them to find it. . . . I've got three more grenades.

BRIGHTWELL: Mr Ryan, this is important. Have you got them with you?

RYAN: No, not with me.

BRIGHTWELL: Where are they?

RYAN: I'm not saying.

BRIGHTWELL: Where did you get the grenades?

RYAN: I bought them from a bloke.

He again asked about his dog. Sergeant Brightwell told him that it was at Hungerford police station, and promised that he would look after it. Ryan asked him to give it a decent burial. He then shouted that he wanted to know about his mother, and said that he had picked up his gun again.

RYAN [*still shouting*]: What about my mother? She's dead – I know she's dead.

BRIGHTWELL: If you come out, we'll find out about your mother together.

The officer then repeated his instructions to Ryan to walk slowly down the stairs, with his hands in the air, and said that he would come to no harm. But Ryan said that he wanted to think about it. Sergeant Brightwell then asked Ryan if he had seen anyone in the school.

RYAN: No, I'm on my own. I haven't any hostages. What time is it?

BRIGHTWELL: 6.24.

RYAN: If only the police car hadn't turned up. If only my car had started.

BRIGHTWELL: Mr Ryan, it happened. The sooner you come out, the sooner we can sort it out.

Ryan asked Brightwell his rank, where he was based, and whether or not he was from the Tactical Firearms Unit. After the officer had answered those questions, Ryan asked if there were 50 policemen surrounding the school.

BRIGHTWELL: No, not that many.

RYAN [*shouting*]: How is my mother? I didn't mean to kill her. It was a mistake.

BRIGHTWELL: I understand that.

RYAN: How can you understand? I wish I'd stayed in bed.

Ryan said that he would come out, and asked if he could go to London. Sergeant Brightwell said that he would be taken to Newbury or Reading.

RYAN: Will I be jailed for life?

BRIGHTWELL: I don't know, Mr Ryan. Obviously you'll go to prison for a long time.

RYAN [*shouting*]: It's funny. I killed all those people, but I haven't got the guts to blow my own brains out.

BRIGHTWELL: Don't do anything silly – do you understand?

Ryan again asked the time and repeated that he would not come out until he knew about his mother. There was silence for several minutes – and then, at 6.52, the sound of a muffled shot came from the room. Sergeant Brightwell immediately called out to Ryan several times, but there was no reply.

It was more than an hour later when armed police, satisfied that Ryan had shot himself, moved into the building.

Sergeant Brightwell afterwards reported: 'I can say that, during the time I remained talking to Mr Ryan, he remained calm and rational. My conversation with him was fairly continuous; there was just the occasional lull, but for no longer than a few minutes. My main concern was to keep him talking so as to prevent him from firing out of the window and to try to keep him calm and hopeful and to persuade him to come out of the school safely. By talking to him continuously, I was

aware that he was staying in the same room – not moving around the school. No shots were fired by the police during the entire incident.'

While the conversation was going on between Sergeant Brightwell and Ryan, another sergeant, 49-year-old David Warwick, often had a clear view of the mass-killer through the telescopic sight of his rifle. At the start, he had asked himself a series of questions: Was Ryan likely to shoot anyone else? . . . Was there any threat to the police or the public? . . . Was he likely to escape?

'Each answer came up "no",' he has since explained. 'If I had fired, then I would have been a murderer – no better than him. You have got to be governed by the law, and you have got to have the justification. The justification was not there. He had no hostage. He was in an empty school. He had thrown one weapon out, and he wasn't going anywhere. All the talk was proceeding as if he was going to give himself up. I and the other armed officers were there to bring that man before a court of law. We were not the judge, jury and executioner all in one. I knew what Ryan had done in Hungerford, but to pull the trigger would have been wrong. If I had taken that option, I would have failed. I know that at least one other armed officer was also watching Ryan, and he came up with the same decision as I did.'

According to a former classmate of Ryan's at the primary school near South View, 'He was more like Bambi than Rambo: his mum, Dorothy, used to give him everything he wanted – the best clothes, the fastest cars, the latest records.' Others who knew him as a child describe him as 'withdrawn, placid, but not particularly bright,' and a man who knew him in his teens says that he preferred guns to girls:

'He used to shoot at birds and tins with an air-rifle, and as soon as he was old enough, he carried a gun everywhere, even to the local pub.'

Neighbours in South View say that Ryan drifted from one casual labouring job to another. A man who was in charge of a group on a scheme for the unemployed says that, while Ryan was a member of the group, 'he showed me a small Bereta gun and another gun in his car. Both were loaded. He told me that he always carried a Bereta in his waistband at night for protection. When two other men in the group took the mickey out of him, he threatened to shoot them, but I didn't take it really seriously – I thought it was more bravado than anything.'

Though he boasted to acquaintances that he had been a crack paratrooper, a spokesman for the Paratroop Regiment at Aldershot states: 'We have been through our records and can find no reference to this man having served with us.'

It has emerged that the gun licence issued to Ryan was approved by a local policeman who had friends killed in the shootings. The officer, whose identity is not being disclosed, made a routine visit to Ryan's home in South View to inspect security for storing firearms, and as there were no obvious problems, the quiet man with no criminal record had his application for a licence referred back to Thames Valley police headquarters. On December 11 last year, Ryan received his licence, No. 6197, permitting him to buy any number of weapons with semi-automatic actions.

He had followed the path taken by many shooting enthusiasts: first joining a club for a three-month probationary period, and then applying to the police for a licence.

During the probation, Ryan's background was checked. The inquiries revealed no 'Rambo' tendencies.

Having become a member of a shooting club at Abingdon, Oxfordshire, he joined one in Wiltshire, where he turned up for the first time on July 13, carrying his firearms certificate and a Chinese-manufactured semi-automatic AK47 Kalashnikov rifle. On a subsequent visit, he brought a 0.9 mm pistol with him, and two weeks ago, on August 8, he used his Barclaycard to purchase a second-hand M1 semi-automatic carbine rifle from the club's shop for £150.

The peculiar excitements of the gun-enthusiast's world, with its mixture of fantasy and deadly reality, are captured in a monthly magazine, *Gun Mart and Accessories*, which, describing itself as 'the market-place of the gun world', is on sale in newsagents' shops at 85p. It shows in detail the arsenal of weapons, ranging from hunting knives to semi-automatic military rifles, which can be bought by mail-order or across the counters of British gun-shops.

The cover indicates the main interests of many of the magazine's readers, with a picture of a rifle referred to as 'the infamous AK47'. Similar to one of the weapons owned by Michael Ryan, and available from British dealers for £295, it is given a two-page 'road test' inside. Throughout the 144 pages, the predominant impression is not of traditional sporting guns, but of military weapons such as the Colt AR15, a semi-automatic version of the M16 carbine used by the American Army.

An arms-dealer in Wakefield who has been importing Chinese AK47s for two years believes that 'they are very popular because of all the TV exposure', and the owner of a gun shop in Hertfordshire who has sold about 200 weapons similar to the AK47 in the past 18 months suggests that 'buyers must have seen such guns in wartime contexts on the telly'.

There are more than 8000 licensed gun clubs, and the Home Office has issued 160,000 firearms certificates, as well as 819,000 shotgun licences. But, as colourfully written adverts in *Gun Mart* make clear, no licence is required to buy any number of replicas which 'load, fire and eject ... just like the real thing'. Also available are crossbows such as the Panzer II – 'unbeatable in any situation' – and a wide range of fearsome knives, including the 'Terminator', which is said to be suitable 'for hunting, stalking and surviving'. In many adverts, the blatant appeal to militaristic fantasy is fuelled by cartoon Rambo-style figures and pictures of armed men in combat kit, flak jackets and other camouflage clothing.

The Hungerford massacre appears to be Britain's bloodiest shooting. Although such mass-killings are becoming commonplace around the world, they are rare in this country.

But domestic feuds have wiped out whole families, sometimes spilling over to claim other victims.

- On September 1984, Jeremy Bamber slaughtered five members of his family with a .22 rifle.

- In October 1978, Barry Williams's hatred for his neighbours in West Bromwich, West Midlands, exploded into violence. He gunned down a building contractor, his wife and son, and then shot dead a couple in a service station at Nuneaton.
- In April 1986, a former Cornish detective, Colin Gill, shot dead his wife and four sons and then killed himself, after learning that his wife was having an affair.
- In September of the same year, Joseph Cleaver, a retired publisher, his disabled wife, son, daughter-in-law and a live-in nurse were all strangled to death at Fordingbridge, Hampshire.
- In January 1977, axeman William Hughes was shot dead by police at a road-block after he had murdered two men, a woman and a little girl at Pottery Cottage, Chesterfield, Derbyshire.

The list of British mass-killers is headed by Mary Ann Cotton, hanged in 1873 for 19 murders. Over 20 years she had poisoned husbands, children, step-children, other relatives, and friends.

Last week, in Melbourne, Australia, a 19-year-old former Army cadet shot dead six people and wounded 18. A year ago in New York, Pat Sherril, about to be sacked as a postman, killed 15 colleagues before shooting himself.

Leading article; Wednesday, September 23:

The Home Secretary's proposals to restrict further the ownership of firearms are welcome. After the Hungerford massacre, we argued that there could be no justification for an ordinary citizen owning the kind of semi-automatic rifle which

Michael Ryan used to murder his 16 victims. The AK47 is not a sportsman's gun: it is a soldier's or terrorist's. The same goes for the 'burst-fire' guns which are also to be banned. Sane people may enjoy pretending to be soldiers by firing such weapons in the safety of licensed shooting ranges. If, however, it will make it harder for a future Ryan to slaughter innocent people, society has a right to deny them this enjoyment by prohibiting the ownership of such weapons. The National Rifle Association argues that 'guns don't kill people; people kill people' and that a car is as much a lethal weapon as a Kalashnikov. But some guns kill people more efficiently than others; and a car is not exclusively a lethal weapon. In addition to an amnesty for illegally-held firearms, and higher penalties for those who ignore it, the Home Secretary [Douglas Hurd] proposes a change to the rules governing shotgun ownership. Sawn-off shotguns are to be prohibited, while pump-action and self-loading shotguns are to be licensed under stricter conditions. That will not satisfy the Police Federation, which wants all shotguns classified as firearms. But it should be acceptable to farmers and sportsmen. The Home Secretary has struck a nice balance. It is sad that it took a tragedy to initiate his reforms.

BANNED: the Kalashnikov AK47 (used by Michael Ryan at Hungerford) and similar high-powered assault rifles will be prohibited. So will conversions of fully-automatic machine-guns such as Uzis and Armilites.

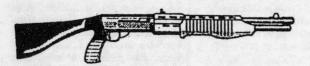

RESTRICTED: pump-action and semi-automatic shotguns, used by 'practical shooting' enthusiasts, will require a firearms certificate.

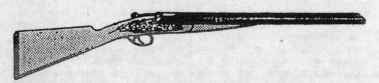

CONTROLLED: all shotguns will have to be kept in the same secure conditions that apply to Section 1 firearms.

1991 . . .

On the night of Tuesday, July 9, 1991, a prostitute named Julie Dart was abducted from the Chapeltown red-light district of Leeds, Yorkshire. Demands for ransom of £140,000 were received by the city's police, who 'played along' till the girl's naked body was found, trussed in a sheet, in a field near Grantham, Lincolnshire, on July 19. On the morning of Wednesday, January 22, 1992, Stephanie Slater, an estate agent, was inveigled to and abducted from a vacant property in Birmingham, Warwickshire. Demands for ransom of £175,000 were received by her employers, and soon after the ransom was paid, Miss Slater was released near her home. There were indications that both crimes, and perhaps others, had been committed by the same man.

Wednesday, February 5, 1992:

PSYCHO-FIT: THE PIECES
TO CATCH A KIDNAPPER

The artist's impression shows a man with staring eyes, but witnesses always remember suspected murderers as having staring eyes, don't they? He looks aggressive, but Stephanie Slater, who says that this is the image of her kidnapper, would hardly remember him smiling. Does he normally wear square glasses and have black hair or are they disguises? A visual image, in short, is an uncertain tool for those seeking a criminal.

There is another kind of image, however, which is safer and less easily camouflaged because the criminal himself is not aware that it exists. His own psychological make-up, his quirks and kinks, his way of handling himself, are as much a give-away as a face, a voice or a handwritten note. What we do not know about this kidnapper, and what the police will have been asking Stephanie, is what he was like. You know, really *like*. . . .

This is one of those cases where the psychological fingerprint of the wanted man looks like being critical. The question is, what is this man in it for? Tony Black, who was chief psychologist of Broadmoor for 27 years, says that all the evidence suggests that the police are dealing in this case with a criminal who is not only guilefully intelligent – a fact plain enough from his tactics – but one who may have convinced himself that there is a kind of 'moral justice' in what he is doing.

In other words, 'they asked for it' – *they* being not his victims but unjust society. On this premise, Stephanie, who was kidnapped and let go, and Julie Dart, the Leeds teenager whose kidnap and murder last July is believed to be the work of the same man, were chosen at random. This chilling theory is related to the psychologist's rubric that those seeking to understand an off-beam mentality must search for common themes and habits.

It is a science of logic and lateral thought, the cerebral alternative to the pavement-plodding and paper-sifting of traditional detective work. The history of forensic psychology throws up numerous cases where this has paid dividends.

Perhaps the best-known recent success was in the case of John Duffy, the double murderer and mass-rapist convicted in 1988. All his victims had been tortured and humiliated and left near railway stations. Psychologists concluded that he probably had a rocky marriage, was a semi-skilled worker, and might be hooked on the martial arts; and they were correct on all three counts. The fact that Duffy had a much-used South-East Region rail-pass added another piece to the jigsaw. He is doing life.

The present case has thrown up its own set of curious clues. For example, the ransom notes in both cases mentioned odd sums: £140,000 for Julie, £175,000 for Stephanie. Does that suggest that the kidnapper harboured a grudge over some such sum – a repossessed house maybe? Was Julie murdered as a demonstration, to prove simply that he had the capacity to kill? The 'mechanical' style suggests, says Black, that these crimes were plot-ted without emotion but with a burning anger.

All this is not good news for detectives working on the case because it removes from the equation such other motivations as the Pimpernel complex, which makes it all a bit of a cat-and-mouse game, or the Moriarty syndrome, which is fired by an intellectual stimulus to worst authority; or sexual or sadistic perversion, with base needs controlling actions.

Taproom debate, not to mention the tabloid press, has presented a welter of amateur psychoanalysis. The kidnapper, speculation has it, eluded the police because he is an ex-policeman who knows the form ... or an ex-VIP bodyguard who has turned his anti-kidnap training to a different use. Suggestions that his notes have taunted the authorities have similarly led to theories that he is a recalcitrant redundant soldier, an SAS man with a per-verted killer instinct.

The existence of an accomplice is an interesting theory that has developed from the imprint of a memo, addressed to 'Mavis', on one of the kidnap notes. Black says that women prepared to support men in violent crimes do exist, as the Hind-ley-Brady relationship showed. 'Some women are fascinated by vio-lent, ruthless men. That's why bat-tered wives stand by their husbands.'

Stories in some tabloid papers that police have interviewed Donald Neilson, the mass-murderer and kidnapper known as the Black Pan-ther, who was jailed for life 17 years ago, are not officially substantiated. Perhaps the notional parallel with *The Silence of the Lambs* was too much to resist. Comparisons between the present case and Neil-son's are inevitable because of the nature of the crimes, the meticulous and ruthless nature of their execution, and the suspected character of the criminal.

As a reporter, I [Maurice Weaver] can remember standing a few feet from Neilson at Oxford Crown Court and seeing his look of disgust when it was suggested that he had snatched 17-year-old Lesley Whittle for sexual purposes. Neilson, a fitness fanatic and collector of militaria, was in it for money. He felt under-valued; his marriage was shaky. The world was against him, he believed, but he would show them how clever he was.

Black suspects from the evidence that the wanted man in the current case must share some of those characteristics. The way that Stephanie was kidnapped smacks of arrogance: the convoluted instructions left for the police; the smart clues, like a treasure hunt; the fact that he showed his face to Stephanie Slater, even if it was disguised. Perhaps the ultimate arrogance lay in letting her live after getting the ransom. History shows that this is a gamble that few kidnappers will take.

Years of experience at reaching inside criminal minds lead Black to envisage a quiet, over-restrained sort of man, probably an unmarried loner who stews on his problems and seldom shares them. 'Most abnormal behaviour is normal behaviour writ large. He could be a man who would not be deemed insane under mental-health legislation but is psychotic in certain aspects of his make-up. Something has happened to trigger his anger and desire for revenge.'

Black suspects that the man might be a job-hopper. A familiar characteristic of the type, he says, is a tendency to get involved in hobbies such as collecting knives and firearms. 'They are the objects of fantasy for people who are socially inept.' Once again, over-commitment to body-building or militaristic hobbies is raised. These can appeal to those seeking to overcome a feeling of inferiority.

The knowledge of the north Midlands displayed by the kidnapper's trail-laying must be important to detectives trying to pinpoint his home or his origins. Stephanie will have been questioned about his mannerisms to see if they indicate his social class; his attitude towards her, to assess if he betrayed any feelings for home and family issues; the method of her incarceration, which might hint at military experience; his moods, to measure whether they suggested mental instability.

Professor Tim Wheeler, of the Department of Psychology at the Southampton Institute, said: 'The victim will not have been able to absorb much information during the first terrifying hours of her ordeal, nor at the end, when she cannot have known whether her kidnapper was preparing to murder her or release her. But in the middle phase she would have a high level of recall – and, remember, the kidnapper was under stress, too. What he said and did would have betrayed quite a lot. He was probably disguised and changed his voice.' But Wheeler says that people are much more observant about these things, even under threat, than we might suspect. 'His arrogance is the factor which registers with psychologists, and it could be his undoing.'

Friday, July 9, 1993:

THE LIES OF MICHAEL SAMS

Many murderers look ordinary, but Michael Benneman Sams looks more ordinary than most. At Nottingham Crown Court this week, he wore the uniform of the dull provincial man: suede-fronted grey cardigan over a shirt and a tie with a Windsor knot, grey trousers and grey shoes. His black hair was brushed flat above the collapsed face in which only his coal-nugget eyes seemed animated; he needed to raise his gold-rimmed spectacles so as to read the wad of evidence against him.

When witnesses spoke of the ordeal he inflicted on Stephanie Slater, the face creased into tears, but there was a hardness as he denied kidnapping and murdering Julie Dart.

He lied about that – little lies, ludicrous lies, spectacular lies; lies festooned with paranoia and conspiracy. They led him into cul-de-sacs where he could only turn on the prosecutor, Richard Wakerley, QC, and mutter: 'I've no explanation for that.'

Yesterday, the jury drew their conclusions.

Sams was driven by two dark ambitions rooted in his earlier life: to commit the perfect crime and to humiliate the police. In the pursuit of those aims, he employed technical skills and a formidable grasp of detail that was otherwise focused on his obsession with railways. They led him, in the darkness of his 17th-century workshop in Newark, Nottinghamshire, to kill a young woman with a hammer. 'She was rendered unconscious by three to four blows to the back of the head,

and then strangled,' he later wrote in one of the extraordinary rambling letters he sent anonymously to tease the police. 'She did not feel a thing.'

Sams was born on August 11, 1941, in Keighley, West Yorkshire – a consequence of a wartime affair his mother had with George Benneman while her husband, Ted Sams, was away. Michael and his brother John grew up knowing that they had different fathers. Ted Sams left his wife when Michael was aged 10, but the boy's saturnine looks made it clear that he was not Mr Sams's son, and he added the name of his real father to his own.

His criminal career did not begin until the mid-1970s, when he was living in Keighley with his wife Susan and two sons, running a central-heating firm. As the business began to founder, the marriage broke up. Sams was convinced that his wife had had an affair.

Becoming involved in a car 'ringing' operation, Sams was caught and charged, and co-operated with the police by naming his accomplices. While he was awaiting trial, his house caught fire. He believes that it was fire-bombed in a revenge attack. While repairing an upstairs window, he fell, exacerbating a weakness in his right leg. In April 1978 he began serving a nine-month sentence at a prison in Leeds. His leg continued to trouble him. After a malignant tumour in his knee was diagnosed, a surgeon amputated his lower right limb.

He blamed the police for failing to protect him from the alleged fire-bombing, and the prison service for lack of medical attention. The possibility of a 'brilliant' crime began a slow-burn that was to last 12 years. Following his release from prison, he began bricking up the cellar of his house, where he kept his 00-gauge model-railway layout, in preparation for a kidnap-victim.

Then he met his second wife, Jane Marks, through a lonely hearts advertisement, and found a new job, maintaining power-tools for Black & Decker. The couple moved to Leeds – but that marriage also failed, in 1981.

Sams's third marriage, to a Birmingham woman, Teena Cooper, took place in 1988. He accepted voluntary redundancy from Black & Decker and used the money to start a tool-repair business in Peterborough, Cambridgeshire. By mid-1990, he had set up another workshop – T & M Tools, standing for Teena and Michael – in a dingy courtyard by the River Trent in Newark. On Wednesdays he would go off train-spotting, afterwards carefully logging the details in albums and on his Amstrad computer.

The couple moved to nearby Sutton-on-Trent – to Eaves Cottage, a whitewashed house with a garden next to the main East Coast railway line. Sams transferred his model-railway layout to the attic of Eaves Cottage.

Before long, he fell behind with mortgage payments, and in April 1991 he began illegally claiming income support. Teena wanted to adopt a child, but the couple were turned down by Nottinghamshire social services as too old. Sams's third attempt at a settled life was falling apart. The house was put on the market and Teena was talking of packing her bags.

In the gloom of the workshop, Sams began to log on his computer

details of the plan that he later admitted he thought was 'brilliant, lovely'. He devised a series of elaborate trails that might be used to collect ransom money, and entered them in a file marked 'Skill'. He learned how to use latex make-up and Clearasil to disguise his complexion, and experimented with artificial warts on his cheeks. He also thought about ways to disguise his red Metro; eventually, he made wooden panels shaped to the rear windows to make the car look like a van, and on these he painted 'Cracked & Broken Drains' and a mobile-phone number; he later added a roof-rack complete with drain-rods.

He had decided that he would kidnap either a prostitute or a female estate agent. As the workshop had no separate back room, he made a chipboard box for his intended victim.

An attempt to kidnap a Leeds prostitute known as Mary failed when she jumped from the Metro as he pulled out a knife. A few days later, a complex plan to abduct an estate agent was aborted when, as he waited for the woman to arrive at an empty house in Crewe, a builder engaged him in conversation; fearing that the builder would be able to describe him, he drove away.

Six days later, on July 9, 1991, he abducted 18-year-old Julie Dart, who had become a prostitute after being turned down by the armed forces, from the Chapeltown red-light district of Leeds. Having inveigled her into his car, he threatened her with a knife, bound and gagged her, and drove to the workshop, where he imprisoned her in the chipboard box.

The police believe that some time during the following night, after Sams had gone home, Julie Dart, who was claustrophobic, tried to escape.

But Sams had installed an infrared sensor to detect movement in the workshop. It was connected so that its pulse would trigger the redial button on the telephone, and he had previously rung Eaves Cottage. When his home telephone rang, he made the 20-minute drive to the workshop. He beat the girl about the head, rendering her unconscious, and then strangled her to death.

He had already posted two letters – one to Julie's boyfriend, saying that she had been kidnapped, and the other to the Leeds City Police, demanding £140,000 as ransom. He subsequently sent other letters to the police. Meanwhile, the naked body, stuffed into a 'wheelie' dustbin, began to decompose. Sams trussed it in a pink and white sheet and dumped it in a field near Grantham, Lincolnshire.

Still planning to obtain the ransom, he set up a 'trail of deception' which was to be followed by a policewoman from the Leicester Forest service area to the M1, to Wakefield, and then back down the motorway to Barnsley. He had taped a series of messages under the shelves of telephone boxes – but, almost at the end of the trail, a telephone box which he was to call with further instructions was out of action. He had intended to lead the policewoman to a motorway bridge near Barnsley at which he had placed an electronic device to detect whether the parcel of ransom money contained a police radio transmitter. Had the policewoman reached the bridge, she would have found a message telling her to leave the money in a receptacle under a nearby pedestrian bridge. Sams had planned to pull the money up by a cord and escape on a motor-scooter

along a disused railway line known as the Dove Valley Trail.

Frustrated by failure, in October he embarked on another scheme, which was to extort £200,000 from British Rail by threatening to derail an InterCity express. Early in November, after sending a series of letters to the authorities at Euston Station, he suspended a concrete block from a remote bridge at Millmeece, Staffordshire, over the main West Coast line. Mercifully, though trains passed every 10 minutes, no damage was caused. The block was found in shattered pieces.

He decided to go back to his original plan. This time he would kidnap an estate agent.

After some reconnaisance, and having coloured his hair, lightened his complexion, and applied three large artificial warts to his face, he visited a branch of the Shipways estate agency in Great Barr, Birmingham. In the computer-diary entry he made later, he recalled his conversation with the receptionist: 'I needed her to see my facial details and hair colour. She hadn't the time or didn't know anything about [the properties available]. The manager was out. I could have screamed. . . . Was it a good thing that I had not been noticed or was it going to prove fatal that my "added" features had not been noticed? However, I had started, so I would finish.'

Twenty-five-year-old Stephanie Slater, who had been employed by Shipways for only five weeks, met Sams at 153 Turnberry Road, a three-bedroom house half a mile from her office, on January 22, 1992. As she started to show him round, he produced two knives from the clipboard he was carrying. He bound, gagged and blindfolded her, secured her to the reclined passenger seat of the Metro, covered her with a blanket, and drove away.

To kill time till it was dark, he went to Millmeece, where he spotted trains for a couple of hours. Then he drove to his workshop. Since using the chipboard box to imprison Julie Dart, he had added other devilish features. He chained Stephanie's hands, led the chain through a hole, and threaded a heavy rod through it; he tied her ankles with a washing line, which also was threaded through a hole. Before dropping the lid, he told her that if she struggled, she would bring rocks down upon the box. Occasionally, he let her out, always insisting that she must not remove the blindfold.

In Stephanie's cool behaviour, based on her decision that she must do as she was told in order to survive, he thought he read the signs of the Stockholm Syndrome, in which hostages become close to their captors. But he was wrong: it was he who was entering *her* orbit. In the opinion of one of the investigators, 'He probably fell in love with her.' Another detective believes that 'he wanted to demonstrate a man's control over a woman. He wanted to show that she was vulnerable'.

Here was a young woman made as clearly biddable as the hundreds of model trains in tea-chests in the attic; a young woman who was tied to him in a way that no other woman had been and who – unlike Julie Dart – seemed compliant: a woman in a box.

In the computer-diary, which must be considered as much a fantasy as a record, he wrote: 'Always before putting her back in the box, I stood opposite her and put my hands on her shoulders or cheeks and promised her she would be OK and unharmed, but on this occasion, she suddenly put her arms around me and hugged me for a while. When she put her arms down, she went back in the box without either of us speaking. I could tell she was choked.' All the time, he marvelled that she did not scream.

In the diary, which he planned to send to Stephanie after her release – his perverse idea being that it would help her if she wrote a book about her experience – he warned that it 'contains serious discrepancies from her account, which could take some explaining if she initially was subconsciously trying to protect me due to the enforced friendship that had built up between us'.

But her passivity was not about friendship: it was about surviving so as to see him in the dock.

The day after the kidnapping, a letter was delivered to the Shipways office. It warned the estate agents not to involve the police – but that had already been done, and a news blackout imposed. The letter said that a ransom of £175,000 was to be paid on January 29; the money was to be in used notes – £75,000 in fifties, £75,000 in twenties, and £25,000 in tenners – made up in thirty-one bundles. Other letters arrived, and also a tape-recording. The Shipways branch-manager, Kevin Watts, was to be the courier.

The ransom-trail followed a 100-mile circuitous route, with directions taped to the underside of shelves in phone-boxes, and wooden pointers and traffic cones marked 'Shipways'. It led Kevin Watts to a bridge over the Dove Valley Trail. The last message instructed him to leave the money on a tray on the parapet of the bridge. Sams, waiting underneath, tugged the tray down with a cord, then sped away on a motor-scooter to where his car was parked.

Soon afterwards, Sams released his hostage in a side-street near her home. His Metro was noticed by a local man who worked as a paint-

The drawing
Stephanie Slater
made of her
'coffin'

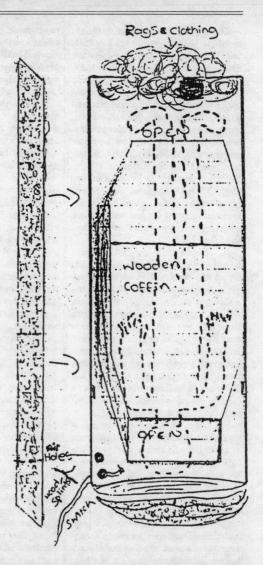

Rags & clothing

OPEN

Wooden
coffin

OPEN

Air
Holes

wood
splint

Switch

sprayer for the Rover Motor Group, and was therefore able to tell the police the exact shade of vermilion on the bodywork.

Even so, it was only after three weeks of further investigation that the police asked the *Crimewatch* television programme to play a tape of the kidnapper's flat Yorkshire voice giving instructions to Kevin Watts.

The voice was recognised by Sams's first wife, Susan, and the following day detectives raided his workshop and found, among other things, a parcel containing £19,000 of the ransom money. Though, following his arrest, he admitted that he had kidnapped Stephanie Slater, he refused to say where he had hidden the bulk of the ransom money. However, during interviews he mentioned that he had recently been in the Stoke Summit area of Lincolnshire, claiming that he had gone there train-spotting.

A 20-strong police team, aided by a former SAS officer and a geologist, spent 15 hours at Stoke Summit before unearthing a polythene-wrapped parcel containing a Black & Decker carrier-bag, a copy of the *Newark Trader* which had been delivered to Sams's home – and £70,000 of the ransom money. A day or so later, a further search unearthed an ice-cream carton containing £60,000 of the ransom money. It occurred to one detective that Sams, the obsessive railway enthusiast, had chosen a hiding place that was especially significant to him: alongside the stretch of line between Grantham and Peterborough where the Mallard had established the world speed record for a steam locomotive in 1938, when it topped 125 mph. Of greater geographical significance was the fact that Stoke Summit is less than two miles from where the body of Julie Dart was discovered.

Though the workshop was, as one of the detectives put it, 'an Aladdin's cave of evidence' that showed that Julie Dart had been murdered there, Sams continued to insist that the crime had been committed by 'a mate' – who had stolen his kidnap-ping plans, used his rope and his pink and white sheet, persuaded him to write the ransom letters, and even used sticky tape on which he, the mysterious 'mate', had accumulated fibres from Sam's clothes.

In the witness-box at his trial, he continued – often tearfully – to blame the 'mate' for the murder of Julie Dart.

There were more tears when Richard Wakerley asked him: 'Is the name of your friend Michael Benneman Sams?'

Michael Benneman Sams, the failed man? The cruel man? The killer?

'No,' whimpered the man in the witness-box. But that was a lie as well.

Found guilty of all the charges, he was sentenced to four terms of life imprisonment.

Tuesday, July 13:

Yesterday, at Full Sutton Prison, York, Michael Sams asked to see detectives who investigated the murder of Julie Dart.

Following the visit, Detective Superintendent Bob Taylor, who headed the inquiry, said that Sams had admitted that his 'mate' did not exist, that no one other than himself was involved in the crime, and that he had killed the girl in his workshop at 6 p.m. on July 10, 1991, after abducting her in the red-light Chapeltown area of Leeds at 11.30 the previous night. He said that he had confessed so that Julie's mother would know when her daughter died.

1991 . . .

HORROR IN MILWAUKEE

Anxious relatives of missing young men yesterday besieged the home of 31-year-old Jeffrey Dahmer, who has confessed to mass-murder and cannibalism, while police and forensic science experts wearing breathing apparatus continued to examine the horrifying evidence.

Dahmer, who had served a 12-month prison sentence for sexually abusing a 13-year-old boy, moved into the flat two years ago. Neighbours complained of bad smells coming from the flat, but these were explained away by Dahmer as being caused by meat that had rotted in a broken refrigerator. The building manager says that he passed on complaints about the smells to his bosses, but took no further action as Dahmer appeared to be a hardworking man, with a job in a chocolate factory, who 'kept himself to himself' and always paid his rent on time. Neighbours now say that they heard scuffles, cries and sawing noises coming from the flat.

The killings were discovered only when a potential victim managed to escape in handcuffs. Telling the police that he had been attacked by a man with a knife, he led a patrol to Dahmer's flat. The policemen are still recovering from the shock of their discovery. 'You think you've seen it all out there,' said Patrolman Rolf Mueller, ten years on the beat, 'and then something like this happens.' They found skulls in a filing cabinet, three torsos of men of different races in a vat in the bedroom, and jars of body-parts thought to be genitals. A dresser in the living-room was crammed with Polaroid photographs depicting the process by which handcuffed young men were dismembered.

The Milwaukee police say that 'part or all of' 11 bodies have been recovered from the flat. They are now investigating whether more bodies have been hidden at other locations.

Court records have revealed a letter from Dahmer's father, Lionel Dahmer, of Medina, Ohio, to the probationary service, pleading for psychiatric treatment for his son when he came out of prison: 'I do feel this may be our last chance to institute something lasting and that you hold the key. . . . I have tremendous reservations regarding Jeff's chances when he hits the streets.' Under a court order at the time of his release, he was to be interviewed at his home once a month, but his probation officer, pleading a heavy workload and fear of Dahmer's neighbourhood, was relieved of the task by the court.

In 1988, while Dahmer was staying with his grandmother, she learned that he was taking men to a den and performing 'rites' with them after he and they had undressed. The family feared that he was involved in satanism. At the same time, Lionel Dahmer saw a bone-filled cooking pot in his son's quarters, but accepted the explanation that the bones were of animals.

Dahmer's stepmother, Mrs Shari Dahmer, says that, two years ago, before he left for Milwaukee, he lured a man into his bedroom and tried to drug him with sleeping pills in coffee, but the man awoke and escaped. 'Since then,' she says, 'we have been on the edge. Obviously he has taken a turn for the worse.' A man who was at school with him in Ohio says that he was 'given a wide berth' by his fellow pupils because 'he was just one generally weird dude'.

'Way of the World' by Auberon Waugh; Saturday, July 27:

MISUNDERSTOOD

Various explanations have been offered for the behaviour of Jeffrey Dahmer, whose flat in Milwaukee was found to contain the half-eaten corpses of 11 murder victims. Childhood trauma – whether sexual abuse or beatings – has been suggested by one expert in criminal psychology. Others have confidently claimed that it was a liking for alcohol which led him to this shameful course of action. Many of us like a bit of alcohol occasionally, of course, without being tempted to murder or eat our neighbours, or keep their heads in our refrigerators, but alcohol remains a front-runner among possible reasons.

It is easy to theorise from thousands of miles away, but I wonder whether anybody has enquired whether or not the Dahmer parents were smokers. If so, it may be possible to win this unfortunate man an acquittal, while giving the victims' relatives someone to sue in the tobacco companies responsible. There is something unbearably poignant in the thought of a bereaved American family with no one to sue.

Perhaps the worst tragedy would be if it turned out that Dahmer's behaviour was attributable to improper diet – not enough fresh fruit, fresh vegetables, fibre and low-fat yogurt – or too much fresh fruit, not enough fibre, or too much fibre, not enough low-fat yoghurt. The permutations are almost endless, and there is no pot of gold at the end of that rainbow. Whatever they say, the United States of America is a very dangerous country.

'Commentary' by Claudia FitzHerbert; Thursday, January 16, 1992:

The news that Jeffrey Dahmer is to plead insanity at his trial has enraged some people, on the grounds that if his plea is accepted, he could, within a couple of years, be considered cured and released from a mental institution.

This response seems somewhat hysterical, if understandably so. For while Dahmer could, theoretically, be released after a year of treatment, it is inconceivable that he will be. The real reason behind the desire to see Dahmer incarcerated in a prison, rather than a mental hospital, is that the latter option is not regarded as sufficient punishment for his crimes.

The Americans, like us, have an adversarial system of justice, and it is now inevitable that in the Dahmer case the shrinks, rather than the defendant, will effectively be on trial.

This is what happened at the trials of the two most notorious serial killers in Britain, Peter Sutcliffe and Dennis Nilsen. In both cases the psychiatrists were given a sound bashing by the lawyers. (Both killers were judged sane and sent to prison – though Sutcliffe was later transferred to Broadmoor after attacking another prisoner for defacing the *Sun*.)

A number of similarities between Jeffrey Dahmer and Dennis Nilsen, who also killed and dismembered men, have already been observed.

Both picked up their victims at pubs and gay bars, plied them with drink (in Nilsen's case) or drugs (in Dahmer's case) and then strangled them. Both committed their first murder when threatened with abandonment, and both derived sexual satisfaction from the presence of a corpse.

It is therefore not surprising that the two cases have elicited similar responses in the general public. 'He must be mad,' we exclaim, distancing ourselves from the monster on first hearing of his horrific deeds. But then 'he must be punished' follows shortly after. And if we think he must be punished, it can only be because we think he must be guilty, and to be guilty, he must be responsible.

The plea of diminished responsibility, born of an unworkable compromise bashed out by the legal and psychiatric professions in the 19th century, makes little sense to the secular mind. Common sense tells us that to be responsible, you have to be sane.

And so it is that while we shudder at the madness of such men as Jeffrey Dahmer and Dennis Nilsen, we shrilly insist on their sanity. It may be that in the dock we would all be judged of unsound mind.

Monday, February 17:

Described by his lawyer as a 'steamrolling killing machine', Jeffrey Dahmer today joins the small penal fraternity of men – Charles Manson, John Wayne Gacy and David Berkowitz – regarded as the most evil in America. He was unable to convince a jury that his cannibalism and necrophilia were the result of madness. Ruled sane at the weekend, the former chocolate factory worker goes before a judge in Milwaukee this morning for sentencing. The jury said that a key fact in their decision to reject the idea that he was crazy was that he, a homosexual, used a condom while having sexual relations with a corpse.

Throughout his sanity hearing, Dahmer remained impassive. His hazel eyes seemed placid and, as one observer put it, he seemed more like a 'spacey nerd' than a notorious serial killer. He smiled only once, when shown a copy of the tabloid newspaper *Weekly World News*, carrying a tale that he had eaten his cell-mate at the Milwaukee jail. 'It's amazing what they come up with,' he said.

In fact, it was silly for the paper to invent stories. The truth was chilling enough. Some of Dahmer's deeds beggared the imagination. He stored the severed head of one of his victims (the official count is fifteen) in a fridge. He had a heart in a freezer. A barrel of acid was kept for the left-overs. In the case of one of his victims, he used a small knife to remove the flesh from the bones so as to bleach the skeleton. According to the defence, he practised a crude lobotomy on the brains of three men in an attempt to create 'zombie-like' companions to help him deal with his loneliness.

The killer chose not to take the witness-stand to defend his actions, but policemen who interviewed him were shocked by his matter-of-fact approach to killing. One detective has said: 'He talks so casually about killing people. To him it was as natural as pouring a glass of water.'

Dahmer is lucky that he was tried in Wisconsin, which has no death penalty. In neighbouring Illinois, John Wayne Gacy, convicted of murdering 33 young men, awaits death by lethal injection at Menard Correctional Centre, where he is kept in a windowless cell for 23 hours a day, spending much of the time painting landscapes and clowns. [*Gacy was executed on May 10, 1994.*]

Charles Manson, now 57, whose 'family' sect killed the actress Sharon Tate and six other people in 1969, is isolated from other inmates at Corcoran Prison, California. His death sentence was commuted to life imprisonment.

David 'Son of Sam' Berkowitz is serving 25 years for terrorising Manhattan with six killings and seven woundings in the mid-1970s. He has turned to religion and is said to spend his days assisting other troubled inmates.

On Monday, February 17, Jeffrey Dahmer was sentenced to 15 consecutive life terms. Before being taken to the Columbia Correctional Institution, there to be isolated in one of six high-observation cells, he said: 'I should have stayed with God. I tried and I failed – and I created a holocaust. Frankly, I wanted death for myself.'

Tuesday, November 29, 1994:

CANNIBAL KILLER BEATEN TO DEATH

Jeffrey Dahmer, the serial-killer who preyed on homosexuals, was murdered yesterday by a fellow inmate while cleaning a bathroom at the Columbia Correctional Institution. He was pronounced dead on the way to hospital with head injuries. A blood-covered broom-handle was found at the scene, where another inmate lay, also fatally injured. Joe Scislowicz, the prison spokesman, said: 'There was a great deal of blood in the area.'

Four months ago, Dahmer was attacked with a home-made knife in the prison chapel, but a US government official said that he was not thought to be in special danger from fellow prisoners.

At his trial, Dahmer admitted to necrophilia and mentioned that he had saved the heart of one of his victims 'to eat later'. His stepmother, Sheri Dahmer, has said: 'He never expressed fear. From the day he was arrested he felt he deserved anything he got.'*

* According to a less reliable paper than the *Telegraph*, it was suspected that Dahmer was killed by a convict whom he was pestering for sexual favours – which is reminiscent of the plea in mitigation successfully advanced by the convict who in 1936 killed Richard Loeb (who, together with his friend Nathan Leopold, was imprisoned for the kidnapping and murder of 14-year-old Bobby Franks in Chicago twelve years before), inspiring a reporter for the Chicago *Daily News* to write the famous opening paragraph: 'Richard Loeb, a brilliant college student and master of the English language, today ended a sentence with a proposition.'

1993

THE KILLER NURSE

Yesterday, at Nottingham Crown Court, 24-year-old Beverley Allitt was given 13 life sentences for four murders, three attempted murders, and six counts of grievous bodily harm. For 59 days, between February 23 and April 22, 1991, she escaped suspicion as she injected children aged between seven weeks and 11 years with massive overdoses of insulin and potassium chloride, or put her hand over their faces to suffocate them, on Ward 4 at the Grantham & Kesteven Hospital, Lincolnshire. She replaces Mary Elizabeth Wilson, who poisoned three husbands and a lover with phosphorus in the 1950s, as Britain's worst female serial killer this century.

Allitt, who suffers from anorexia nervosa, had not attended court since March 12 because she was considered to be too weak, having lost six stone since her arrest. Wearing jeans and a mauve jumper, she stood during the sentencing, staring straight ahead and with her hands clasped in front of her. She showed no emotion as relatives of her victims screamed at her from the packed public gallery: 'You ought to hang,' 'I want you dead,' and 'Lock her in a cage.'

Her downfall was hastened by a combination of science and routine detective work.

A telephone call from Dr Derrick Teale, a biochemist, told the police that tests showed that one of her victims, five-month-old Paul Crampton, had been injected with the second highest dose of insulin ever recorded in Britain: the child had 43,147 milli-units of insulin for every litre of his blood, whereas the normal level is 12 to 15 milli-units. Paul survived only because doctors gave him glucose as soon as the results of the blood-test were known. Dr Teale also found evidence that nine-week-old Becky Phillips had been injected with insulin before her death.

The triumph for police routine came from checks on duty rotas that were ordered by Detective Superintendent Stuart Clifton. These showed that in each of 25 cases of unexpected collapse on Ward 4, Allitt was on duty.

Yet at no time had she aroused suspicion. Other nurses, concerned that she might suffer stress caused by the coincidence of heart-attacks and respiratory arrests when she was present, had offered commiseration.

Manufacturers of insulin told the police that an overdose was easily administered and difficult to detect. As detectives checked who had access to both hypodermic syringes and insulin, Allitt's name cropped up time after time. They discovered that pages relating to

Paul Crampton's stay in hospital had been cut from the Ward 4 notebook. A book recording the allocation of nurses to patients vanished, but was subsequently found in a wardrobe at Allitt's house.

At first, her answers seemed plausible – but, according to Superintendent Clifton: 'As we collected more evidence, we discovered that she had been lying. There was a dawning realisation that something was terribly amiss.'

No one knew then of the obsession driving Allitt. Specialists who have examined her since her arrest believe that she was suffering from Münchausen's syndrome (lying so as to receive unnecessary medical attention) and Münchausen's syndrome by proxy (making people ill in order to care for them).

Allitt's reputation as an attention-seeker followed her from childhood. One of four children brought up in the Lincolnshire village of Corby Glenn, she is remembered by some of the residents as a child who longed to be noticed, dressing unusually and making a lot of noise. School-friends recall that she often complained of minor injuries: 'She would come to school wearing bandages and plasters. We could not actually tell if she was hurt or not.' When she was released on police bail following her arrest in May 1991, she went to live with the family of a friend, and, during that short time, money disappeared from the house, curtains caught fire, a knife was found embedded in a pillow, bleach was poured over carpets, and the family's pet dog coughed up tablets. Allitt suggested that poltergeists were at work.

Detectives say that she showed no remorse when she was charged.

Friday, October 15:

Beverley Allitt, who had consistently denied murdering four children and attacking nine others in her care, has admitted nine of the attacks, including three of the murders, during interviews with detectives at Rampton top-security hospital, where she is being detained. The statement issued by the Lincolnshire police goes on to say: 'She is continuing to co-operate with doctors who have requested information relating to medical problems still being experienced by some victims. At this stage, neither the police nor Mr John Kendall, Miss Allitt's solicitor, intend to identify which offences she has admitted.' Detective Superintendent Stuart Clifton defended that decision, saying: 'I know some of the parents would like us to disclose our information, but I take the view that it would be unfair to the four remaining families.'

1994

Friday, August 5:

TRIPLE EXECUTION 'CARRIED OUT WELL'

Three convicted murderers were successively put to death in Arkansas yesterday in America's first triple execution in 32 years. The executions by lethal injection were completed in two and a half hours on the same trolley at intervals only long enough for the bodies to be carried out and for the needle to be changed.

Forty-three-year-old Darryl Richley and Hoyt Clines and James Holmes, both aged 37, had been sentenced to death for the murder of a businessman in a house robbery that netted $1,200 in cash; they had beaten their victim with a motorcycle chain before shooting him. A similar sentence passed on a fourth man had been reduced to life imprisonment because some of the evidence against him was obtained by hypnotising the victim's daughter.

The triple execution in Arkansas comes as no embarrassment to the state's former Governor, for President Clinton scheduled the deaths of Richley, Clines and Holmes three times during his reign in the 'dogpatch' Southern state. Indeed, the issue of the death penalty was among his earliest U-turns from liberal idealist to pragmatic politician. Now, as then, there is no doubting the popular sentiment on the ultimate penalty: Hang 'Em High.

As the three men were declared dead by volunteer doctors whose fees for attendance were cut by the economies of scale, the state is congratulating itself, not only for efficiency, but also for saving taxpayers' money. A defence lawyer damned the event as 'hogs to the slaughter' while civil rights groups and specialist capital punishment opponents gathered beyond the razor-wire of the Cummins Jail at Varner – but the objectors were outnumbered, as usual, by common folk who always congregate, as they once did at the gallows at Tyburn, to be in the presence of justice done to their satisfaction.

These latest executions – numbers 24, 25 and 26 this year, 250, 251 and 252 since the death penalty was restored in 1976 – have created more interest than usual. The obvious reason has been the sensation of the mass execution: the last triple execution was in California in 1962.* History books reveal that multiple executions were not

---

* On August 8, 1962, an obsessively son-loving woman, Elizabeth Ann Duncan, and the two men, Augustine Baldonado and Luis Estrada Moya, whom she had hired to beat her daughter-in-law to death, were executed in the gas-chamber at San Quentin Prison.

uncommon until the 1930s: in 1862, 38 Sioux Indians were simultaneously hanged in Minnesota.

That is an eye-catching detail, for one of the themes behind the Arkansas executions, and the national acceleration in carrying out death sentences, is a feeling of a return to frontier justice. Americans are *afraid* of violent crime – and with good reason. Statistic after statistic shows crime soaring to levels unimaginable in other Western nations, and it is crime largely based on a gun culture. The danger of coming face-to-face with the barrel of a gun is real, and so is the idea of killing the killers. However, there is no statistical evidence that the rise in executions has yet had any impact on the rise in crime.

On the day the three men died, Clinton's blockbuster Crime Bill, the central component of his pledge to clean up America's streets, stalled in Congress, which was unexpected, for it was clearly popular among the electorate. What brought it to a halt was an unlikely coalition of the Right, objecting to the banning of semi-automatic rifles, and the Black Caucus, demanding laws allowing blacks to appeal death sentences on the grounds of racial discrimination.*

The carrying out of Clinton's old gubernatorial orders puts him in good standing on that one: the three men executed in Arkansas were white. As evidence of equal justice, their deaths give the Administration a new lever to reopen the old arguments about racial discrimination on Death Row. Figures compiled last year showed that there were 2,785 Death Row inmates:† 50 per cent were white, 40 per cent black, 7 per cent Hispanic, 2 per cent Native American, and the remaining 1 per cent Asian or of unknown ethnicity. Of those executed since the restoration of capital punishment, 55 per cent were white, 39 per cent black, 6 per cent Hispanic, with one Native American also put to death.

Given that blacks make up a disproportionate percentage of the entire prison population – and carry out a percentage of crime far higher than their 12 per cent of the total population – the figures seem to argue against racial discrimination in the death chambers of American jails. But there is another, revealing way of looking at the execution statistics. In 85 per cent of the cases where the death penalty was imposed, the *victims* were white. That points to the cultural roots of the boom in executions: the South.

The old Mason–Dixon line still marks the axis of national cultural swings. There are 14 states which still resist the imposition of the death penalty: Alaska, Hawaii, Iowa, Kansas, Maine, Massachusetts, Michigan, Minnesota, North Dakota, Rhode Island, Vermont, Wisconsin and West Virginia. Only the last considers itself a Southern state, and then one with a differ-

---

* On August 11, the Bill, which had eventually been passed by the Senate, was rejected by the House of Representatives. A fortnight later, Congress approved a 'diluted version' which provided for, *inter alia*, 50 new Federal types of capital crime, including treason, murder of high Federal officials, and homicides committed in the furtherance of 'carjacking'; a ban on the sale or possession of 19 makes of assault weapon and 'copycat' models (650 kinds of sporting rifles are exempt); mandatory life in prison for criminals convicted of three violent felonies or drug offences if the third conviction is for a Federal crime.

† By the start of 1995, the number had risen to 2948, including 38 women.

ence. And the five states responsible for the majority of the executions are Texas, Louisiana, Arkansas, Florida, and California. The last is complex, as southern and northern California have such disparate cultures that moves are afoot to divide the state, but the others are clearly Southern.

Since the 1960s and the Civil Rights movement, the South has increasingly conformed to the common American culture, from the neon strips of the national food and motel chains to the new Sunbelt industrialisation. But as the gun culture grows, along with the fear of crime, the rest of America is seeing sense in the Southern tradition of retributive justice.

1994

Tuesday, August 9:

DINNER FOR FOUR – MURDER FOR TWO

The Family

Nicholas and Elizabeth Newall gave their two sons everything that wealth and privilege could buy, but never showed them the slightest sign of affection. Family life was characterised by simmering resentments and ferocious rows.

The Newalls, both former teachers, left an estate of nearly £1 million, but they had spent a great deal of money – accumulated from industries associated with Scottish shipbuilding – before they died.

Mrs Maureen Ellam, a family-friend who lives in the Newalls' former home on the Channel Island of Jersey, says: 'They treated their sons so coldly that, if you treated your dog like that, you would be reported to the RSPCA. I don't think the boys ever had a kiss and cuddle from their parents all their lives. Nick was utterly cold towards both boys. They did not exist to him, apart from white knuckles and real hate. They were four very different and volatile people.'

She describes Mrs Newall as 'excitable, aggressive, and without doubt a spendthrift,' while Mr Newall was 'arrogant and pompous'. His sons saw him as a Victorian-style disciplinarian. He referred to them as 'Elizabeth's boys'.

When Roderick asked him to film him in a school race, he seemed unable to rcognise him and focused on another fair-haired boy. When the error was pointed out, he handed the film to the other boy's family without a word to Roderick.

Mrs Ellam says: 'The boys watched their parents go through their inheritance and even sell this house, which had great potential, and buy one which had nothing. I see many rich people on this island. The idea is that if you inherit something, you tend to add to it and pass it on to your children. Nick and Elizabeth were not like that. When money came to them, it was the end of the line.'

Nicholas Newall and Elizabeth Nelson met while working at New Park School, St Andrews, and married in December 1963. Roderick was born in Glasgow on April 11, 1965, and Mark in St Andrews on June 22, 1966.

The Newalls settled in Jersey by chance after leaving Scotland while the boys were infants. Setting sail for the West Indies on their yacht, they stopped in Jersey to pick up a nanny. They were forced to turn back when she fell ill on board, and they decided to stay, buying a house called Martello Lodge in St Brelades Bay. The family later moved to Crow's Nest, a large property with panoramic views over the bay of Greve de Lecq.

In 1985, the Newalls' capital came under threat from calls from Lloyd's as a result of multi-million-pound settlements of asbestosis cases. Mr Newall faced demands of £25,000–£30,000 a year. He had an estate-protection policy which meant that the debts would be settled on his death.

About a year before they were murdered, the Newalls sold Crow's Nest for £240,000 and bought a modest bungalow at Clos de L'Atlantique, St Brelade, for £85,000.

By now, Mark had taken control of his parents' financial affairs. He transferred £155,000 from the house-sale into shares and options to give himself an income of 30 per cent of capital gains and Roderick 10 per cent.

Nicholas Newall was to have been the joint main beneficiary, with his identical twin Stephen, of an £800,000 trust fund set up by their uncle Kenneth, an eccentric bachelor who lived on the Channel Island of Sark. In the event of Nicholas's death, his share would go to Elizabeth and be disposed of according to their will.

The Elder Son
Roderick Newall cut a dashing figure as the archetypal handsome young Army officer in a fashionable regiment. He had girlfriends around the world and a love of the great outdoors, including sailing the oceans.

After attending the best prep school in Jersey, he was sent to Radley College, near Oxford, in 1978, with his brother arriving the following year.

They had diametrically opposed personalities and fought viciously. Their relationship was so poor that they were sent home separately for school holidays to prevent them from fighting en route.

Roderick, an NCO in the school cadet force, nursed an ambition to join the Royal Green Jackets. When asked why by friends, he replied: 'Because I want to kill people.'

Mr Tony Hudson, his housemaster at Radley, remembers an 'atmosphere' when Roderick and his parents were together. He says: 'To get the best out of school and enjoy it, there has to be teamwork between parents, teacher and boy. Maybe Roderick did not have the full teamwork.'

He was given a one-way ticket to Australia by his father because of his unruly behaviour, but returned a few months later.

After he had gone on an outward-bound course in Scotland, his mother arranged for him to enter Sandhurst. When commissioned, he joined the Royal Green Jackets at the regimental headquarters in Winchester. He is remembered by women who hung around junior officers as 'immensely charming', although his contemporaries raised eyebrows at his red Toyota sports car. Fellow officers recall him as a show-off; one said he expected that Roderick would either get the VC or end up in prison.

He was chosen for his regiment's winter expedition to St Moritz for the annual 'Swift and Bold' handicap in 1988, and claimed to have made a descent of the Cresta Run on a tea-tray after recording one of the fastest official times on the run that year. While stationed in Germany, he tried to impress his fellows by driving down an autobahn near Hamburg at 140 mph in fog and performing handbrake turns.

He served briefly in Northern Ireland, was promoted to lieutenant, and commanded his own platoon before resigning after his parents' deaths to become a man of leisure.

He became a regular user of cannabis, experimented with other drugs, and was jailed for a month in Jersey for possession of cannabis.

The Younger Son
Mark Newall is 14 months younger than Roderick but intellectually his superior. His overriding passion was making money and he was never without a personal computer on which he monitored the world markets.

He is remembered as an aloof boy who, in his late teens, dismissed his parents as 'grossly negligent and utterly incompetent'.

A fellow-pupil at Radley, where Mark became head boy, says: 'He really was unpopular, arrogant and extremely unpleasant. He used to have fits of anger and punch holes through the plasterboard walls with his bare fist. I remember that he once walked around with a leather strap wrapped round his fist because he was scared of being set on. I think he was roughed up by the bigger boys when he first arrived, and never forgot it.'

According to his aunt, Mrs Nancy Clark, he was content with his own company. A knee-injury developed into a permanent disability that restricted his sporting activities to scuba diving and martial arts. He became proficient in both.

At 18, he entered the world of banking with Barclaytrust in Jersey, and two years later became a trainee Eurobond dealer with the Banque Arabe et Internationale d'Investissements group. Transferred to the head office in Paris, he spent the next two years travelling between France and the United States. In Paris, he was chauffeured in a white BMW and had a two-storey, two-bedroomed apartment with a roof garden. He travelled by Concorde to New York, where he had a flat overlooking Central Park, and a girlfriend, the daughter of a BBC executive. He also had a personal shirt-maker, an account at Harrods, and a regular reservation at Blakes Hotel in South Kensington. By 1993, he had built up a fund with a colleague that earned him £150,000 a year in addition to his six-figure salary.

The Dinner Party
Mrs Elizabeth Newall was five days from her 48th birthday when her two sons flew into Jersey unexpectedly in 1987 to take her out for a candlelit dinner.

A table was booked for the evening of Saturday, October 10, at the Seacrest Hotel restaurant in Petit Port. But first both Roderick and Mark had some business to attend to.

Earlier in the day, it later emerged, a young man fitting Roderick's description spent £103.42 in cash at Normans' builders' merchants in nearby St Helier. On his shopping list was a blue and green tarpaulin, heavy-duty red refuse sacks, two trenching spades, two torches and batteries, a pick-axe, two small modelling knives, a saw, some rope, and a can of upholstery cleaner. In the afternoon, Mark accompanied his father to hire a red Renault Trafic van in order to move furniture between Mark's rented flat and his new house. Both the equipment and the vehicle were to play a part in the horrific series of events that followed.

That evening, champagne flowed at table 17 as Elizabeth was lavishly entertained by Roderick and Mark. Nicholas Newall completed the apparently harmonious gathering of a wealthy family. Mrs Newall complained about her starter and main course of gambas and deep-sea lobster. Mark, who was driving, did not drink.

At around midnight, the four left together for the brief drive back to the Newalls' bungalow. The parents were never seen alive again.

The Alarm
The following morning, Maureen Ellam delivered a bouquet for Elizabeth's birthday. Mark's Toyota MR2 sports-car was parked outside. Roderick answered the door and told Mrs Ellam that his parents were asleep. Mrs Ellam joked: 'Lay the flowers on the bed. When she opens her eyes, she'll think she has died.'

That evening, the brothers returned to their jobs on the mainland. Friends of the Newalls grew concerned when they failed to appear at social engagements. Six days after the Seacrest dinner, Mrs Ellam's husband, David, arrived at the house to find the central heating on full and no sign of the Newalls.

The Ellams contacted Mark, and the brothers returned to Jersey to report their parents missing. They were interviewed on October 19 by Detective Inspector Jimmy Adamson, a tenacious Scotsman who played a key role in the investigation, and told him that their parents had been alive when they left.

The Clues
A police search unearthed a number of items, including a spade bought at Normans, in undergrowth on Noirmont Common, near Mark's Jersey home. Blood spots were found on a poker in the lounge at the couple's bungalow, on a pair of Roderick's jeans in the spare bedroom, on the doorframe of the master bedroom, and in the rear of the hired van.

Detectives used dogs and underground radar, and checked on spy-satellites that might have been passing overhead. The bedroom carpet was taken away for examination after Mrs Ellam, described as something of a 'Miss Marple', recalled seeing a stain on it.

On November 9, Mr David Northcott, a senior forensic scientist, found a large number of tiny blood specks around the lounge fireplace and just inside the master bedroom door, on dark surfaces that had been missed during cleaning.

The following March, a dog-handler chanced upon the remains of a fire on a footpath leading from the Newalls' former home, four miles away at Greve de Lecq. Among the debris was Mrs Newall's partly-burnt handbag, her husband's spectacle-lenses, and the remains of his pipe.

The Odyssey
Roderick, meanwhile, had left the Army to sail the world in his father's 32-foot yacht, *Chanson de Lecq*. He went to Spain, Morocco, the South Sea Islands, New Zealand, the Falklands, Antarctica and South America.

In the Falklands, he became part of an anarchic group known as 'The Black Pig' crowd, named after a rusty tug owned by a fellow-yachtsman. He intended to start a yacht-chartering business but sailed on to Brazil. While tying up at the Beleiros do Sol Yacht Club in Porto Alegre, Roderick – who by now resembled a Viking, with his long blond hair and ginger goatee beard – met Helena Pedo. She invited him to the 30th birthday party of a friend, Eloisa Endres, and he later took both women for a champagne dinner, telling them: 'I have become a millionaire today.' Mark had earlier told him that their parents had been declared dead and they had inherited their wealth.

Newall later told Miss Pedo of his secret, choosing to make his confession in literary mode. Sitting by the fire in her flat in September 1991, he asked her to fetch a book called *Magister Ludi* from the bedroom. He opened it and read aloud: 'Oh! he thought in grief and horror, now I am guilty of his death. And only now, when there was no longer need to save his pride or offer resistance, he felt, in shock and sorrow, how dear this man had already become to him.'

Weeping, he grasped Miss Pedo and repeated: 'I am a murderer.' He told her that he had killed his parents. When she asked why, he would say only that he had never forgiven them for sending him to boarding school. He refused to see a psychiatrist but said that he wanted her to help him come to terms with his guilt. He decided to return to Britain to see relatives.

The Trap
Newall called on his mother's sister, Mrs Nancy Clarke, in Fulham, west London. When she asked about his parents, he replied: 'Even if you knew exactly what happened, you would still not understand.... I don't understand myself.'

He bought a £150,000 yacht, the 66-foot *Austral Soma*, and went to Scotland to meet Stephen Newall, his father's twin, and his wife, Gay.

It was at this meeting – on Sunday, July 14, 1992, in room 138 of the Dunkeld House Hotel, Perthshire, where the couple were celebrating Gay's 60th birthday – that Roderick made a second confession, breaking down as he looked into the familiar face of his father's twin.

Unknown to him, it was a set-up. Police had traced his movements and bugged the hotel-room.

Detective Inspector Adamson had charted Roderick's movements around the world with the help of Interflora, because of his habit of

sending flowers to his paternal grandmother in North Berwick, Scotland.

Roderick had not seen his uncle since the funeral in 1987 of his eccentric great-uncle Kenneth, who had told the family that he planned to split his £800,000 between the twins, Stephen and Nicholas.

Newall chatted for four hours to his aunt and uncle, initially about his voyages. Detective Chief Inspector Jim Smith, of the Scottish Crime Squad, recalls: 'Everybody got bored and took off the earphones, except the technicians. Then all of a sudden it was there, the truth coming out. Everyone grabbed their earphones.... There was particular reference to bodies wrapped in plastic and camouflaged graves, and that was pretty spine-tingling stuff.'

The Escape
Despite the confession, the police could not yet act. There was a two-day delay in obtaining an arrest warrant because Mr Philip Bailhache, QC, a cautious man who was then Jersey's Attorney General, insisted on hearing the tapes first. Newall left Scotland, using tactics learned in the Army to give police the slip at a motorway exit near Warrington, Cheshire.

He returned to London on July 15 before leaving for the South Atlantic aboard the *Austral Soma*. Despite an alert through Interpol, there were no reported sightings of the vessel. A fortnight later, however, Mark Newall checked into his favourite London hotel, Blakes, in South Kensington.

Scotland Yard detectives suspected that he had come to Britain to collect registration papers for the *Austral Soma*, which Roderick needed to start a chartering business.

When Mark made a telephone call at two o'clock in the morning, details were passed to Jersey CID. Detective Sergeant Charles Mac-Dowall dialled the number, which turned out to be Air France, and was told that Mark had booked flights the next morning to Paris, Madrid and Tangier.

The Capture

Roderick was traced to Tangier. Top-level talks were held between Britain's Ministry of Defence and the police forces of Jersey and Gibraltar. When Newall set sail at 8 p.m. on August 4, 1992, Operation Snowbird swung into action.

Within three and a half hours, the *Austral Soma* had been spotted by Ranger, a Royal Navy patrol vessel. On board was Sergeant MacDowall with the warrant.

The frigate Argonaut teamed up with Ranger 160 miles south-west of the straits of Gibraltar. Sergeant MacDowall and five armed police officers from Gibraltar moved on to the frigate. The Argonaut's Lynx helicopter was sent to verify the identity of the yacht.

Captain Bob Stevens, the frigate's commander, says: 'The whole idea of the operation was to make Newall think we were simply carrying out a routine check. We called him on the VHF radio, he responded, and we asked him to come across for a document check. He got into the tender on the stern of his boat and rowed himself across, carrying his passport and vessel-identification papers.'

The boarding officer who helped Newall on to the Argonaut said to him with a smile: 'Have we got a surprise for you, old boy.'

The warrant was read to Newall by Sergeant MacDowall, and he was manacled to a grille in the brig for the journey to Gibraltar. He said later that he would have rammed the frigate with his reinforced-steel hull had he known that he was going to be arrested.

Mark's movements, meanwhile, were traced through his bank transactions, and he was arrested at his Paris penthouse on March 17, 1993. The receipt for his parents' last supper was found in a desk in his study. He was flown to Jersey by private jet six weeks later. He closed his eyes when the plane took off and reopened them only on landing.

The Threats

Attempts to have Roderick extradited from Gibraltar to Jersey took 15 months and cost about £2.5 million.

In the intervening time, he was held in the medieval Moorish Castle Prison, perched high on the rock, where intercepted telephone calls to him fuelled fears of a terrorist-style attempt to 'spring' him. In one, a woman told him: 'We have the best shots on the Rock and more are on the way. Money is no object.' A man later called, saying: 'We have got one shot at this. There are people working for you in London, Gibraltar and Jersey.'

An air-exclusion zone was set up around the prison, and security surrounding Newall's court appearances was drastically stepped up.

Newall also made several apparent suicide attempts, using items smuggled into his cell. He slashed his wrists and groin and swallowed sleeping pills that he had hoarded. A syringe containing a potentially lethal cocktail of drugs was found concealed in an orange. A razor-blade was found in the spine of a book and a surgical knife under the seat of a van taking him to court.

Another twist came when Mr Desmond de Silva, QC, hired by the

Crown to head the extradition battle, recognised a man staying in the same hotel as the prosecution team as a former MI6 agent. Checks with the intelligence services revealed that the man, who had flown to Gibraltar on several occasions, each time arriving the day before Newall's court appearances, was now classified as a 'security nuisance'. When arrested, he was found to be carrying £240,000 in cash.

A bug was discovered in the seventh-floor suite in the hotel used by the prosecution team, and Inspector Adamson's room was burgled.

The Denouement

Mr de Silva knew that he had won when Newall sent him a copy of Michael Ondaatje's novel, *The English Patient*, with a note telling him to look at page five. After studying the text, he held the page to the light and noticed pinpricks under the first letter of a series of words. They spelt: 'I will plead guilty.'

Roderick was flown back to Jersey, where he led detectives to the woodland grave in which the bodies of his parents had lain for six years and one month. They were still in the clothes they had worn to dinner. The Rolex on Mrs Newall's watch was ticking on her wrist. They had been virtually 'vacuum wrapped' in tarpaulins, preserving their bodies so well that a toxicologist found phenobarbitone, potentially fatal when mixed with alcohol, in the body of Mr Newall.

Both had been hit on the head with a blunt weapon, possibly a martial-arts rice-flail. The murder-weapon has never been recovered.

Roderick later testified that he killed his parents in a heated argument – during which 'many old wounds were re-opened' – after Mark had left the bungalow. He

claimed that his father pushed him and he fell down beside a box containing a rice-flail. He said that he struck his father with the flail and that his next memory was sitting on the hall-floor. He went into the lounge and saw his father's body. He then discovered his mother's body in the bedroom, which triggered his memory of attacking her with the flail.

Mark told police that he returned to the house the following morning to find Roderick holding his father's shotgun and threatening suicide. He said that he agreed to help because of fear that Roderick would kill himself.

Entries in a filofax found on Newall's yacht led the police to Helena Pedo's home in Brazil, where she told them of his confession.

The police say that his probable motives for the murder of his parents was hatred of them and the financial incentive. Detective Inspector Martin Fitzgerald, of the States of Jersey Police, says: 'There is absolutely no doubt in our minds that Roderick planned to kill both of his parents that night.'

The Sentence

The brothers, who had pleaded guilty to the respective charges, showed no emotion in the Royal Court of Jersey yesterday as Bailiff Sir Peter Crill sentenced Roderick to life imprisonment and jailed Mark for six years for helping to dispose of their parents' bodies and destroying other evidence. Sir Peter commented: 'Throughout the ages, crimes of patricide and matricide have attracted particular odium. This court shares that view.'

Detectives have traced the murdered couple's money through bank accounts in London, Spain, Switzerland and Andorra. Of the brothers' inheritance, hundreds of thousands of pounds have been paid out in lawyers' bills. Stephen Newall and Nancy Clarke are challenging their right to the inheritance as a result of the crimes, and a civil action is planned to replace the brothers as beneficiaries.

1994

Thursday, September 15:

THE FANTASY TRAP THAT FAILED

When Colin Stagg was charged in August 1993 with the murder of Rachel Nickell, it appeared that an extraordinary undercover operation involving a young policewoman had helped to solve one of the most horrific murders in British criminal history.

At 8.45 on the sunny morning of Monday, July 13, 1992, Rachel had waved goodbye to her boyfriend André Hanscombe as he left their home in Balham, south London, for work. Shortly afterwards, she drove her two-year-old son Alexander and her black mongrel, Mollie, to Wimbledon Common, a journey of about three miles to the west.

Whether the killer pursued his victim or chanced upon her, he chose a relatively secluded spot to pounce. After 'compelling her to silence by fear', in the words of Mr William Boyce, prosecution counsel at the committal proceedings, he forced her to kneel and inflicted a neck-wound of such severity that she would have been incapable of crying for help. Despite the ferocity of the attack – Miss Nickell suffered 49 stab wounds and, probably just before she died, a brutal sexual assault – no one heard anything. The killing took no more than three minutes.

At 10.35 a.m., a retired architect, Michael Murray, came across the harrowing sequel as Alexander, stained by his mother's blood, held her head and pleaded with her to get up.

By that time, the killer had escaped. No weapon was found, and the murderer left no fingerprints, semen or fibre in the vicinity of the crime.

Yesterday, at the Old Bailey, the man accused of the murder was freed after a judge condemned police attempts to lure him into making a confession. Thirty-one-year-old Colin Stagg was befriended by an undercover woman constable calling herself Lizzie James, who encouraged him to exchange increasingly violent sexual fantasies with her.

Mr Justice Ognall ruled that evidence obtained in that way was inadmissible. He singled out the sending of a sexually explicit tape-recording to Stagg as a 'wholly irresponsible' attempt to incriminate by 'deceptive conduct of the grossest kind'.

Mr John Nuttall, prosecuting, then announced that the Crown was left with insufficient evidence against Stagg to warrant a trial, and the judge entered a formal verdict of Not Guilty.

Stagg, an unemployed labourer living in a council flat in Roehampton, south-west London, became a suspect during the early stages of the investigation, and was charged after Mr Paul Britton, a forensic psychiatrist, had studied Stagg's exchanges with the policewoman and concluded that his responses showed him to be in the same rare sub-class of sexual deviant as the killer, whose 'psychological profile' Mr Britton had compiled earlier, without reference to Stagg or any other suspect.

Of the prosecution's claim that the police had no route other than through the 'Lizzie James' scheme of testing whether or not Stagg matched Mr Britton's 'profile' of the killer, the judge said: 'So be it. But if that route involves trespass into the territory of impropriety, the Court must stand firm and bar the way.' Speaking of another prosecution claim, that although Stagg had made no direct admissions regarding the murder of Rachel Nickell, he had betrayed knowledge of the state and position of her body that he could only have gleaned as her killer, the judge supported defence arguments that the key details he had given were wrong. The judge added that even if he had allowed material obtained during the undercover operation to go before a jury, the prosecution would have faced 'formidable difficulties' when seeking to have Mr Britton's opinions admitted as expert evidence.

As the court cleared after the ruling, Rachel's mother, Monica Nickell, sat with her husband Andrew, tears streaming down her face. Just a few feet away, Stagg waved to relatives in the public gallery as he left the dock.

Immediately afterwards, in the street outside the Old Bailey, Andrew Nickell raised questions about the extent to which defendants enjoy protection in the courts:

'I am sure that the law has been upheld – but where is the justice? We have an impasse which may – and I emphasise *may* – put other daughters and wives at risk in the months and years ahead. When my daughter was murdered on Wimbledon Common, I believed, like many other citizens, that the law was even-handed and that justice was available for all. What appears to have been lost over the last thirty years is the principle that everybody is equal under the law and entitled to justice. The pendulum has swung too far to the side of the criminal. The suspect is allowed to remain silent, and the prosecution during a trial cannot draw attention to that fact. The whole of the evidence of the police inquiry in this case – 10,000 pages, I believe – is given to the defence for them to study and to find an answer. The defence does not have to give the prosecution anything until the trial commences. The prosecution has no appeal whatsoever against today's decision. If it had been the other way round, then Colin Stagg's lawyers could have taken his case to the Court of Appeal. If the defendant has that right, then why not let the case be heard before a jury?'

Mr Nickell also spoke about his grandson, Alexander, who, now aged five, is living in France with his father, André Hanscombe: 'He clung to my daughter while her killer murdered her in the most foul way. He will spend the rest of his life remembering those dreadful moments. He is under a life sentence.'

Stagg, who may receive as much as £225,000 in compensation, spent the rest of the day celebrating with his lawyers and giving television interviews in a £300-a-night suite at the nearby Waldorf Hotel. He said, among other things: 'I am innocent – and I have always been innocent – of this horrible crime, and I am pleased that this has finally been proved. I hope that the police will now go out and find the real killer. My life has been ruined by a mixture of half-baked psychological theories and some letters written to satisfy the strange sexual requests of an undercover police officer.'

The Crown Prosecution Service said that it was satisfied that the prosecution was brought in accordance with the Code for Crown Prosecutions, which requires the CPS to be satisfied that there is sufficient evidence to give a 'realistic' prospect of conviction. CPS officials considered that their position was vindicated by the fact that the case was committed for trial by the stipendiary magistrate in Wimbledon. The CPS knew that the undercover operation was being mounted, and offered legal advice to the police.

THE UNDERCOVER OPERATION

'Lizzie James' was created as the dream partner for whoever murdered Rachel Nickell.

According to the 'psychological profile' drawn up for detectives by Paul Britton, the killer was a sexual sadist consumed by fantasies involving the ritualistic domination of women, and capable of carrying them out to the point of murder, and the undercover policewoman who posed as Lizzie James became the key to attempts to establish whether – as detectives believed – Colin Stagg fitted that description.

She sought Stagg's trust, encouraged him to share violent sexual fantasies with her, and pretended to have participated in the sacrificial murder of a woman and a baby, so as to give him the impression that, unless he had been concerned in some similar crime, they could never form the relationship he came to crave. It would be 'brilliant,' she told him, if he was Rachel Nickell's killer and had got away with it.

During the exchanges, Stagg repeatedly denied murdering Rachel. On one occasion, in the hope of meeting Lizzie's demands, he invented a story that he and a cousin had strangled a girl in the New Forest when he was 12; but even when Lizzie said that she disbelieved this, he did not admit murdering Rachel.

But he did tell Lizzie that he found it exciting to think about the Wimbledon murder and that he had been sexually aroused when shown a police photograph of the body.

In one taped telephone call, Stagg said that he felt 'a bit two-way' about the murder. 'It does turn me on, you know, thinking about it,' he said. 'You should not feel turned on by something like that ... that's why I feel confused.'

As Lizzie steered Stagg towards increasingly extreme material, she also sent him a tape-recorded message containing what his counsel, Mr William Clegg, QC, condemned in court as 'the most hard-core pornography one could imagine,' adding that for a police officer to send such a tape to a suspect was 'something happily without precedent – and, frankly, a disgrace.'

It accompanied a letter which the policewoman and two male detectives had composed, though Lizzie said that the contents were agreed within guidelines set by Mr Britton, who not only drew up the original 'profile' but also orchestrated the undercover operation.

WPC 'James', who was allowed to keep the pseudonym during court proceedings, was accustomed to clandestine roles. A combination of her experience and physical characteristics made her an ideal candidate for the operation, with Mr Britton constructing a suitable lifestyle. Lizzie was to be white and aged between 20 and 40, with fair, shoulder-length hair. She would be sexually sophisticated, but not promiscuous. She had belonged to an occult or satanic group for most of her teenage years before withdrawing in a state of emotional turmoil 10 years before. She believed that she could only enter fully into a sexual relationship if the man had comparable experience.

Lizzie wrote to Stagg from an accommodation address in Slough, where she said she worked with cats. Mr Britton analysed the exchanges and decided on the timing and nature of each development.

The officer first contacted Stagg in January last year, saying that she was fascinated by letters he had sent to a 'friend', Miss Julie Pines – who, approached by Stagg after she had placed a lonely-hearts advertisement, had found his third letter 'totally disgusting' and, when she became aware that he was a murder suspect, handed it to the police.

In her first letter, Lizzie explained that her friend was 'a little old-fashioned'. Stagg replied immediately, saying that he liked his own company and walking with his dog, Brandy, on Wimbledon Common, but admitting that he did sometimes get 'painfully lonely'. He wrote warily, unsure whether Lizzie was genuine, telling her later

that he had suspected that she was a journalist.

On January 27, Lizzie wrote again. Dismissing Miss Pines as a 'boring old bag,' she said that the fantasy her friend had found so disgusting was 'revealing in more ways than one'. Even at this early stage, the defence said, Lizzie was implying that a sexual relationship could develop.

Stagg referred in his next letter to his sexual inexperience and enclosed a collection of fantasies about open-air sex. She responded with a Valentine's Card, followed with praise for one of the fantasies: 'If I close my eyes, I can almost feel you sat astride me, and feel your weight pressing me into the ground. . . . I bet this is just the tip of the iceberg when it comes to your thoughts.'

Mr Clegg said that Lizzie, who enclosed a photograph showing that she was very attractive, presented herself as sexually experienced. 'She knows that Stagg is a virgin and is promising future sexual experience.'

Stagg wrote back: 'I yearn to be with you, to hold your hand, to feel your warm, sexy lips against me. I am glad you liked my letters and that you are as broad-minded and uninhibited as me.' He enclosed a story about sex in public, and promised a fantasy with each letter.

But before she could reply, he wrote again and apologised for making himself 'look a right prat': 'If I have turned you off, I am sorry. I will understand if you do not want to know me any more. I know I said I can be a bit possessive. That's because I have never really had anyone in my life to cherish and love, especially a beautiful woman like you. That is why receiving your first letter was like a dream come true. I have never really been attractive to women. They don't want to know. That's why I have all these passions and fantasies inside.'

To the defence, Lizzie's reply was a clear signal for Stagg to be more extreme. 'Please, please, please,' she wrote, 'don't worry about anything you write ... you are filling me with more confidence each time. My fantasies hold no bounds and my imagination runs riot. Sometimes this worries me, and it would be nice to know that you had the same dreams as me. Sometimes I scare myself with what I really want. I hope I am not sounding unnatural, but sometimes normal things just aren't enough and my demands are greater, not just straight sex.... Sexually, people don't use their imagination, but I am sure you do and can, Colin, my darling. Tell me something that will really drive me crazy.'

Mr Clegg said that the exchanges were marked by a series of steps by which the policewoman introduced themes of dominant and group sex, anal intercourse, ritual abuse, and murder involving knives. She was, he said, effectively inviting a confession to the Wimbledon murder in return for sex and a lasting relationship.

In one such step, she suggested that he was showing restraint and added: 'I want you to burst. I want to feel you all-powerful, and overwhelming, so I am completely in your power, defenceless and humiliated.'

Mr Clegg said that when Stagg failed to send a sufficiently uninhibited and deviant fantasy, she 'punished' him by withholding an answer. Each escalation of the fantasies was prompted by the officer. Despite her repeated hints that he needed to divulge something shameful from his past, he at first offered only a minor homosexual encounter. In desperation, she mentioned the satanic group, the killing of a young woman whose throat she had cut, and the murder of a baby.

Mr Clegg said that this brought together a woman and child, and a method of killing, to match details of Rachel Nickell's murder.

In response to the officer's requests for more bizarre fantasies, Stagg wrote: 'I now have some idea of what you want. I want to dominate you, take your body as my plaything. You will be left humiliated and dirty. You're going to be left sore and exhausted. Lizzie, I'm going to make you pay for what you have done to me. I'm going to make sure you are screaming in agony when I abuse you. I'm going to destroy your self-esteem.'

When the couple began to talk by telephone, he made his first reference to his previous arrest on suspicion of murdering Miss Nickell. He denied involvement, blaming neighbours' lies.

On May 20, they met at her suggestion for lunch in Hyde Park. Here, Lizzie told him that it might be easier for their relationship, because of her own past, if he really was the killer.

Stagg also wrote a fantasy which, Mr Britton said, included details associated with Rachel's murder – a local common, sunny weather, trees, and a knife used to trace marks on the victim's body.

At a second meeting in Hyde Park, on June 4, Lizzie told him that she did not believe his story about the New Forest killing. At their third meeting, when she again said that she wished he had murdered Rachel Nickell, Stagg admitted having been close to the scene of the crime and showed signs of sexual arousal. He said that he would like to take Lizzie to the scene but was discouraged by police interest.

On July 1, Stagg apparently became aroused while telling her on the telephone that he would like to take her to the common and creep up on her with a knife. He afterwards sent her a fantasy story about forcing sex upon a 'tall, sexy, blonde woman'.

But Mr James Sturman, defence counsel at the committal proceedings, attacked the police 'manipulation' of Stagg's responses. Referring to an early letter in which Lizzie said that she wanted a man who 'really shows me who is boss', Mr Sturman said: 'You'd need to be a moron not to realise that this woman wanted to be dominated.'

Police had found no hard-core pornography at Stagg's flat; only magazines such as *Razzle* and *Escort*. 'This is not a man with a dungeon and an S & M [sadism and masochism] collection,' Mr Sturman remarked.

It seemed to the defence counsel at the Old Bailey that Lizzie had neatly summed up Stagg's predicament when she wrote: 'You seem so perfect to me that if you fit my criteria, there is no going back for us and we will be together for ever.' She was promising 'the one thing he wanted more than anything else in the world: a relationship with a woman for ever'.

The problem, Mr Clegg pointed out, was that Lizzie's criteria required Colin Stagg to be Rachel Nickell's murderer.

THE UNSEEN POLICE FORCE

Mr Justice Ognall's judgment has brought unwelcome publicity to the work of one of Scotland Yard's most secretive units: SO10 – so named because it is part of the Yard's Specialist Operations Department. Its officers perform some of the most hazardous tasks in policing, and are understandably keen on anonymity. Drawn from different racial and linguistic groups, many of these officers are diverted only occasionally from normal duties for specific SO10 assignments. The unit develops and executes strategies for the full range of covert intelligence-gathering, as well as handling major informants and 'supergrasses', protecting vulnerable jurors and witnesses, and providing 'hostage negotiators' in sieges.

As well as sometimes being physically dangerous, the work of SO10 is often close to the edge of legality. In almost every operation, the head of the unit, Commander Roy Ramm, must decide *ad hoc* – usually after consultation with the Crown Prosecution Service – where legitimate intelligence-gathering ends and illegal incrimination, or entrapment, begins. That is an onerous responsibility, given the scrutiny to which police methods are subjected in Crown Courts. The decisions are not helped by a lack of clear legal guidance. There is no basic defence of entrapment in English law, but trial judges are entitled to exclude covert police evidence if they believe that it threatens the fairness of a trial, and that discretion has led to a patchwork of judgments and legal precedents, not all of which appear to correlate.

According to a senior SO10 officer: 'It is an abiding problem in all undercover cases to determine just how far we can go. A detective investigating a particular crime will come to us for covert help, telling us what he wants, and then we have to decide whether it can be done legitimately. The CPS is reluctant to get too involved at the investigative stage, which means, in effect, that we have to make our own decisions and see what happens when the cases come to court.'

In the Wimbledon Common case, Colin Stagg, an unemployed loner with an interest in pagan religion, living on a council estate bordering the common, was the 27th of 32 men arrested during the investigation. Stopped by a constable as he was walking towards the common with his dog within a few hours of the killing, he said that he had also been on the common until about an hour before the crime, and his details were passed to detectives. A number of women gave the police descriptions of a man – alleged by the police to have been Stagg – who was acting suspiciously near the scene of the crime, and one of them picked him out at an identity parade.

Two months after the murder, he was arrested and held for three days. While answering all questions, he denied involvement in the killing, saying that he had been asleep in front of his television at the time. His flat yielded no incriminating evidence.

He appeared in court at this stage, but on an unrelated charge of indecent exposure on the common on an unspecified date within a few days of the murder. He pleaded guilty, though explaining his behaviour as 'nude sunbathing', and was fined £200. In consultation with lawyers from the Crown Prosecution Service, the police concluded that they had insufficient evidence to charge him with murder.

All operational decisions were ultimately the responsibility of Detective Superintendent John Bassett, a veteran of numerous successful murder inquiries, who has since retired. Superintendent Bassett and his colleagues agreed that Stagg remained their 'best suspect'. A month after Stagg's first arrest, the police received what they took to be further circumstantial evidence against him: his lonely-hearts letter to Miss Julie Pines. Superintendent Bassett turned to Paul Britton, who had previously compiled a 'profile' listing what he regarded as the killer's main characteristics, and then asked SO10 about the possibility of using an undercover female officer to befriend Stagg and, by encouraging him to expose his innermost sexual thoughts, determine whether he could be the murderer.

There is some conflict between the police and the CPS as to the extent to which they worked together, but CPS officials have indicated that, even before the Lizzie James operation began, there had been a lot of informal discussion about its propriety. According to Scotland Yard, the police followed CPS advice 'to the letter' throughout, several times updating the authority on progress.

Superintendent Bassett decided that, with the Lizzie James material, there were sufficient grounds for charging Stagg, and he was re-arrested on August 17, 1993. On the advice of a solicitor, he exercised his right to remain silent. The case-file was sent to the CPS soon afterwards, and lawyers there took the view that the evidence achieved the criterion of being strong enough to offer a realistic prospect that Stagg would be convicted.

However, it was appreciated both by the CPS and by Mr William Boyce, the Treasury counsel instructed to act for the Crown, that the policewoman's evidence was 'at the edge of admissibility'. Although Stagg had not confessed, it was believed that he had let slip details known to only a handful of people, including the culprit. The decision to proceed seemed to be vindicated in February when Mr Terry English, a newly-appointed stipendiary magistrate, sent the case for trial. The stipendiary had listened to long legal arguments as to whether or not Mr Britton's evidence should be admitted, and found that, while the defence argument held attractions, these affected the weight to be attached to the evidence rather than its admissibility; he had also heard other evidence from many witnesses.

Mr Justice Ognall's condemnation of the Lizzie James operation has wounded Commander Ramm and his colleagues in SO10, but they point out that other court judgments have given legitimacy to even more obvious 'sting' operations that they have conducted.

The most blatant, and arguably the most audacious, happened early in 1991, when they went into the jewellery business in an attempt to snare underworld fences in north London. The local police, who had had success against habitual burglars but had been unable to uncover the handlers of the stolen goods, approached SO10, and a decision was made to open a jeweller's shop in Tottenham, where the handlers were known to be based. An empty property was leased and stocked; undercover detectives were brought in to serve behind the counter; and word was put about in criminal quarters that the owners of the shop – Stardust Jewellers – were in the market to buy loot. In three months, the shop's detectives bought £25,000's worth of stolen goods from five men they had identified as important fences – though only after they had haggled over prices, asked where the goods had been stolen from, and demanded itemised receipts. Every exchange was recorded on video and audio machines concealed around the shop.

The five were found guilty in October 1991, but appealed against their convictions on the grounds that the police had acted as *agents provocateurs*. The Appeal Court agreed that the men had been tricked into incriminating themselves, but ruled that they had 'voluntarily applied themselves to the trick', and that 'not every trick resulted in unfairness'. And so the appeals were dismissed and an entrapment operation vindicated.

Comparing this judgment with that of Mr Justice Ognall, the difficulty for the police in wondering what the courts will admit as evidence and what they will regard as unacceptable is apparent.

The work of SO10 will certainly continue, despite the latest setback. Lessons have been learnt. The unit is still one of the police's most effective weapons in the fight against serious crime.

PSYCHOLOGICAL PROFILES

'White, middle-aged male, often with a beard, usually in an academic or a public-sector post, possessing a degree in psychology, and demanding millions of pounds of government money to continue profiling.'

That less than complimentary pen-picture of a typical specialist in 'offender profiling' was published in the *Criminological and Legal Psychology Newsletter* earlier this year. Its tongue-in-cheek tone is in contrast to the reverential media coverage. After modest contributions to several recent murder cases, the profiling psychologist is widely portrayed as the Sherlock Holmes of today.

Graham Davies, professor of psychology at the University of Leicester, believes that the media have become 'mesmerised' by a field of study that is largely untested. One recent survey of criminal cases in Holland concluded that none of the profiles had led directly to a conviction. 'What profiles do is to give the police some suggestions,' says Professor Davies. 'Where I feel more uncomfortable is when these investigatory methods then become evidence at trial.'

It was the evidential value of the profiler's art that was at the core of the Colin Stagg case. Without the contribution of Paul Britton, the police would not have attempted to bring Stagg to trial. Mr Britton, head of the Trent Forensic Psychology Service, has said that his original profile of the unidentified killer was 'indistinguishable' from his conclusions about Stagg. The inference that Stagg was therefore the killer was attacked at the committal proceedings, where defence counsel said that Mr Britton's findings were 'speculative and unsupported by anything other than his instincts. . . . It boils down to: "I am Paul Britton, therefore I am right." What is worrying is how often psychologists have got it wrong. You have only to remember the number of times a mental health tribunal or other body has released a disturbed person into the community only to kill, rape or maim. . . . We simply do not know what lunatic was loose on Wimbledon Common that day. Mr Britton is trying to prove possible guilt by giving an opinion. The prosecution cannot quote a single case in which a psychologist has pronounced guilt. You are being asked to create legal history.'

Professor Davies's view is that 'profiles are so general that they fit large numbers of people. When profilers try to be more specific, they can be quite spectacularly wrong.'

'Notebook' by Claudia FitzHerbert; Friday, September 16:

Colin Stagg, despite months of pornographic provocation from an undercover policewoman, always maintained his innocence of Rachel Nickell's murder, and his arrest and imprisonment present an extraordinary saga of stupidity on the part of the police and the Crown Prosecution Service.

Perhaps the case will sound the death-knell of psychological profiling of criminals, which has caused a great deal of trouble down the years. Not only can psychological profiles lead to the wrongful arrest and imprisonment of innocent persons simply because they fit some nonsensical quasi-scientific picture, but they can also have the effect of blinding police officers to the obvious in their search for the deviant.

In America in the early 1960s, the Boston Strangler escaped detection for years, so taken were the police by the premise that the killer had a deep-seated hatred of his mother (many of his victims were elderly women). Before the arrest of the Strangler, Albert de Salvo, a psychologist suggested that the police should be looking for a flamboyant homosexual with an accomplice – but de Salvo was aggressively heterosexual and worked alone.

Similarly in Britain in the 1980s, the determination on the part of police officers that they were looking specifically for a killer of prostitutes rather than 'ordinary' women meant that two of Peter Sutcliffe's attacks were not recognised as the work of the 'Yorkshire Ripper', and Sutcliffe was interviewed several times without being arrested simply because he did not fit the psychological profile in the policemen's heads.

In both cases, the killers' victims, elderly women living alone in flats, and prostitutes walking the streets at night, were easy prey, and it is a thousand pities that the police officers involved saw fit to muddy the clear waters of common sense with costly and unproven psychobabble.

Monday, September 19:

Paul Britton broke his silence on Saturday when he issued a written statement: 'I am confident that I have acted professionally throughout my involvement as an adviser to the Metropolitan Police in their investigations.'

Mr Britton has recently been called in to help Warwickshire Police in a current murder inquiry.

Tuesday, September 20:

The Metropolitan Police face a bill of more than £1600 after Colin Stagg collected his dog, Brandy, from kennels yesterday. The 13-year-old bitch went into the care of the Battersea Dogs' Home last September, a month after Stagg was arrested in connection with the murder of Rachel Nickell. The daily cost of keeping the 'mainly labrador' dog at the home's country kennels at Old Windsor, Berkshire, until the case against Stagg was dropped last Wednesday was £4.55. A spokesman for the home said: 'Mr Stagg was very happy with his dog's condition. We would have thought a little donation might have been nice. We are a charity. Strictly speaking, he was liable for the dog's daily keep after being discharged.'

LETTER TO
THE EDITOR

SIR – Setting aside the unbearable
tragedy of Rachel Nickell, what is
so worrying is that the police officer
in her undercover role encouraged
Colin Stagg to confess to committing a violent act.

He denied that act throughout.
One can only thank God that he did
not commit one to satisfy her.

(Mrs) JEAN ROOKE
Shalford, Surrey

1994

Wednesday, November 2:

BRITAIN'S LAST HANGMAN DIES

Sydney Dernley, apprentice hangman to Albert Pierrepoint, and Britain's last surviving executioner,* died at his home in Mansfield, Nottinghamshire, yesterday, aged 73.

A former welder at Sherwood Colliery and treasurer of his local Conservative club, Mr Dernley took part in the execution of 28 men between 1948 and 1953.

'He would come home from the colliery and there would sometimes be a letter waiting for him from the Home Office,' said Mrs Joyce Dernley, his wife of 51 years. 'Then he would go off when they told him to and be back the next day.'

Unlike Pierrepoint, who campaigned against hanging after his retirement, Sydney Dernley never lost his faith in capital punishment as a deterrent. 'He never had any qualms about hangings,' Mrs Dernley said. 'But normally he was a great big softie.'

He was particularly proud of having carried out, with Pierrepoint, the fastest hanging on record (of James Inglis, who murdered a prostitute in Hull) in just over seven seconds from the condemned man's arrival at the gallows to the opening of the trapdoor.

'He was a bit of a joker really,' said Jonathan Goodman, who visited Mr Dernley last week. 'When he answered his door, he sized me up and said: "How much do you weigh?"'

Sunday, November 6:

THE GALLOWS HUMORIST
by Byron Rogers

I spoke to him just over a month ago, so it was a shock to hear about the death during the week of Syd Dernley of Mansfield. I can remember as though it were yesterday, and always will, the afternoon six years ago when we met, and how Mr Dernley in the neat little bungalow talked about his old job, while Mrs Dernley made scones for us.

* Other, less well-known hangmen are almost certainly still alive. (Reports on the executional careers of Albert Pierrepoint and his successor Harry Allen, both of whom died in 1992, form the final chapter of *The Daily Telegraph Murder File*.)

Popular appeal: the public hanging of William Palmer the poisoner in 1856

(The *Telegraph*'s reporting of the Palmer case, which gave a great boost to the paper's sales at the start of its second year of publication, makes the first chapter of *The Daily Telegraph Murder File*).

She kept emerging with fresh batches, chiding me for my lack of appetite, while her husband, brisk and informative, produced a length of rope for my inspection, or sat, lost in nostalgia. And believe me, if there is anything more terrifying than a hangman, it is a nostaglic hangman. . . .

We met because he had taken exception to something I had written about a hangman my grandfather knew, who had decorated his front room with nooses and portraits of his Victorian colleagues, and whose life, the *Carmarthen Journal* noted in its 1901 obituary, had been dominated by just one thing, 'a deep-seated longing to participate in the infliction of capital punishment everywhere'. The paper had begun the obituary with a remarkable sentence: 'He has at last "shot his bolt", as he himself would put it.'

His name was Robert Evans (though on occasion he called himself Anderson) — a solicitor's son from Carmarthen, who, by a bizarre coincidence, lived in a house that has subsequently become a symbol of lost innocence to generations of Eng Lit graduates: Dylan Thomas's Fern Hill. The hangmen Calcraft and Marwood were his guests there, and successive Home Secretaries must have groaned at seeing that address on the eager letters they received from him most months.

'The doomed one should be addressed firmly and, as far as can be, cheerfully assured that he will not be hurried into eternity without being allowed proper time and means to prepare himself, and he should be made to feel confident that no unnecessary punishment be inflicted on him. . . .'

Evans, or Anderson, built a gallows in his garden, on which he would sit his neighbours, my grandfather probably among them, and ply them with strong drink. When I wrote about him, I made the point that this nut would have been none the worse for some urgent medical attention; and in the post a few days later there was a letter. Why, enquired the writer, should a hangman not be allowed a sense of humour? He himself had been a hangman, and he had a sense of humour. Mr Dernley asked me to tea.

But writing about 'Y Crogwr' (The Hangman), safely tucked away in Victorian Wales, or reading about such men in Thomas Hardy, was worlds away from this jolly man, hopelessly addicted to practical jokes. At one point he produced a safety razor stuck into one of the old round-socket electric plugs ('Know where I can get this fixed?'), and a little later, a wobbly, lifesized rubber hand which he had in his sleeve ('Shake'). Had it not been for the friendly presence of Mrs Dernley — and my own curiosity — I should have run howling into the spring afternoon in the first minutes of that meeting.

Syd Dernley was in his late sixties then, a good-looking man with wavy hair, who could have been anybody's grandfather, with his pipe and cardigan and slippers. Indeed, he *was* somebody's grandfather, and must have been that somebody's despair with his practical jokes. I had to keep reminding myself that here was a living practitioner of something the Anglo-Saxons had brought with them out of the forests. Abolition was not even 25 years old, yet it felt as though I was sitting in a room with Jack Ketch, the 17th-century hangman notorious for his barbarity.

At the time, Syd Dernley did not want his name used, even though (he gave a leer) it might be worth it just for the shock it would give her next door. But he felt that the shadow of the Home Office still fell on him: it had treated its hangmen like jobbing gardeners, paying them half their fee on the morning after an execution, and half a fortnight later – a sophisticated device which ensured that they did not gossip.

The Civil Service was also determined that they should never achieve the social cachet of their French equivalents, the Messieurs de Paris, as they were called, who were sub-contractors and owned the guillotine. This meant that they could supplement their incomes by showing tourists over the thing. However, the third generation of the Sanson family, whose grandfather had briskly decapitated royalty, was so unnerved by young English women tourists, who not only wanted to see the terrible thing but to pose grinning under the knife, that he took to drink, and pawned the French guillotine: thus creating chaos in the courts.

Syd Dernley recalled that his own fee per execution was just three guineas, although later this was raised to five; there were perhaps eight executions in a good year, and travel warrants were always third-class, although his chief, Albert Pierrepoint, travelled first. Someone in the Home Office had decided that an assistant hangman was not a gentleman.

The job was never advertised. Syd Dernley himself applied for it, in the hope, as he told me, of meeting criminals. He was a miner who had an obsession with the books of Edgar Wallace ('Wrote 123 books, he did, and I've got 80 of them. It were all Edgar Wallace's fault.'). Unfortunately, Wallace forgot to mention one small fact that might have made all the difference: the average length of time between the

moment the hangman enters the cell and the moment the trap falls is ten seconds. There was always a locked door which, if a prisoner enquired, he was told was a store for old furniture; but beyond that, just fifteen feet beyond it, was the gallows. Mr Dernley never did get to meet his criminals socially.

'If he were honest ...' His wife had brought in another plate of scones. '... if he were honest, he applied just to get out of the colliery.'

The Home Office replied with brevity, telling him that no vacancy then existed, but a year later wrote again, just as briefly, requesting him to present himself for interview at Lincoln jail.

'Governor were a tall bloke, and he wanted to know my hobbies. I said I liked shooting. Where did I shoot? Up at Castle. He were a bit taken aback at that, and asked, did I shoot with the Duke, then? No, I said. I generally shot after the Duke had gone to bed. That were it, really. He was so tickled, he called the doctor in. "Got a poacher here, says he wants to be a hangman."'

There followed something so bizarre, no black comedy could hope to match it: the Class of '48 – Syd Dernley and three others – was sent on a week's training course to Pentonville Prison. Of his colleagues, Dernley remembered two: a mathematician from ICI ('He were just interested in mathematics of hanging') and an ice-cream salesman from Birmingham.

They spent the week in the condemned cell, doing long-division sums. ('You divided 1,000 by the man's weight. What for? For the length of the drop'), sum after sum, scribbling and puzzling, puzzling and scribbling ('Important that. You get yer sums wrong, and you can take a man's head clean off').

They had hoped to have Pierrepoint as a tutor, but it was an elderly warder. The practical aspects they tried out on each other, the pinioning and the strapping, and they took turns on the lever ('Pushed forward, just as in a signal box').

No knots. 'The noose is already there.' He had dropped his voice to a whisper. 'Hang on, I think I've still got one about the place somewhere.' What? My host had skipped lightly past me to a drawer in a sideboard, from which he produced a length of rope, the inside of which was bound in leather ('to stop rope burns, that') and one end of which had a metal loop, through which he passed the rope.

'Just a souvenir,' he told me.

I did not ask many questions of him as he told me of the time the four of them had attended their first execution at Shrewsbury Jail. He had a photograph of them with Pierrepoint, taken outside the railway station, and it could have been any works' outing, except that after it was over there were only three left.

'The maths chap, he wet himself in the taxi and emigrated. But me, I were impressed. The clock struck nine, Pierrepoint and his assistant went into the cell and, as I told you, eight seconds later it were all over. Mind you, me and him got it down to seven when we hanged James Inglis. Fastest hanging ever, that.

'And what's more, the condemned man has no time to be frightened. People talk about electric chairs; but that's cruelty. They talk about the guillotine; that's quick, but it's a bloody mess. Here, I've got one of them as well, made it meself.' And from somewhere, the extraordinary being had produced a tiny working model with a little blade which he pulled up and released. Click.

'But hanging's humane. I timed it

from the time that clock in Shrewsbury struck nine. Eight seconds.'

'Perhaps you find this shocking,' murmured Mrs Dernley.

'Nothing shocking about it,' said her husband, before I had time to say anything. 'I'd come home, and the wife would say: "All right?" and I'd say: "All right". That were all. It were an accepted way of life, and we both believed it had to be done.

'Of course, I tried to keep it secret at first, but we weren't on phone, and the old postmaster had to come puffing up the hill whenever a telegram announced a reprieve. So it was suggested we had a phone put in, only there were a two-year waiting list, so then I had to say what me other job were. We had the thing put in in two days. But being I were a miner, we lived in a Coal Board house, and the phone people must have had to install an extra pole or something, so they got in touch with the pit manager. He told his clerk, and after that it were like dropping a stone in a puddle.

'For six months there was a hush every time I went in pub. But after that it were all right. Some of the men even made jokes about it when we were playing dominoes: "Whose drop is it?" "I dunno, ask 'im. 'E's the expert". But nobody said anything adverse.

'I've never regretted it. It were a very interesting time in my life, when I got to see a lot of the country and met some very interesting people I should never have met in pit.'

But one of the others had regrets. News of the ice-cream salesman's other job leaked out in Birmingham, and this affected sales to the point where one day his boss called him in. 'Harry, ice-cream and hanging, they don't mix, boy.' Which left two of the Class of '48, though Syd

Dernley forgot what became of the other man.

He himself went his busy way, helping to hang Timothy Evans, of whose guilt he remained convinced, as you might expect, for even hangmen aspire to sleep at nights. At one point, I hesitantly touched on the more lurid aspects of folklore, but he was not in the least embarrassed. No, he said, he had never seen hanged men with erections, and it had been part of his job to undress the corpses in the execution pit.

Pierrepoint, in his autobiography, talked of hanging as a moment of intimacy, when it was just him and 'the poor broken body' of his victim. The last thing he wanted on the gallows was gallows humour, and the day inevitably came when Syd Dernley cracked a joke. Through the post a letter came, as brief as its predecessor, informing him that there would be no further need of his services.

He felt the disappointment, which was why, for old times' sake, he told me solemnly, he had bought a gallows. He bought it off a doctor who had it out of the old Cambridge jail, and it came in a Pickford's van. He sprang to his feet again, and rummaged in that drawer out of which I was by now convinced anything might come.

He showed me a photograph of the gallows which he had installed in his cellar, with two green spotlights trained on a tailor's dummy, which he had got from John Collier's. It had come without a head, so he had arranged a white bust on its shoulders – at which I started, for there was something familiar about that gaunt profile.

'Hey, that's Dante you're hanging.'

'Who?'

'Dante. Italian poet.'

'That's. who it is? I often won-

dered. Doctor threw it in when I bought gallows.' His cellar was not high enough for this to be assembled with the drop beneath it, so he put two blocks of wood under the thing, just enough, he smiled, just enough for the trap to creak.

These were social years. 'Word got round, and all sorts turned up. A managing director came. "I understand you have a gallows in your cellar." I took him down. "I understand you have a rope." He stood there. "Excuse me, may I have the rope round my neck?" Mr Dernley took flashlit photographs and had certificates printed, some of which his graduates had framed and hung up on their walls.

He was keeping a post office then, and time passed merrily enough. Until, his wife being taken ill, her cousin came to keep house for him. She, of course, did not know where anything was. One morning, a man came to read the electric meters. Syd Dernley was busy in his post office, but he noticed the man walking up his garden path. Five minutes later, he saw the man come running down it, running faster than he had ever seen any man run, down the path and up the street until he was lost to sight. His wife's cousin had not known where the meters were, so the man had said to leave it to him, and had opened a few cupboard doors before opening the one leading down into the cellar. He must have switched the lights on, at which point the two spots had illuminated the gallows and Dante, his head in a noose.

'You know, I can't remember anyone coming to read our meters after that. It were all estimates.'

At the time, I was writing a column for the *Sunday Express* and thought hangman Syd an ideal profile for the paper. But no, they wouldn't touch it with a bargepole;

it was explained to me that, however much the paper's readers might approve of hanging, it would be far too much of a shock to confront them with a hangman.

Their ancestors were not so squeamish. Hangmen, along with their victims, were the first authentic working-class heroes (and hangmen had a longer shelf-life). Crowds met them when they arrived on business in county towns, and newspapers scrupulously noted their tastes in dress. 'Mr Berry,' recorded the *Carmarthen Journal*, 'unostentatiously dressed in a plain suit of dark clothing *and wearing a red Turkish fez*.' (The italics are mine.)

I kept in touch with Syd Dernley, a helpful man, who at one point sent me a table of weights and drops, a sort of hangman's ready-reckoner. He also sent me various ideas for feature articles. In return, I read and tried to help him with a memoir he had written about his poaching days, and I must have kept this for some time, as I remember an irritated reminder coming from him ('If you don't want to find yourself dangling from one of your apple trees'). I never could cope with his humour.

When we spoke last month, he told me that the last gallows of all had finally been taken down ('You know, the one they had at Wandsworth for blokes that had a mind to run off with the Queen'), although it had subsequently been reassembled at the Prison Officers' Museum near Rugby. He urged me to go and see it; he himself, he said, had already been twice. Thomas Hardy had some bleak fancies in his time, but not even in these did a wistful hangman surface.

'Notebook' by Claudia FitzHerbert:
Friday, December 2, 1994:

> The recent deaths of Buster Edwards and Jeffrey Dahmer* have provoked a heated debate about the rights and wrongs of obituarising criminals. As an occasional contributor to the noble obituary columns of this newspaper, I veer towards thinking that we should have given some space to the notorious cannibal of Milwaukee.† An obituary should not be seen as some stamp of approval for a life well spent; it is, rather, a record of any life deemed significant for any number of reasons.
>
> Dahmer's life of crime, like that of Dennis Nilsen's before him ... haunts our collective consciousness, and stamps, in small and depressing ways, our sense of the times we live in. As such, it is worthy of record.

Which has brought on a touch of déjà vu.

From *A Book of Remarkable Criminals* (London, 1918) by H.B. Irving, actor-manager, crime historian, and one of the half-dozen founding members of Our Society, which certain non-members call 'the Crimes Club':

'Charles Peace told a clergyman who had an interview with him in prison shortly before his execution that he hoped that, after he was gone, he would be entirely forgotten by everybody and his name never mentioned again.

'Posterity, in calling over its muster-roll of famous men, has refused to fulfil this pious hope, and Charley Peace stands out as the one great personality among English criminals of the nineteenth century. In Charley Peace alone is revived that

---

* Ronald 'Buster' Edwards, the Great Train Robber, hanged himself on Tuesday, November 30. Jeffrey Dahmer: see page 168.
† While no national newspaper had published an obituary of Dahmer, several – but not the *Daily Telegraph* – had obituarised Edwards.

good-humoured popularity which in the seventeenth and eighteenth centuries fell to the lot of Claude Duval, Dick Turpin and Jack Sheppard. But Peace has one grievance against posterity; he has endured one humiliation which these heroes have been spared. His name has been omitted from the pages of the *Dictionary of National Biography*. From Duval, in the seventeenth, down to the Mannings, Palmer, Orton, Morgan and Kelly, the bushrangers, in the nineteenth century, many a criminal, far less notable or individual than Charley Peace, finds his or her place in that great record of the past achievements of our countrymen. Room has been denied to perhaps the greatest and most naturally gifted criminal England has produced, one whose character is all the more remarkable for its modesty, its entire freedom from that vanity and vaingloriousness so common among his class.

'The only possible reason that can be suggested for so singular an omission is the fact that in the strict order of alphabetical succession, the biography of Charles Peace would have followed immediately on that of George Peabody. It may have been thought that the contrast was too glaring, that even the exigencies of national biography had no right to make the philanthropist Peabody rub shoulders with man's constant enemy, Peace. Remorse should overtake those responsible for this grave omission – for so undeserved a slur on one of the most unruly of England's famous sons.'

Index